Summer 2017: computer screens go blank in 150
countries. The NHS is so affected that hospitals can only
take in patients for A&E. Ambulances are grounded.
Computer screens turn on spontaneously and warnings
appear. Employees who desperately pull the plugs are
too late. Restarting is pointless; the computers are locked.
And now the attackers ask each victim for money.

This is hijack software. It is just one example of how
vulnerable the digital world has made us.

Based on the cases he investigated over a period of six
years, award-winning Dutch journalist Huib Modderkolk
takes the reader on a tour of the corridors and back doors
of the globalised digital world. He reconstructs British-
American espionage operations and reveals how the
power relationships between countries enable intelligence
services to share and withhold data from each other.
Looking at key players including Edward Snowden,
Russian hackers Cozy Bear and Evgeniy Bogachev – 'the
Pablo Escobar of the digital era' – Modderkolk opens our
eyes to the dark underbelly of the digital world with the
narrative drive of a thriller.

THERE'S A WAR GOING ON BUT NO ONE CAN SEE IT

THERE'S A WAR GOING ON BUT NO ONE CAN SEE IT

HUIB MODDERKOLK

TRANSLATED BY ELIZABETH MANTON

BLOOMSBURY PUBLISHING
LONDON • OXFORD • NEW YORK • NEW DELHI • SYDNEY

BLOOMSBURY PUBLISHING
Bloomsbury Publishing Plc
50 Bedford Square, London, WC1B 3DP, UK
29 Earlsfort Terrace, Dublin 2, Ireland

BLOOMSBURY, BLOOMSBURY PUBLISHING and the Diana logo are trademarks of
Bloomsbury Publishing Plc

First published in September 2019 in the Netherlands as HET IS OORLOG MAAR
NIEMAND DIE HET ZIET by Uitgeverij Podium b.v.

First published in Great Britain in 2021

Copyright © Huib Modderkolk, 2019
Translation © Elizabeth Manton, 2021

This publication has been made possible with financial support from the Dutch
Foundation for Literature

Bloomsbury Publishing Plc does not have any control over, or responsibility for, any third-party
websites referred to or in this book. All internet addresses given in this book were correct at the
time of going to press. The author and publisher regret any inconvenience caused if addresses
have changed or sites have ceased to exist, but can accept no responsibility for any such changes

A catalogue record for this book is available from the British Library

ISBN: HB: 978-1-5266-2933-3; TPB: 978-1-5266-2934-0; EBOOK: 978-1-5266-2937-1;
EPDF: 978-1-5266-4546-3

2 4 6 8 10 9 7 5 3 1

Typeset by Newgen KnowledgeWorks Pvt. Ltd., Chennai, India
Printed and bound in Great Britain by CPI Group (UK) Ltd, Croydon CR0 4YY

To find out more about our authors and books visit www.bloomsbury.com
and sign up for our newsletters

CONTENTS

PROLOGUE

It's a Friday morning, spring 2015. Dutch Prime Minister Mark Rutte is seated across from his three security chiefs. Once a month they meet to brief the PM on their latest intelligence. Rutte receives them with his main cabinet ministers in the Blue Room of the Binnenhof, the Dutch parliament, surrounded by portraits of all the prime ministers going back to the Second World War. The meeting is a state secret. The minutes are classified and the participants aren't allowed to disclose anything beyond these walls.

'This is making me nervous,' one of the security chiefs tells Rutte. 'What we were afraid of is actually happening.' What's happening is that the Dutch Military Intelligence and Security Service (MIVD) has just discovered Russian hackers are mounting attacks from a computer server in the north-eastern town of Meppel. They're using the server as a base from which to infiltrate and implant viruses in power stations in countries hostile to Russia. They're attacking the networks of TV studios in Eastern Europe, erasing videos and documents. And they're trying to locate the control systems of Western European bridges and other water infrastructure so as to disable them in case of a conflict.

The three experts outline the potentially disastrous effect of this. As they see it, the prime minister has little choice. 'We have to act,' says one of them. Russia's attempts at sabotage are a red line. 'Our warnings aren't theoretical any more. We're now seeing the first waves in practice.' The security and intelligence directors propose €340 million in investment as the 'absolute minimum' to keep the Netherlands from falling even further behind in the global digital war.

Such investment is vital to secure the safety of vulnerable systems like power plants and waterways, to scan Dutch internet traffic and train digital specialists. 'Everybody agreed something had to be done,' one of those in the room later confirmed.

But with the amount of money at stake, Rutte starts to waver. There are practical obstacles. The Ministry of General Affairs has virtually no budget, Defence has already been cut and Foreign Affairs would rather finance education abroad. In the end, he disregards the warning.

Why didn't the prime minister take action? Did he doubt his security chiefs? Or was he afraid that extra spending on cybersecurity wouldn't go down well with his voter base?

*

Imagine you live in a nice house in a pleasant town. You're close to your work, there's a good local school for the kids and you have family nearby. One day, a man shows up at your door. 'I'm here to warn you,' he says. 'We've carried out some surveys and found evidence of severe subsidence in this neighbourhood. We're not yet sure why.'

You look at the man in disbelief. This is the first you've heard anything about subsidence. What on earth is he talking about? You call your family up the street. Yes, they say, that man came knocking on our door, too. Like you, they have no cracks in the walls. A few weeks pass and you forget about the whole thing. But then the man returns, this time with a colleague. 'We have new findings and the ground is sinking faster than we thought. It's becoming hazardous for residents. To reduce stress on the area, we're asking people to move out.'

You're not usually quick to panic, but now you can't help it. Signs go up around the neighbourhood with warnings in big letters: SEVERE SUBSIDENCE. Neither you nor your family have noticed anything unusual. Should you be able to see that buildings are sinking? In the media, experts comment on the surveys, but that's no help. Mostly it's just speculation. Some say the problem isn't all that serious, others that houses will start collapsing before the year is out. A popular tabloid headlines *Subsidence Set to Sink Whole Neighbourhoods!* Should you upend your life because of an invisible threat? Take your kids out of school, leave your nice house behind and wave your neighbours goodbye?

*

Warnings about digitisation are met with the same doubts and uncertainty. All day long we go around calling, sharing and liking. We enjoy the convenience the digital era has brought us – the smartwatches that monitor our heart rates, the smart meters that clock our energy consumption and the smartphones that let us navigate wherever we want to go.

And, sure, we hear the warnings. Beware: these devices are minutely tracking your routines. Watch out: new threats are looming. States are increasingly using the internet to control and influence. Spying is easier than ever. Such convenience comes at a price: our anonymity and privacy are being compromised, fake news is fuelling our distrust and cyberattacks are pulling at the seams of society.

Yet despite these alarming signals, we keep calling and messaging, strapping on Apple Watches and sharing baby photos on Facebook. Is it because we don't see the dangers, or because we can't fathom them?

Even the prime minister of the Netherlands shrugged off a clear warning from the directors of his security and intelligence agencies. That intrigues me. How can we remain so indifferent when the consequences could be so serious and destabilising? Why do we apathetically go on as normal when our civil liberties hang in the balance? What has to happen to make us, politicians and the public, truly see the dangers? And if we do see them, will we go off Facebook, put away our smartphones and change our behaviour?

These are the questions I wanted to answer. To do that, I had to find out how big the dangers really were and what else might be lurking out of sight. I had to make invisible threats visible, and descend to the places where I could see for myself the risks of the modern age.

PART I

The Situation

1

An Uninvited Guest

There's an intruder in my house and he is watching me. He's sitting in the corner of the room, next to the TV stand; a guest who sneaked uninvited into my Amsterdam-West apartment.

He probably didn't intend for me to notice, but he got careless and gave himself away. And although I can't look him in the eye, I feel intimidated. He can see me, but I can't see him. What does he know about me? How long has he been there? And who else is watching with him?

That's what was going through my head as I paced my apartment on the morning of Saturday 2 November 2013, casting glances towards the corner of the room.

Six months earlier, I'd struck out on a new path. I worked for *NRC Handelsblad*, a big Dutch daily newspaper, where I was an investigative journalist reporting on domestic stories ranging from high-speed railway proposals to Dutch foreign affairs policy. My boss, Jan Meeus, encouraged me to think about big societal issues. 'Privacy and surveillance,' I told him, 'that's a topic I'd like to dig into.' From where I was standing, it looked like individual privacy was being eroded in all kinds of ways. Cellular technology was taking over more and more of our lives, email had put paid to telephones and now we were all hooked on WhatsApping for free. With smartphones, the outside world had infiltrated our private lives. How was all this affecting our safety?

Then onto the scene came Edward Snowden, a twenty-nine-year-old American who made off with tens of thousands of top-secret documents from the US National Security Agency (NSA) and leaked them to journalists in 2013. Just like that, the secrets of the world's most powerful agency became public knowledge. It was a terrific scandal, setting off a media storm around the globe and revealing that the digital era had also brought new forms of espionage.

Suddenly everyone in the world knew the NSA was procuring data from Google and Facebook. As many as 230 million internet records a year and everything from a single email to the chat histories of hundreds of people, as well as daily copies of the complete telephone records of 120 million Americans.

My boss Jan Meeus assigned me to cover the Dutch and European angle. Were agencies in Europe as invasive as their US counterparts? Did they work together? And did Dutch intelligence always keep within the law? 'This,' he said, 'is your chance.'

I was keen to meet Edward Snowden in person but hadn't the faintest idea how to make that happen. Could I contact him directly? Could I phone the journalists to whom he gave classified documents? Had you told me that six months later I'd be sitting across from Snowden in the flesh, albeit incognito, I would have laughed.

This world was entirely new to me. Like everybody else I gobbled up the latest technologies, I was all over social media and I owned an iPhone. I was awed by the speed at which messages were sent, but couldn't begin to explain how it's done. There was something both elusive and unsettling about this world. Who else was browsing my holiday snapshots? Who else was listening in when I called my girlfriend?

As a novice to the world of technology, I hardly knew where to begin. Another journalist suggested getting in touch with Erik Bais, the owner of an internet company in Purmerend, just north of Amsterdam. In the summer of 2013, I paid him a visit. His firm occupied a bland office block made up of modular ceilings, glass cubicles and desks with big monitors, staffed entirely by men. As we drank coffee – filter, from big mugs – Bais, wearing a creased shirt, began drawing lines and arrows on a whiteboard. He rattled off words like 'protocol', 'hashes', 'switching' and 'redundancy'. I asked him to back up a bit.

'Imagine it's like an ordinary traffic network,' Bais began again, 'with roads, on- and off-ramps and interchanges. This network lets cars drive from town to town and people get around. Basically, the internet works the same way.' So, beyond our computer screens and smartphones stretches a vast traffic network. And although we barely see it, this network also consists of physical components: wires, cabinets, buildings, cell towers.

Every email or chat message that enters this network makes a trip past seven stops: the modem of your internet service provider (ISP), your ISP's local switch, your ISP's data centre, an internet exchange, the data centre of the receiving ISP, that ISP's local switch and finally the recipient's modem. That's it.

I tried to picture this journey. You type an email, hit 'send' and the message gets parcelled into tiny data packets, each with a label identifying what's inside it, where it's coming from and where it's supposed to go. Each packet selects the shortest distance to your service provider's modem – say Verizon – and from there whizzes along cables to their data centre. Most cables consist of optical fibres, so the packets have to be converted into light signals. The data centres are bricks and mortar buildings filled with endless racks of computers, all humming away.

Computers in the data centre forward these packets to a big interchange, or internet exchange, in search of the recipient's ISP. Often, that's a different company. The fact that this is where all providers worldwide interconnect is what makes these exchanges so vital.

One of the world's biggest internet exchanges happens to be in Holland: the Amsterdam Internet Exchange, or AMS-IX for short. Though technically a single hub, it's made up of several vast data centres. Two of them are tall, windowless towers visible alongside Amsterdam's ring road, piled high with computers processing millions of data packets per second.

You could think of internet exchanges as being like giant spaghetti junctions, with twenty-lane roads providing lots of links and loads of capacity. Big carriers like Netflix, Google and YouTube all want wide highways because that means fast connectivity. For the Netherlands, having a massive internet exchange in its capital is a major economic trump card. But its presence also attracts prying eyes, as the wealth of information passing through makes it a honey pot for criminals and investigative services.

From these exchanges, data packets continue on their way to the data centre of the recipient's ISP. That might be in the same country or it might be halfway around the world, in which case the packets speed across the oceans along thick, multi-layered, black cables on the seabed. Some of those undersea cables enter Europe through the Netherlands, at Beverwijk and Katwijk on the west coast and in the north at Eemshaven in the province of Groningen. The location of that last cable was enough to persuade Google to build a data centre in Groningen, conveniently close to the transatlantic superhighway. At points where these massive cables come ashore, bunker-like landing stations stand guard with fences and cameras.

It's also because of these cable landings that Beverwijk and Katwijk were added to a US list of 'critical sites' in 2010 – sites that, if they were ever attacked or damaged, could seriously endanger American security. The biggest cable station of all lies just outside New York City. In 2012, when Hurricane Sandy bore down on the state of New York, its safety was given top priority, meaning it was first in line for emergency assistance. Under no circumstance could it be allowed to fail.

That, in a nutshell, is how all those data packets speed their way around this network of cables and buildings. Bais set down his coffee mug. 'Got it?' he grinned. Hesitantly, I nodded: I now understood the basics of how the internet works.

*

But Bais's explanation also left me with new questions. Such as: who's powerful online? Who's attacking data, and who's protecting it? What are intelligence services doing with these new technologies? There lay my next step. Unfortunately, secrets don't divulge themselves. I couldn't just pick up the phone and call Edward Snowden in his hiding place in Moscow. I had to go in search of the insiders who knew this world.

As a journalist I'd learned that my phone was my main weapon. Whenever you hit a wall, try to think of who can help you out. So I made some calls and arranged to visit internet service providers, meet with telecom professionals and talk to former intelligence workers and security experts. All, without exception, were friendly. Most were men aged thirty to fifty who opted for T-shirts, jeans and sneakers rather than suits. They tended to work in buildings in industrial parks. It was a world of company canteens and lobby turnstiles.

Those who'd worked for government or intelligence preferred to meet on neutral ground. They wore blazers, as though to emphasise their former status.

Weeks passed in this way, with a series of visits and meetings. Everyone I met was happy to tell me about the internet – about the dangers, the traps and even about the spying and the privacy threats. Time and time again I heard the same story: that there's a colossal trade in data, that the Americans are all-powerful online, masters at snooping; that the Dutch have specialist knowledge but also strict laws on fibre-tapping; and that the British are both knowledgeable and professional at hacking. That besides these players there are also legions of shadowy but no less interesting middlemen such as hosting providers, SIM card manufacturers, service agencies and transit providers. And that developments are moving so fast it's virtually impossible to keep up.

After that basic introduction, however, most people clammed up. It was evident that a lot was going on. We live in exciting times, and everybody's vying to get more and more data. But *how* they did this was still a mystery to me. People would tell me about the technology, the infrastructure and the theory, but not about how it's being put into practice. When pressed, Erik Bais in Purmerend admitted he sometimes gets tapping orders from Dutch agencies like the AIVD – the Dutch General Intelligence and Security Service – ordering him to wiretap someone's internet connection. I wondered how he did that. Did he sweep up all their data packets? What does a tapping order look like? 'Could I see one?' I asked. No reply.

Everywhere I went it was the same. When I asked service providers if they'd ever actually seen American, Russian or other agents nosing around their system. When I asked investigators if they knew how or where Facebook keeps its data, and who has access. When I asked if agencies could trace a person's search history in Google Maps.

The more specific my questions, the more silent and awkward these conversations became. Suddenly, the other person would want to know how I'd travelled to our meeting, if my mobile phone was switched on and could I please stop sending them questions by email. An industrial espionage specialist refused to give examples of his work. 'Absolutely out of the question. If anyone found out, I'd lose my job,' he insisted as he nervously eyed me out of the room. The former intelligence officer would only talk about possibilities within the law. But what do agencies *actually* do? That was a secret – he wasn't at liberty to say. More than one person didn't respond at all to my follow-up questions and requests to meet.

Journalism didn't provide any answers either. There were stories about incidents, but no solid context. Nothing I read told me anything about how technology is impacting our security.

This was the first time in my career as a journalist that I'd encountered walls like this. I decided to ask a lawyer friend with ties to the hacker scene for tips. Visit OHM2013, was his advice. That didn't ring any bells. 'Observe. Hack. Make,' he explained. 'It's a festival that attracts thousands of people including ex-spies, hackers and whistleblowers.' It was also the first time since the Snowden revelations that this kind of event was taking place in Europe. An additional bonus: it was being organised in Holland, on festival grounds outside the northern city of Alkmaar.

When I arrived, the grounds were chaotic with people milling about, bales of hay and banners scattered here and there and clumps of tents thrown up at random. Golf carts rode to and fro. The area was divided into clusters with names like Rainbow Island and Noisy Square. The latter was the domain of hardcore hackers, of men and women in black T-shirts with sticker-covered MacBooks. As I stood taking it all in, a four-propeller quadcopter, aka a delivery drone, zoomed by on its way to drop off a pizza.

I listened to speeches. I watched a video interview with WikiLeaks founder Julian Assange, in which he talked about a fast-proliferating system of surveillance by corporations and governments trying to control the internet. Assange called the system 'the national security state', talking in terms of 'us' and 'them'. 'It's hurtling towards a dystopia,' he predicted, and 'it is dragging many of us along with it.'

The common consensus among festivalgoers was that the internet is no longer a refuge. Where once it was a space for exchange beyond state authority, now big capital and governments had staked their claims. These days the internet isn't just about connecting, networking and communication. The more it penetrates people's private lives through smart TVs, smartphones, smart electricity meters and digital IDs, the more it's about security.

This digital traffic network is changing rapidly. Google and Amazon have started providing the signage, producing the transit mechanisms for data packets and erecting their stores at every exit. Meanwhile, the number of service providers is shrinking every year, from dozens in the 1990s to just a few behemoths now. Power is shifting from the demand side – from the users – to suppliers like

Google. Fed by the data of billions of people, these companies are directing and dictating all internet traffic.

Within this network, all kinds of entities have started putting up digital cameras. The United States at cable stations, the Netherlands at ISPs, at Apple, Google and Facebook, or covertly somewhere in between. These days, not a single data packet crosses the ocean unseen.

The OHM2013 festival was suffused with a weird mix of optimism and defeatism. There was an almost childlike delight at eighties-era arcade machines and old computer games revived in 3D. But there was also a sense of gloom about the power of big companies and entities like the NSA. In one presentation, former NSA senior executive Thomas Drake condemned the conduct of security agencies, saying, 'The surveillance state is taking away citizens' sovereignty.'

This power play was reflected in two conflicts that coloured the festival. OHM2013's main sponsor was Fox-IT, a Dutch security company owned by the eccentric cryptographer and entrepreneur Ronald Prins. Fox-IT monitors systems and networks for client companies around the world. It had been growing fast and customers now included banks in several countries. At the festival, Fox-IT guests got the VIP treatment, with golf carts to drive them around the grounds.

But among hackers Fox-IT had a dubious reputation, embodying the powerful surveillance industry they said was restricting internet freedom. The internet was an invention of the US military. For security reasons, emails and other communications are broken up into smaller packages so as to be unreadable if intercepted. But now firms like Fox-IT had designed smart software that could recognise which packets belonged together. That was ideal for governments seeking to tap the internet and find out what was inside all those data packets.

Besides selling its software to Western countries, Fox-IT had also been giving digital forensics training in places like Egypt. Little wonder, then, that Fox-IT's sponsorship generated fierce debate before OHM2013 even began. Most vocally opposed to any affiliation with the firm was a group of German hackers called the Chaos Computer Club. They wanted to buy out Fox-IT's contribution, amounting to several tens of thousands of euros. That idea was promptly rejected by the foundation behind the festival's organisation. But, then, both the foundation's chair and another board member worked at Fox-IT.

The sponsorship went ahead, and the German hackers boycotted the festival. That wasn't the end of it, however. During the event someone spray-painted 'NSA' in red letters on the Fox-IT tent. People mocked Fox-IT's golf carts. Hackers hurled insults at and catcalled the firm's staff. Walking around the grounds, the tension was palpable. And then something else happened that I would never have thought possible: it turned out that even secret services were on the prowl.

During OHM2013 I met Jurre van Bergen. A twentysomething who helped set up the festival, he'd pitched his tent at Noisy Square, the rowdy activist camp at its fringes. Van Bergen was a smart tech head who developed software for idealistic organisations so that people in countries like Iran could communicate safely and anonymously online. At the time, he was working on Tails, an operating system that guarantees anonymity and privacy. It has a secure internet browser that obscures a user's IP address, almost like sending data packets onto the digital superhighway without a number plate.

On the very first day, Van Bergen noticed something odd: the battery power on his mobile phone, a Samsung Nexus, dropped 50 per cent in just a couple of hours. Amid the flurry of festival set-up, he didn't give it much thought. Then, on the second day, his phone went missing. Not until weeks later did it resurface at the lost and found.

The following Tuesday, Van Bergen was at the library in Haarlem, a city just west of Amsterdam, when his dad called. 'Don't freak out,' he said, 'but someone from the AIVD is looking for you.' His father said a middle-aged man, who introduced himself as Hans Turksema from the Ministry of the Interior, was standing on the doorstep. Alarm bells went off in his dad's head. 'Let me guess – the AIVD?'

Claiming he wanted to talk to Jurre 'to improve the agency's image among hackers', the man left a telephone number. Back home, Van Bergen looked at it and saw he'd received calls from the same number

11

during OHM. It made him feel uncomfortable. After all, he had ties with people he wanted to protect. People like activists. Dissidents.

And it wasn't an isolated incident, Van Bergen told me. 'It was an open secret that they approached a whole bunch of people at the festival.' The agency had targeted OHM in a charm offensive. Its aim: to recruit hackers as informants to get access to their know-how. The AIVD needed to modernise; shotgun microphones and breaking into cables weren't cutting it any more. These days, they were dealing with smartphones and Wi-Fi routers. This new age required new insights. And Van Bergen and his friends were the gateway.

Bit by bit, I was beginning to make out the contours of a battlefield, with on one side security agencies that wanted to harness hackers' knowledge, and on the other hackers who felt their freedom was under threat from big business and spying states. If I wanted to unravel the significance of this struggle, I'd have to find a way to get closer to the crossfire.

*

A few months later, fellow *NRC* journalist Steven Derix and I were in a car on our way to Germany. It was Sunday 15 September 2013. We'd been in touch with news magazine *Der Spiegel*, which had copies of Snowden's leaked documents. I'd had no luck so far penetrating the intelligence world on my own, and that's where Steven came in. A frequent traveller to Afghanistan and long-time military reporter, he had good sources at the Dutch Ministry of Defence.

Part of the difficulty was down to culture. Dutch security services are markedly more secretive than US counterparts like the CIA and FBI. The US agencies are many times larger and work with more outside contractors. They're also tied up in adversarial politics and have a culture that's more open, all of which is conducive to leaks. Also, where CIA policy is to declassify documents after thirty years, the Dutch AIVD and MIVD – the respective civilian and military intelligence and security agencies – don't even provide access to material from just after the Second World War. American intelligence officers routinely publish memoirs, and CIA staffers and former employees talk to the media from time to time. They also leak documents. In the Netherlands, that's all but inconceivable.

Steven and I had lots of questions. Were the AIVD and MIVD also hacking telephones? What *really* happens with the user data ISPs sometimes store? Is a home connection ever totally safe? What does Facebook do with all that personal information? Even as a team, Steven and I weren't making much headway. People refused to speak about it, as if bound by a code. It didn't exist. 'Sorry, I can't tell you anything about that.' But the secret documents leaked by Edward Snowden had shown that all sorts of things were going on.

We wondered if it was because of the way we were communicating. I knew nothing about sending secured emails or encryption techniques: I just phoned or texted sources asking if they would meet me. Could that be scaring people off? I realised it was a distinct possibility, because the more I read and heard about this new world, the more I, too, saw the risks.

For a start, every interaction leaves digital tracks. Pick up the phone and your telecom provider stores metadata about the call: what number you dialled, for how long, where from. Law enforcement and even intelligence agencies can request that data. When you send an email, your data packets travel through data centres and internet exchanges, some in the United States. There, all kinds of entities have access. Email providers store information as well. If they're American, like Google, then they also come under American jurisdiction.

Steven and I decided to change tack. Reasoning that our sources' biggest objection was likely to be our phones, we bought prepaid mobiles on which we could use anonymous SIM cards, thus shielding our identity from agencies. But that created a new problem: with prepaid phones, how would we let each other know we were using them? If we called from our mobiles to a prepaid phone, any government or provider could follow the trail to the anonymous prepaid number.

There were other practical hurdles, too. Keeping our prepaid and regular phones together would mean they'd communicate via the same cell tower; with both numbers taking the same routes, an observer could detect a pattern. To be absolutely safe, I switched my own phone off and walked a couple of hundred yards before using the prepaid phone on which I had Steven's number under a pseudonym.

We also had to rethink how we emailed. It turns out that regular email can't be trusted. It was the same story for computers. We bought a couple of refurbished second-hand machines, to be connected to the internet only in emergencies. Either we sent emails encrypted, or not at all. And we chatted over secure channels, which meant sticking a USB drive in the computer, launching a separate operating system and then opening a browser to shield our unique IP addresses. From there, we used a chat program with end-to-end encryption.

This, we hoped, would let us get closer to the right people.

*

From the Netherlands we took the autobahn to Hamburg, where *Der Spiegel* occupies a vast, shimmering edifice on a branch of the Norderelbe. The German newspaper had been working with Laura Poitras, an American documentary filmmaker. It was to her and the American journalist Glenn Greenwald that Edward Snowden handed over those thousands of secret NSA files in Hong Kong. Poitras in turn shared them with *Der Spiegel*, and now we had invited ourselves to the paper's head office in the hope that they might want to collaborate on the Dutch angle.

But our meeting was a bust. The journalist we had arranged to meet was annoyed that I'd started following him on Twitter a couple of days earlier. Now our connection was suspicious, he said: anyone could infer we might meet. Next time, think first, he advised as he showed us out. That seemed a little paranoid to me.

Disappointed, we turned back to Holland. But on the way home our luck finally changed: a source called up with a tip. It was someone we'd come into contact with only a few weeks before. Now he had information that something was going on at Belgacom, a Belgian telecom provider. It was up to us to find out what.

This was the first time an insider had actually approached me. Evidently, we had a foot in the door. And then we got more good news: the *NRC* correspondent in Brazil, Floor Boon, had managed to get an interview with Glenn Greenwald, the journalist who had access to all the Snowden documents. Afterwards, she asked him if he would be willing to collaborate with the *NRC*, thus giving us access to the NSA documents. He said he would.

But Glenn Greenwald proved difficult to reach. Talking to him was all but impossible. His phone was always busy. He didn't reply to emails. We sent an endless stream of them, encrypted; we called, we sent text messages. We became frustrated.

After two months of fruitless endeavour, I decided to take my chances and booked a flight to Rio de Janeiro. A lesson I'd learned from former spies is that meeting in person works best, because before you agree to co-operate with someone, you want to look them in the eye. My gamble paid off. When Floor informed Greenwald that I'd flown to Rio expressly to meet him, he agreed to make time for me.

We met in the lobby of a chic hotel in Leblon, Rio's answer to Beverly Hills. Around us, beefy men stood conspicuously talking into their mobile phones while looking in our direction. It made me nervous. Greenwald didn't seem at all fazed, though, as he bustled in and loudly greeted me and Floor. I told him about the *NRC* and what I'd come to know about Dutch intelligence operations. Greenwald set out how he envisaged our partnership. First, he wanted authorial credit on all the articles, thus making him a co-author. That would give him the legal protection afforded journalists who publish state secrets. Second, since he'd be contributing and credited as an author, he wanted to be paid as a freelancer. That was it. Relieved, Floor and I bade him goodbye.

*

From the moment I got back to Holland, something was different. Steven and I had arranged to meet a Dutch former intelligence source in a café on the outskirts of Amsterdam. He was someone who knew a lot but, like most of his colleagues, wasn't very forthcoming. Truth be told, we weren't sure we could trust him. Had the agency sent him to find out how much *we* knew? Carefully, we sounded him out: say we got our hands on those NSA documents, would he review them with us to verify information?

His reaction was one of fury. 'I can't trust you. I'm wasting my time with this,' he spat back. Apparently, he'd expected us to hand him the documents there and then. He wanted loyalty from our side and was sick of 'being treated this way'. The meeting was over almost before it began. Shaken, we downed our coffee and sparkling water.

As we were leaving, the man paused and gave us a look. 'Why are you flying to Brazil through Portugal?' We stared back at him in shock. Now that I'd connected with Greenwald, Steven and I had to work out how to exchange the documents. No one, not even our families and friends, knew when and how we were flying to Rio. We hadn't booked our tickets through the newspaper and didn't have them sent to our email addresses. How could our source possibly know our itinerary? Before I could ask, he was gone.

The incident left us both with a bad feeling. This source seemed to be after information from *us*. But on whose behalf did he want it? It also seemed strange for him to demand loyalty from us after talking only a couple times.

That Saturday morning, 2 November 2013, those uneasy feelings returned. This time, in my own home.

The evening before, my internet had suddenly cut out. Steven and I were messaging over a secure channel, me on a purpose-bought, old, reformatted Windows laptop with basic word-processing capability and little else. From a USB drive I launched the Tails OS and an anonymous internet browser, and then a messaging application with encryption. I signed onto a chat channel where Steven could find me under an alias. At his end, Steven followed all the same steps. Then, abruptly, the connection was lost.

I texted Steven to say I couldn't talk any more. But my internet didn't come back. Not the next day either, although there were no known disruptions. My modem was still working fine, only the white router that beamed a Wi-Fi signal into my living room had flatlined. Resetting it had no effect, nor did randomly pressing buttons. I didn't get as much as a flicker – it was stone-cold dead.

When I called Steven to tell him about my internet, he immediately interrupted me. 'Weird, mine stopped working, too. My modem's dead.' Steven had no separate router, so his modem – a Siemens – transmitted the wireless signal. But now he was in the same bind, with no known network issues and a modem that was suddenly about as responsive as a rock.

What were the chances? Two devices fail at the exact same moment, one in Amsterdam, the other in Rotterdam, a week before our second flight to Rio to get the documents from Greenwald. Everyone I mentioned it to agreed it couldn't be a coincidence. Like Belgian cryptographer Bart Preneel. 'They probably tried to install malware on your Wi-Fi routers, made the same mistake twice and broke something.' Unnerved, I asked, 'And who are "they"?' Preneel's guess: 'A professional hacker working for an intelligence service.'

Security experts suggested the NSA. Someone had copied hundreds of thousands of top-secret documents, after all, and they wanted to assess the damage. Back then, I couldn't imagine the full ramifications for the NSA and its relations with European counterparts. Still, it didn't seem far-fetched to think this powerful agency would want to keep tabs on any journalist with potential access to those files, and so wound up in a flat in Amsterdam-West.

Gradually it was dawning on me that this was a whole different world. Now, just before my second trip to Rio de Janeiro, I'd personally experienced agencies' spectacular ability to remotely infiltrate, hack and tap machines anywhere in the world. And, apparently, they had a thing for routers. Which makes sense: routers occupy a prime spot on the network, where all internet traffic passes through. But that's not all. Plug *any* device into the internet and a decent intelligence outfit can always crack it, wherever it may be. Distance no longer matters.

My questions about the NSA documents instantly made me a person of interest to these agencies. The head of the AIVD came to the *NRC Handelsblad* in person to warn that possession of state secrets could have consequences for us. The MIVD filed for an injunction to block us from publishing a story. From oblivious spectator, I'd suddenly become somebody in this world.

The Snowden documents spelled out what nobody was willing to tell me: that technology has made it impossible to keep information safe. That the American NSA had been infiltrating hundreds, soon to be millions, of foreign computer systems. That the Dutch AIVD started hacking operations as far back as 2000. Even before the introduction of the euro, before 9/11, Dutch government agencies were intercepting and reading people's emails in places far outside the Netherlands. And, even then, virtual identities were being used to spy. Later, the AIVD started covertly infiltrating web forums that were spreading jihadist texts. Meanwhile, its military counterpart the MIVD had access to over a thousand foreign computer systems. Nobody ever noticed.

This new world, I realised on that Saturday in November 2013, is digital. It's a world in which the possibilities are boundless and the rules are unclear. What are the implications for security? That's something we'd experience after our second trip to Brazil.

2

Total Blackout

I was back in Rio, where Steven and I had just met Greenwald for the handover. When we went to open the first Snowden files in our hotel room at Rio's Benidorm Palace, we were bursting with excitement. This was it. Finally, we would read what was never meant to be revealed. The door to the hotel room locked, we opened our laptops.

But instead of typing, we found ourselves frowning at diagrams and descriptions, at terms like 'PSTN', 'MySQL', 'CNE', 'Sigad', 'Thuraya' and 'CERF Call'. The frustrating thing about stepping into a new world is that you find out how little you understand. What we were looking at was technical jargon – mostly, we eventually surmised, code names and techniques. What they referred to depended on the context.

Their sheer complexity became apparent when we pulled up a file about a tool that Dutch intelligence specialists had presented to their American colleagues. The Americans were obviously impressed. They wrote that the Dutch tool was 'at a very high level'. But what exactly was it that the Dutch could do?

The document says they were acquiring 'MySQL databases via CNE access'. We googled some more. MySQL turned out to be an application for building and managing databases. It saves all a user's messages together with their login times, IP address and password. With that information, the agency could track down users' real identities. CNE is short for computer network exploitation, which is IT-speak for hacking. So, basically, this document described how the AIVD was gaining access to a web forum, vacuuming up the whole database and then picking through it to see who was active there. We were pretty sure that was illegal. It was just one of the many loose ends we had to verify.

And that wasn't all. The AIVD was also using the database for other things. According to the NSA notes, 'They're looking at marrying up the forum data with other social network info, and trying to figure out good ways to mine the data that they have.' Data mining. Yet another new term. It means the automated analysis of data to discover user patterns. And, more crucially, to track down the individuals behind those usernames.

One way to do that is to combine so much data that cross-links emerge, such as when someone logs onto Facebook and a particular web forum at the same time, using their real name on Facebook and an alias on the forum. The more data, the clearer the correlation.

When we published the document in the *NRC* on our return, the ensuing public debate centred on one question: was the AIVD allowed to do this? Privacy and legal experts said no. The agency was gathering the data of thousands of users, including people who hadn't done anything wrong. The AIVD said yes. A year later, after conducting its own inquiry, the Dutch regulatory body that oversees the agency found multiple instances where it had acted 'unlawfully'.

Our front-page story and the controversy it sparked were characteristic of the pieces I'd write over the following months. Most concerned legality and the impacts on citizens who weren't breaking any rules. The question being: is this allowed? And, what's the scale of the privacy violations? For a journalist these were the central questions to ask. And yet they rang hollow, because they focused on the abnormal rather than the everyday. They didn't illuminate the underlying causes: how the internet is put together, how that makes it attractive to spies and how it puts ordinary users at risk.

This is partly a weakness of journalism. Journalists like to write about what's new and original. It's new that the AIVD is hacking web forums, and if what they're doing is illegal it's also a scandal. All kinds of people and politicians want to weigh in with an opinion, and that's followed by measures (which means more news) and possibly political consequences (still more news).

It also has to do with a big societal blind spot. Reading these documents and talking to people was opening my eyes to all the weak links in this traffic network, and to the fact that everything we plug into it – telephones, laptops, security cameras – can be monitored by others. Like a magnet, this worldwide network attracts organisations, corporations and governments eager to tack on their products and services. That introduces even more weak spots and throws even more interests into the mix – security agencies first and foremost.

But does anyone care how this thing actually works? Or about the impact on society? It reminds me of a famous clip Dutch cinematographer Frans Bromet recorded back in 1998. In his distinct nasal voice he asked people on the street how they felt about mobile phones, still a new phenomenon at the time. Did they want one? Almost unanimously, nobody did. 'I'd hate it if people could reach me all the time,' one lady replied. But mobile phones arrived anyway, and smartphones soon after. They were a stupendous success. And that's how it's gone with all kinds of advances in this digital age: we're resistant at first, but hesitation swiftly gives way until we end up with broad-based acceptance. Say, of electronic personal health records.

As I worked my way through the NSA documents at home or in a separate office in the newspaper's editorial department, and as I tried to get my head around the technical terminology, it felt as if I was entering a room with all the lights turned off. Somewhere inside that darkness was a web of technology in which an invisible war was raging.

The more I read, the more questions arose. How do hackers hack? How could the AIVD sneak from its headquarters in Zoetermeer onto a web forum somewhere else? What did this mean for the contract between citizens and government, and for democracy? The topic had wormed its way under my skin. When I went out for a jog, when I lay awake long past midnight, these questions continued to go around in my head.

In the conversations I had in the following months and years, one story came up time and time again. It's a story that took place in Holland, in 2011.

*

The story begins with Aart Jochem. A forty-six-year-old computer specialist and national government crisis adviser, he's the kind of man who doesn't panic easily. He heads a team of IT experts at GovCERT, the Dutch government's Computer Emergency Response Team.

Aart Jochem studied computer engineering at The Hague's technical college in the 1980s, followed by a graduate degree in electrical engineering and computer architecture at Delft University of Technology. Those were the days of the first Macs and the fall of the Berlin Wall.

When he joined the team at GovCERT in 2007, it was a rather stuffy organisation tasked with drafting security recommendations for Dutch government ministries. Aart Jochem was a serious, level-headed professional. Colleagues liked his affability, innovative drive and terrific knowledge of information security. And that he'd held on to the idealism of the eighties and nineties, believing technology exists to give the people more freedom.

In the four years, eight months and thirty days Jochem had worked at GovCERT, he never felt things were sliding beyond his control – until the evening of 31 August 2011. It was parents' evening at his kids' school. Jochem felt bound to attend, but when he arrived he couldn't think what had possessed him to come. His body was pumping with adrenaline, yet he couldn't tell anyone what was going on.

Flashback to two days earlier. Jochem is sitting in GovCERT's oval conference room when Hans Petri, a co-worker, walks in. Instantly, he knows something is wrong. Petri has been on watch duty and manning the helpline. He's white as a sheet, moustache trembling. Jochem has never seen him like this.

Petri tells him about a post on a Google forum. An Iranian is reporting that when he went to open Gmail he got a Google Chrome message warning him it wasn't safe. The man doesn't know what's wrong exactly, but suspects someone is posing as Gmail.

Specialists at the German CERT, GovCERT's counterpart, have seen the post, too, and they also think it looks suspicious. According to them, however, the source of the problem isn't at Google in Iran or the United States, but in Beverwijk, North Holland. More specifically, at a company called DigiNotar. The Germans notify GovCERT straight away.

Jochem and his team are at a complete loss. He takes a whiteboard and writes *Information we have?* and *Possible scenarios?* at the top. 'Anyone?' Silence. For what seems ages, the whiteboard stays blank. Meanwhile, the team rushes to find out what DigiNotar does and how important it is. Slowly, information starts to trickle in. DigiNotar, it turns out, is in the business of issuing digital certificates. Extremely important certificates. Evidently someone has managed to duplicate these certificates so well that it's impossible to distinguish the fakes from the real thing. And that, Aart Jochem knows, is bad. Because digital certificates are the building blocks of the internet: take one out and the whole thing could come tumbling down.

*

The internet is a chain of computers held together by websites, search engines and browsers. The problem is, not all websites in that network can be trusted. What looks like the national tax authority's website might belong not to the tax authority but to criminals trying to steal login data. We have a system to solve that. Whenever a user goes to a website, their web browser checks if the site is legitimate.

Google (Chrome), Microsoft (Explorer) and Firefox (Mozilla) don't actually perform this check themselves: they outsource it to companies, like DigiNotar, that issue certificates. The system is comparable to a notary who verifies that parties to a transaction are who they say they are. DigiNotar is a digital notary firm that checks who the website you visit belongs to and if that website can be trusted.

Now, there are hundreds, if not thousands, of these certificate authorities, or CAs for short. Big players like Google trust a couple of hundred. They are known as root CAs, and have extra status that lets them not only certify whether any website can be trusted but also confer trusted status on other CAs – almost like super-notaries. DigiNotar belongs to that exclusive group. Giants like Microsoft and Google are wholly reliant on their authority. And therein lies a vulnerability. If someone manages to fake a super-notary's certificate, that person can pose as a trusted website and steal internet users' communications and data.

That's something Tony de Bos knows, too. A big man whose gelled crewcut lends him a boyish look, De Bos was one of DigiNotar's co-founders in 1998. As the country embraced the internet, his company grew, from a handful of employees, to twenty-plus, to fifty. In that time, the organisation traded its first modest premises in the heart of Beverwijk for a spacious office building at the edge of town.

It's here that from 2008 onwards De Bos had his best years. Digital communication was expanding with online buying, internet banking, e-government portals and interconnected devices. Where the work of traditional notaries was diminishing, De Bos's business was booming. Everybody needed his certificates.

DigiNotar was a reputable organisation. Its impressive security measures earned it high marks and never failed to impress its customers and visitors. In light of the importance of its certificates,

DigiNotar carefully guarded the process of issuing them and designed an almost military system to keep intruders out. All incoming internet traffic was scanned. The computer network was split up into several closed clusters. All certificate requests were subject to the 'four-eyes principle', meaning separate approval by two employees.

Once approved, the certificate was issued in a secure environment and authenticated with a digital seal, which required an employee to physically stick a smartcard in a computer. That computer stood in a high-security area about half the size of the average living room. To get inside, the employee had to proceed through a series of doors operated by special electronic passes. For each successive door there were fewer people with access authorisation. The innermost room was protected by reinforced steel doors that could only be opened using hand biometric authentication and entry of a PIN code. This futuristic vault constituted the centrepiece of DigiNotar.

Precautions had been taken for every worst-case scenario. A generator would take over if the power went out. There was even a complete replica of the system inside a secured bunker at Schiphol Airport – in case an aeroplane ever crashed onto the building.

*

Suffice to say, when Aart Jochem and his team hear there's a fake certificate in circulation, it comes as a shock. Even worse is that it's for Google: clearly, this hacker is playing for high stakes. While Jochem and his colleagues try to learn more, the Iranian's post begins to spread. That's when Ronald Prins sees it. Prins is the founder of Fox-IT and a Twitter devotee who's never without his mobile phone. His cryptographic expertise has made him an authority on cybersecurity and his penchant for wading into online discussions has been great for business. On Twitter, Prins hints at the potential repercussions of this Google post, observing that if someone has managed to falsify DigiNotar certificates, the damage will be off the charts. It would be, says Prins, 'a catastrophe'.

Tony de Bos sees the Twitterstorm, too. Earlier in the year he'd sold DigiNotar to US-based Vasco for €3.7 million. It was a stellar deal and another testament to his firm's increasing value. As one of its two shareholders, the sale will bring De Bos a tidy sum, and on paper he's a millionaire. He has already received a portion of the payment, just over €1.4 million, and the rest will follow in a couple of months. That is, barring any catastrophe.

Phone calls start flooding in. Customers are upset and want to know what's going on. Briefly, De Bos thinks back to a few months earlier. While he was away on holiday, there was some kind of fuss at the office. A hack was mentioned. He had asked if he should cut short his trip. 'No need,' came the reply; the incident had been dealt with. Now, customers want to know if DigiNotar can still be trusted. 'Of course,' he reassures them. De Bos has absolute faith in his organisation and all the safety precautions in place. Nevertheless, that evening he phones Ronald Prins and asks him to investigate. Just to be sure. An authority on this sort of business, Prins is just the man to confirm there's nothing strange going on at DigiNotar.

The two men haven't yet formulated a plan when Google issues a public statement. Visitors to all websites that use DigiNotar certificates will receive an alert warning them that the site's security certificate is not trusted and that someone is impersonating Google to intercept emails and documents. The impact of Google's statement could hardly be worse. Now the whole world knows there's a problem at DigiNotar.

At precisely nine o'clock on Tuesday morning, Aart Jochem calls Tony de Bos. It turns out he's sitting right next to Ronald Prins. The Fox-IT boss wants DigiNotar to be absolutely open about what's going on. Reluctantly, De Bos has taken his advice to immediately publish Fox-IT's findings. By now there's a crowd of people poking around the office. Fox-IT research staff have been questioning De Bos about the network structure, installing sensors and examining the vault, and the first lawyer has arrived to take stock of the effects on the acquisition.

Aart Jochem is desperate for answers. What does this all mean? He and his team are still fumbling in the dark. They know the Google post is serious. They know someone has managed to fake a DigiNotar certificate, get inside its heavily guarded vault and sign a certificate using the smartcard. But who? It could be anyone: a mole inside the company itself, or a hacker, or a hostile state. They have to figure out fast how this could have happened.

But until they have answers, the only thing Jochem can do is try to limit the damage. That means getting all DigiNoUtar certificates replaced so that people can still safely access government websites.

The escalating crisis is a reality check. The Dutch government is caught totally unprepared. It's 2011, and nobody knows how vital this one company is for the nation's internet. OPTA, the independent governmental body tasked with enforcing Dutch law on telecommunication, post and cable TV services, ought to know. But it has outsourced DigiNotar audits to PricewaterhouseCoopers, and they mainly look at a company's organisational structure, not its technology.

Aart Jochem will have to improvise. He has no mandate whatsoever. His team doesn't even know if they're allowed to talk to Ronald Prins. Officially, GovCERT is only supposed to provide solicited assistance to government organisations – a curious limitation for an entity charged with overseeing and advising national agencies. Now the phone's ringing off the hook and the team is feeling the heat from all sides. The Ministry of the Interior wants to know which government websites use DigiNotar certificates, software providers like Google want to know if their users are still safe online and other CERTs all over the world want to know what to tell *their* governments.

Erik de Jong, who handles communication with GovCERT's major partners, has no idea either what he can and can't disclose about DigiNotar. What he does know is that if Google and Microsoft decide to blacklist the firm and its certificates, the damage will be untold. As it stands, he can't even get a handle on which organisations in Holland rely on DigiNotar. Thankfully, De Jong has built up good ties with Microsoft and Mozilla. He's been on the phone to them daily, begging them to hold off just a tiny bit longer. Please, he says, don't pull the plug on DigiNotar all at once: 'We don't know yet what the consequences will be for this country.'

That's an understatement. Officials at every level are clueless. One asks Erik de Jong who owns Firefox. Firefox is an open-source project; it has no owner. And Erik Akerboom, the national counter-terrorism co-ordinator and chair of the Cyber Security Council, doesn't even know what digital certificates are.

As if that's not enough, this digital crisis is also sparking a culture clash. On the one hand are hierarchical government agencies accustomed to imposing decisions from the top, and on the other are organisations of technical experts like GovCERT, where management relies on specialists who know what's what.

*

On Wednesday, two days after the incident is first reported, it's still anybody's guess who broke into DigiNotar's vault. In The Hague it's another early start for Aart Jochem, who has barely slept. At 9 a.m. he's back on the phone with Tony de Bos and Ronald Prins in Beverwijk. They're joined by Fox-IT researcher Frank Groenewegen. The hacking expert with the distinctive curly hair and thick-rimmed glasses was onsite until after midnight, only to return to Beverwijk in his Seat Altea this morning. He's placing sensors to monitor internet traffic and trying to get an impression of the network. He's also been up to the second floor and inside the building's futuristic vault.

Then a colleague draws his attention to a network cable stretching the length of the office: a grey internet cable of the kind used to connect computers to modems. It's lying on the floor, neatly tucked under a cord cover. Following the cable, Groenewegen discovers that one end runs to a computer inside the vault. The other is plugged into workstation DIGIWS146.

DIGIWS146 is a special workstation, sitting at the precise dividing line between the office network and the secure network of the vault. This computer initiates the issue of certificates by sending an encrypted request to the secure network. An employee then enters the vault to check and sign the digital certificate and sends it back to the same workstation. In the interests of security, it's all strictly one-way traffic, with a direct link from the vault to DIGIWS146, but not the other way around. A firewall makes sure of that.

And yet, lying at Groenewegen's feet is a second grey cable leading straight from DIGIWS146 into the vault. That cable means two-way traffic. It lets anyone who can access this computer hop right onto the vault's secure network. A firewall won't stop them. And inside the vault is the computer that issues and authenticates certificates. This single network cable renders all those security measures useless, enabling a hacker who can infiltrate workstation DIGIWS146 from outside to slip in and out of the vault as they please. Groenewegen stares at it in dismay.

When he asks office staff how the cable came to be there, they explain that the physical steps involved in the vault procedure were too time-consuming. Getting in and out took ten to fifteen minutes every time. Plus, they complain, it's freezing inside. They decided to make it easier on themselves by hooking up another cable and configuring workstation DIGIWS146 to directly access the secure network and 'sign' certificates from there. And the smartcard needed to sign certificates inside the vault? They solved that by leaving it in the vault computer.

The discovery of the additional cable puts the situation at DigiNotar in a whole new light. For one thing, it makes a digital break-in more likely. It's also bad news for Tony de Bos, because he must have known about this flouting of security procedures. Later, old emails will surface revealing lots of internal discussions about workstation DIGIWS146. It doesn't look good for the company's sale. A judge will eventually rule that tampering with network cables voids the guarantee, meaning De Bos has to repay Vasco the money he'd already received.

De Bos will barely recover from this blow. Years later, he's still struggling to come to terms with his company's downfall. He refuses to answer questions, citing a 'confidentiality agreement'. All he's prepared to say is that these events affected his life in ways that 'influence my actions to this day'.

Forty miles away, Aart Jochem has also received some bad news. After convening a meeting of a group of specialists from the Dutch Tax and Customs Administration and Port Authority of Rotterdam to clarify where DigiNotar fits into the scheme of things, he learns the firm is considerably more important than anybody realised. Take tax returns. Businesses use DigiNotar's certificates to sign their returns. If the returns can't be processed, they can't settle their VAT. Or take government salaries. Certificates are needed to pay the government workforce. That means national finances are in trouble.

Without digital certificates, the Port of Rotterdam will be frozen, too. A truck that comes to collect a container of mangos can't take the shipment if customs can't process the registration. For that, customs uses DigiNotar certificates. Since the container can't go anywhere, the mangos will be left to rot.

Aart Jochem can't shake off the image of those mangos rotting away in a container. My God, he thinks, the whole country is dependent on those certificates from Beverwijk. If Microsoft or Google suddenly decide to revoke them, all computer communication in Holland will cease. Companies won't be able to file VAT returns, debit cards will be useless, trucks won't be able to supply goods. The entire system will be paralysed. It would be a national disaster.

Yet, despite all that, Aart Jochem goes to his son's parents' evening. He and Erik de Jong have arranged to take turns so they can both get some rest, and they jokingly agree that whoever's on duty at midnight will compose a haiku for the morning shift – to provide a little levity. But levity is the last thing Jochem is feeling. Sitting among the other parents, his mind's a complete blank.

*

Two days later, Aart Jochem is looking into the frowning face of Interior Minister Piet Hein Donner. It's 10 p.m., Friday 2 September 2011. Outside, it's hot and humid. Inside the Ministry of Security and

Justice tower, next to The Hague's central railway station, several floors are still lit. Minister Donner has just arrived, dropped off by his driver, after receiving an urgent summons to the National Crisis Centre.

Jochem is seated across from the minister in an office off the crisis conference room, where dozens of officials are scrambling to prepare press releases and documents. He has ten minutes to tell Minister Donner what he knows, in the clearest possible terms. The minister, a starchy jurist, isn't exactly noted for his knowledgeability about this part of his portfolio.

After the network cable was discovered, things started moving quickly. Signs of a breach were found on DigiNotar's web servers, which were operating software that hadn't been updated in six months. That let the hacker infiltrate the office network and workstation DIGIWS146, from which – probably to his own surprise – he could slip right into the vault. On 10 July the hacker created his first fake certificate. A further 530 followed. He went straight for the biggest fish, making counterfeit certificates for Amazon, Microsoft, Google, the website of the British MI5 security service, the CIA, a host of Dutch organisations and Mossad, Israel's national intelligence agency. All courtesy of Beverwijk.

DigiNotar had been compromised at every level. The hacker also obtained access to computers that issue certificates for the Dutch government, including the Ministry of Security and Justice, and the Dutch Bar Association, Renault and Delft University of Technology. Not only is internet traffic to and from government sites now suspect, but so is all communication between Dutch government services.

That idea triggers panic among government personnel. For them, this is an intangible crisis. Aart Jochem is one of the few people who understands the repercussions. Another is the Interior Ministry's director general Uijlenbroek, and together they take the lead. But then, on Friday, after consulting with the state advocate, Uijlenbroek decides to take the reins from GovCERT. Just like that, the cyber support team is sidelined.

For Erik de Jong this comes as a shock. All week he's been on the phone to Microsoft, Google, Mozilla, pleading with them to put off revoking the certificates just a little longer. He has had a constant feed on the deteriorating situation at DigiNotar. Then, just as they get a handle on the disaster in store, he's closed out. The state advocate forbids GovCERT from even speaking to anyone.

Nevertheless, De Jong makes one last round of calls. To Mozilla, telling them he's no longer allowed to talk. Then to Microsoft, where concerns are greatest. The American software giant's credibility is at stake. For days, customers and users have been asking why Microsoft isn't revoking DigiNotar certificates when it's clear the Dutch tech firm is in chaos. De Jong knows this conversation is critical. So, defying the state advocate's orders, he tells them the whole story. He explains the severity of the situation, what the Dutch government plans to do and what the impact of revoking the certificates would be. That the whole country would crash to a halt. A total blackout. All he can do now is appeal to their better natures. Please, he says one last time, wait just a little longer.

At 4.30 that afternoon Aart Jochem gets on the phone to the country's chief security officer, Erik Akerboom. Over in Delft, Fox-IT has just presented an initial report on the situation at DigiNotar, and it's alarming in the extreme. DigiNotar is leaking like a sieve.

Akerboom immediately activates the national crisis plan. This will be the first time that the National Crisis Centre, established in 2004, has been mobilised in a cyber-emergency. At 5 p.m. Aart Jochem steps off the tram at Schedeldoekshaven in The Hague for a crisis meeting at the Ministry of the Interior. There the plan is explained to him: the Dutch government will take control of DigiNotar and replace its certificates to prevent system failures. In the meantime, web users will receive a warning that sites protected by DigiNotar certificates should no longer be trusted.

Aart Jochem then spends the next few hours explaining to government officials what a digital certificate is and why DigiNotar's downfall is bad, potentially catastrophic. Director General Uijlenbroek makes multiple calls to DigiNotar's owner, Vasco, trying to convince the company to 'voluntarily' cede control. If they don't, the mess at the tech firm will bring the government to a crashing halt and it will be up to Vasco to clean it up. Finally, around midnight, the Americans give in.

So now Aart Jochem is sitting across from Minister Donner and Security and Justice Minister Ivo Opstelten. He has ten minutes to brief them on how certificates work, before Donner goes out to hold a press conference. Jochem pauses, thinks, looks Donner in the eye. There are no houses on fire, no tunnel has collapsed, no one has died. Somehow he has to make it clear why the government must intervene at DigiNotar.

He starts his explanation to the two ministers with a metaphor: paper passports. All over the world we've all agreed to trust them. They contain security features to guard against forgery. Now imagine, he says, that a trusted issuer of passports is hacked and can produce fakes that are indistinguishable from the real thing. As a result, none of the passports they issue can be trusted any longer. That's the situation we're in. Only in our case it's systems and websites. You don't know if the website you're on is real. Or whether the electronic signature you put on a document is authentic. Donner listens attentively.

A couple of hours later, at around midnight, Jochem watches anxiously from the sidelines as Minister Donner launches into the press conference, reading from some papers. He says the government is taking control of DigiNotar because it can no longer guarantee the security of crucial government certificates. Then come the questions and he has to respond off the cuff. When a reporter from the country's biggest news network insists on details about the impact of the hack, the minister draws a comparison. 'It's a system whereby you can be sure that the postbox you use on the internet really is the postbox of the organisation you want.' And because the government can't vouch for its reliability right now, Donner advises against using government websites.

Aart Jochem relaxes: the minister understood. Satisfied and exhausted, he takes a taxi home.

*

And that's how Minister Donner, a politician in his sixties with a slightly stuffy image, becomes the face of the country's first digital crisis. He convincingly makes the case that the government is taking over DigiNotar and that it's in control. Behind the scenes, though, panic still reigns. The State of the Netherlands officially asks Microsoft to postpone revoking DigiNotar certificates. The American company agrees, taking the unprecedented decision to do an update but to skip all Dutch computers. Holland is given a week and a half to replace the certificates.

A nationwide blackout has been narrowly avoided, but the aftershocks will be felt for a long time to come. DigiNotar exposed the fragility of the worldwide network: a single weak link endangers the entire system. It doesn't matter where the weak link is, whether in Beverwijk, Buenos Aires or Beijing. The story of DigiNotar helped me better to grasp the complexity of this traffic network. How impossible it is to monitor. How hopelessly outdated the government's knowledge and understanding. And how vulnerable its users.

In the years after this, Google, Microsoft and Mozilla will all build additional safeguards into their systems so as to be less dependent on firms like DigiNotar that issue certificates on their behalf. As a consequence, Google and Microsoft grow even more powerful. In the Netherlands, GovCERT will be reorganised into the National Cyber Security Centre (NCSC). The Dutch government will decide it needs an overview of critical infrastructure – a map of key points in its traffic network.

The NCSC's mandate hardly changes. It's still restricted to an advisory role, like a referee who's allowed to blow his whistle but can't hand out red or yellow cards. A year after the DigiNotar incident, the Dutch Safety Board trots out the usual government recommendation: administrators need training. They need to better understand the digital world.

In all that time, one question goes unanswered. Who broke into DigiNotar, and why? Subsequent years yield no more than partial answers and possible scenarios. The full story goes untold.

*

The first clue lies within DigiNotar's own network. Whenever we visit a 'secure' website – indicated by a padlock icon in the address bar – we're using what's called an SSL certificate. This certificate creates a secure channel between the user and the site. These days most sites have SSL certificates, but in 2011 only trailblazing companies and organisations with a real need had them, like the tax authorities and banks, and Google.

When you go to a site with an SSL connection, such as Google, your web browser performs a superfast check with the certificate issuer if that certificate is still valid. A so-called OCSP responder takes care of this. It comes back with a status: the certificate is good, or it's been revoked, or it's invalid.

Researchers at Fox-IT knew a fake Google certificate existed and could see in the OCSP responder which web users had checked for such a counterfeit. Altogether, 300,000 IP addresses in one month. When the researchers then looked at where those IP addresses were located, they got a shock. Almost all were in Iran.

In 2011 Iran witnessed an unprecedented number of demonstrations. It, too, was affected by the Arab Spring that swept through the Middle East. The country's leaders responded to the unrest with a violent crackdown, censorship of the internet and by blocking Western services such as Twitter, Facebook and Gmail. All to suppress the incipient uprising. Dozens died.

The Dutch researchers discovered that someone had forged a Google certificate, so 300,000 Iranians who assumed they were surfing on Google wound up on a fake Google site. As a result, another party had access to their logins, emails, locations and documents. It's almost certain that those 300,000 Iranians included individuals critical of the regime. They thought they were communicating securely through Gmail, but walked straight into a trap. All because of an extra cable in Beverwijk.

For the National High Tech Crime Unit, a specialist division of the Netherlands' police created in 2007, DigiNotar was its first major espionage case. Copies of the firm's computer servers were loaded into their vans for examination at the national police headquarters in Driebergen, near Utrecht.

Tracking down the culprit was complicated. And dull. It meant hours of scrolling through logs – through series of numbers stored in computers that recorded everyone who had connected to DigiNotar – and then trying to spot irregularities. Essentially, the method wasn't all that different from solving a physical break-in. It was all about hunting for clues.

The High Tech Crime Unit knew the attacker got in through DigiNotar's website, which had outdated software. Picking through the web server files in search of traces left by the hacker, investigators ultimately identified three suspicious addresses: one in Iran, a second in England and a third in Russia. Which immediately created a problem, because in none of those three countries was the Netherlands allowed to conduct its own investigations. The internet may not be constrained by national borders, but the police most certainly are. Investigation services are not free to go nosing around in foreign data centres. All they could do was send a mutual legal assistance request for a copy of the computer server. Though the Netherlands had no mutual legal assistance treaty with Iran, it did with England and Russia.

The National Crime Agency in the UK swiftly delivered a copy of the computer in England. The Russians agreed to prepare a copy to download from the Netherlands but, for reasons never explained, never did. Weeks later, specialists in a delegation from Russia's Federal Security Service, the FSB, dropped off a physical copy on a visit to Driebergen.

The investigators were closing in. Data from the English and Russian computers showed they'd both occasionally also connected to a server in the Netherlands. These three computer servers outside Iran appeared to constitute the tools of the hacker's attack. The Dutch IP address was traced to Leaseweb, one of the biggest internet hosting services worldwide. And that was a stroke of luck for the Dutch police, because a server in the Netherlands was a server they could tap.

In the autumn of 2011 a police team set out for an industrial park just outside Haarlem, to a grey warehouse with a serious fences and cameras above the entrance. Inside, the data centre's 430,000 square feet were sectioned into aisles of racks piled with humming computers. In the event of a power failure, three fuel tanks filled with 13,200 gallons of diesel stood ever ready to feed a generator for up to forty-eight hours.

It was familiar ground for the police. They even had a server with tapping software set up and waiting whenever the need arose. Making the connection was child's play: just a matter of locating the server in question, plugging in some cables, rerouting internet traffic and then directing it to their own headquarters in Driebergen. And with the court having already approved the tapping order – containing only an IP address – Leaseweb was obligated to co-operate. At lunchtime they all went out for a bite together, the police officers and the technicians from Leaseweb, to a local pub with slot machines in the same industrial park.

Over chicken and chips, talk turned to what was going on. The hacker had leased a server at Leaseweb and connected to it through a virtual private network. VPNs are widely used both in business and privately to encrypt data as it travels over public networks. A VPN tunnel creates an anonymous connection between a private network and an external network. You and I might use it to, say, watch Netflix series that aren't available in our home countries. You connect to a VPN server back home, which fools Netflix into thinking you're still in your own country. In this case, the hacker had trusted his VPN connection to shield him in the same way. What he didn't realise was that Dutch law enforcement had located the VPN server and was now monitoring all his traffic.

Also, the hacker got sloppy. Looking at the tapped data, the High Tech Crime Unit noticed he'd gone on Facebook using the same VPN tunnel. Furthermore, the IP address used matched one found in the server data from the UK, where on one single occasion the hacker logged in from his own computer. A fatal misstep, it turned out. When the police laid the two IP addresses side by side they could see both used the same browser (Firefox) in the same version and with the same language settings (Persian). They could also see which

Facebook profile the user was logging into: it belonged to an Iranian man in his twenties. From there, it took seconds to track down his name and address.

A lone wolf, the investigators initially concluded. They forwarded his name and address to the FBI in the United States and to the services in Israel, where the hacker had also targeted companies. The profile appeared to fit. Under an alias, the same individual had previously claimed responsibility and that he'd been operating alone. He'd also left behind a message in Persian in DigiNotar's systems. 'I will sacrifice my soul for my leader,' it read.

But when investigators went to map his IP address in Iran, suddenly things no longer looked so clear-cut. They discovered the hacker had been working out of a building on Imam Khomeini Street in downtown Tehran. This building wasn't on a university campus or in some residential neighbourhood, but on the grounds of the AJA, the army of the Islamic Republic of Iran.

The discovery immediately posed all kinds of new questions. Was this hacker working for someone else? How had he got into an Iranian army building? The police wanted to send a mutual legal assistance request to Iran to obtain information about the suspect. And that's when the High Tech Crime Unit was abruptly ordered to cease operations. Apparently, an AIVD staffer in charge of liaising between the police and the agency – a cunning and clever veteran of the service, not to mention the son of Second World War resistance fighters and a devout Christian – had balked. He informed the head of the National Crime Squad, Wilbert Paulissen, that he didn't want the police investigating any further. 'An absolute no go,' he told the team, without revealing what the AIVD knew.

The Ministry of Foreign Affairs was also opposed to continuing the investigation. It didn't want the hacker's name to be made public. Case closed, members of the High Tech Crime Unit were told. So, was all their work in vain? Answers weren't forthcoming. At least, not yet.

3

The Switzerland of the Surveillance World

Normally, I head out with my dark brown leather laptop bag strapped to the handlebars of my bike, iPhone in my inner coat pocket and earbuds in my ears. Not today. My bag was back at the *NRC Handelsblad*'s editorial office downtown, with my phone tucked in a side pouch.

I was on my way to meet a source. He was someone I'd spoken to on two previous occasions, but our last meeting had ended on a mysterious note. Next time he'd be able to explain something to me, he'd said. But there were conditions. I couldn't bring my mobile, I couldn't contact him by text or email, I had to meet him at the same place at the same time, I couldn't take notes and, if we saw anyone who looked suspicious, our meeting would break up.

We ordered a sparkling water and an iced tea. Whenever a waiter passed too close to our table, our conversation stopped abruptly.

My source glanced around warily, then leaned in again. The thing he wanted to explain to me concerned the AIVD. They had bugged the Iranian ambassador to the Netherlands, he said. Speaking in a whisper, he continued, 'We even knew when the poor guy was going to the bathroom.'

I felt a twinge of unease. This was the first time anyone had shared information with me about a covert operation. *So, this is how it works*, I thought. Once someone trusts you, you can learn secrets. I thanked my source and promised I wouldn't divulge his name anywhere.

It was a small step. The NSA documents had given me a firmer handle on the technology. We're dealing with a traffic network in which emails pass seven points on their way from a sender to a recipient. This network is growing increasingly congested and more complicated and the government doesn't necessarily know where the weak spots are. That's precisely what makes us vulnerable. Knowing this, it's logical to ask if agencies are combating these vulnerabilities or exploiting them. But to answer this question you need to find someone who's actually willing to talk.

My meeting with this source gave me hope. Evidently it was possible to expose a covert operation. But it wasn't enough; every journalist knows that one source doesn't make a story. However confident I personally felt about what my source had revealed, I couldn't print it in the paper until I had another source to confirm it. Another source who, like the first, would be bound by a non-disclosure agreement and could face years in prison for breaking it.

I spent weeks trying my luck with all kinds of people. The problem, though, is that agencies compartmentalise. To minimise the risk of leaks, employees can only access their own domains. And they can't go digging around in agency systems. Their every action is logged.

Once again, I reached out to people with inside knowledge of intelligence, inviting myself over or getting together for coffee at lay-bys and tennis clubs. I always guaranteed anonymity up front, promising their names would never appear in print. Frustrating as it was, there was no other option: without such an assurance they wouldn't even see me. Those that did agree to meet could barely bring themselves to talk. To break the ice, I'd tell them about my research and stress that I realised the possible consequences our conversation could have for them.

Finally, after weeks of fruitless meetings, my search paid off. Someone who could reasonably be expected to know seemed to corroborate what my source had said. Only he did it in such a roundabout way that it felt shaky. He spoke in hypotheses: 'Say the AIVD wanted to know what the Iranian ambassador was getting up to, then this would be an excellent method.' It was confusing. I went back to take another shot. But he answered in the same way. I talked it over with my boss, Jan Meeus. What were my options? Jan's conclusion: 'It must be a way to confirm the information *without* actually saying so.'

That had to be it. It let him confirm my information without implicating himself. This way, the disclosure couldn't be pinned on him. When I asked other sources about it, they laughed: it was an old trick. Finally, the piece could run. *AIVD Spied on Iranian Ambassador for Months*, the article's headline read. Years later, I would find out this had been just one thread in a much bigger story surrounding Iran, and a much bigger, invisible conflict. A conflict that had everything to do with DigiNotar and the aborted police investigation into the hack.

*

Before DigiNotar prompted a national crisis in 2011, two other situations were unfolding that, though apparently unrelated, would prove extremely significant.

The first was a mysterious attack on a nuclear facility in Iran. Over a period from 2007 to 2009, an advanced computer bug modified the controls of Iranian ultracentrifuges in a plant near the city of Natanz, some 200 miles south of Tehran. First, it caused pressure inside the centrifuges used for uranium enrichment to spike for no apparent reason. Plant technicians who saw it happen were baffled. Why hadn't their systems signalled a failure? Next, the bug caused hundreds of centrifuges to speed up. One by one, they spun themselves to pieces before the technicians' horrified eyes. Several Iranian scientists were sacked and it is estimated that Iran's nuclear weapons programme has been set back years.

This digital attack was a joint operation by US and Israeli intelligence. They worked on it for years. They came up with and wrote the sabotage virus, dubbed Stuxnet by analysts who studied it afterwards. Thought to be the first-ever offensive cyberweapon, Stuxnet inaugurated a new phase in digital warfare. Without a single American or Israeli soldier having set foot on Iranian soil, it launched a precision attack every bit as destructive as bombs dropped from a plane. In time, the virus would spread beyond the plant and run amok to infect thousands of computers.

The background to this operation was considerably more complex than is generally reported. The US and Israel weren't the only two countries interested in the facility at Natanz. In the early years of the new millennium, pretty much every Western agency had its attention trained on the nuclear plant buried beneath this rugged stretch of desert, including the Dutch AIVD and MIVD, reliable sources informed me in confidence.

These two Dutch agencies have separate roles. Where the AIVD is concerned with national security, the MIVD gathers intelligence for military operations and national defence. Internally, their cultures are different enough to cause frequent clashes. Mutual distrust makes both agencies reluctant to share information, but they do work together in some areas. One is the collection of nuclear intelligence.

The Netherlands has a long history in nuclear intelligence. Back in the 1970s, Pakistani atomic expert Abdul Qadeer Khan came to Holland to study nuclear physics. He worked at a research laboratory in Amsterdam for years, building a life in the Netherlands with his South African wife, making Dutch friends and learning the language. From time to time he also visited the eastern city of Almelo, where a uranium-enrichment facility operated by the British–German–Dutch consortium UCN used a process known as ultracentrifugation. Ultracentrifugation was a unique technology. No other country knew how to do it. Exporting the technology was therefore prohibited and surrounded by tight restrictions, but there were equally persistent attempts to dodge them.

In 1975, Khan failed to return from what was meant to be a short trip to Pakistan. Three years later Pakistan suddenly had the capability to build an atomic bomb. Khan went on to sell his atomic know-how to North Korea and Libya as well as Iran. Evidently, the man who'd embraced life in the Netherlands had turned against the West, and agencies in the Netherlands were mystified as to how it could have happened.

Thanks to Dutch ultracentrifugation expertise, by this time the AIVD and MIVD had decades-long experience with the process and materials used in uranium enrichment. According to my sources, the AIVD kept close tabs on the market, especially freight carriers that sometimes shipped falsely declared goods to countries like Pakistan and Iran. The agency had several partners in this effort, notably the American CIA, German BND, British MI5 and Israeli Mossad.

Whenever the AIVD noticed that one of these carriers – many of which were being tapped – was attempting to ship materials, an employee would notify it of the goods' true destination. In some cases, the agency would tamper with the shipment itself. So many products travelled through Schiphol Airport and the Port of Rotterdam that cargo or a container was easily detained. Say Iran purchased some aluminium pipes in the United Kingdom and had them shipped through Rotterdam. The AIVD might intercept the shipment, make minuscule, undetectable perforations in the pipes and then send them on their way. Because those pipes were designed to create a vacuum, a tiny hole rendered them useless, but the Iranians wouldn't discover the problem until after the pipes had been installed.

Another trick the AIVD used was to hide GPS trackers in packaging in order to see where goods went. In, for example, shipments of air pressure gauges, an essential component in missiles that not a single Middle Eastern country had the capability to make. Any time air pressure gauges bound for a country like Syria or Iran passed through Schiphol or Rotterdam, the agency would slip a tracker inside where it wouldn't be noticed. In exceptional cases, it would even tamper with the equipment's functionality. But that's risky with something like air pressure gauges, which are also used in passenger aircraft.

That Dutch security services engaged in sabotage surprised me. To my mind, that was something other countries did, such as the US, the UK, Israel and France, alongside China and certainly Russia. Apparently, the Netherlands was doing it, too.

Sabotage wasn't the AIVD's only tool. It also kept a close eye on Khan and his network. Like his daughter, who lived in Amstelveen, near Amsterdam. People who worked at the network's supply companies informed the agency whenever orders were placed. The CIA infiltrated the network as well, and there's every indication that by around the year 2000 the Western intelligence community was in on the plans for Natanz.

What set things in motion was an incident that took place in September 2003. A ship called MV *BBC China* was intercepted by the UK and the US en route from Dubai to Libya. On board they found thousands of ultracentrifuge parts. The world's media had a field day reporting how, in the nick of time, a Western intelligence coup had prevented Libya from launching a secret nuclear weapons programme. Muammar Gaddafi had been caught red-handed.

What went unreported is that this eleventh-hour foiled smuggling attempt owed everything to the Netherlands. As it happens, it was the Dutch AIVD that alerted UK intelligence to the shipment, which quickly devised a pretext for diverting the vessel to a southern Italian port. Also mostly unknown is what happened to the centrifuge parts after that.

The US wanted to seize the goods. The Netherlands objected, not wanting knowledge of the uranium-enrichment process to be exported, even to an ally like the United States. But the Netherlands had no one at the scene and the UK didn't care one way or another, so the Americans took everything home.

A few months later, the AIVD got a request from the CIA and Mossad. Such requests are made through official channels – through liaisons who act as links between their respective embassies and the Dutch agencies in The Hague. As partners of the AIVD, with profiles that are roughly the same, communication between these agencies tends to be direct. Now the CIA and Mossad liaisons wanted to know: could the Dutch help them at a facility south of Tehran? Or, in intelligence terms: could the AIVD 'generate access' to Natanz?

*

That this request would culminate years later in broken ultra-centrifuges in an underground Iranian plant was something no one could yet have foreseen. The year was 2004. The US, under President George Bush, had invaded Iraq the year before. Although the Iraqi invasion relied on conventional weapons – such as bombs and tanks – US intelligence had already started to undergo a transformation. Before it bombed Baghdad, American hackers had infiltrated Iranian army computers to pave the way.

This transformation began back in the late nineties, when the intelligence community discovered the internet. In 1997, when not even 2 per cent of the world's population had access to the World Wide Web, the NSA was putting together its first team of hackers. Other global superpowers swiftly followed. A year later, hackers in the former Soviet Union succeeded in infiltrating the computer systems of the Pentagon, NASA and other organisations in the US, swiping thousands of sensitive documents. Moonlight Maze, as this operation was called, took place the same year that Dutch people on the street told documentary maker Frans Bromet they couldn't imagine a life with mobile phones.

These years also saw the AIVD taking its first, albeit tentative, steps into the digital arena. Agency veterans had little affinity for the potential of this new technology and the impetus came mainly from outside – from newcomers such as a young hothead named Ronald Prins, whom the agency employed in 1998.

Prins was thoroughly enmeshed with computers and the emerging internet. Fascinated with scanners, eavesdropping and coded messaging, in the late eighties the maths student spent entire nights tuning his personal scanner to police channels in the precincts of The Hague. He even managed to snatch encrypted AIVD communications, to learn about criminals under police surveillance and about other covert operations.

When the lanky Prins arrived at the AIVD in 1998 with a degree in cryptography and expertise in encryption, he was taken aback. The agency was just making its first forays onto the internet, and, with a department staffed by a grand total of three people, it was obviously lagging behind in digitisation. That same year saw the agency carry out its first ever internet wiretap, of a suspected terrorist in coastal Zeeland. Technically, Prins could already access targets' mailbox content, but doing that wasn't yet legal. With a new intelligence and security services act in the making, Prins recommended adding provisions on hacking. Because hacking, as he informed colleagues, could become big.

Prins didn't stay long at the AIVD: just a year later, he was gone. But his presence flipped a switch and made people realise that a new era had dawned. Then, as now, the agency had directorates organised around democratic law and order, state security and special intelligence. Special intelligence was spread across several teams, including special operations and technology. Interception – eavesdropping – was the job of the technology team, and it was here that the biggest change was taking place.

Up until now the AIVD had recruited a large part of its workforce at universities, employing students still in their second or third year. The trick was to tempt those who had yet to graduate with a generous starting salary. That they'd never get paid more anywhere else helped cement a life-long commitment to the agency. But in 1998 the AIVD also began employing graduates who had taken their degrees. Erik Akerboom, who went on to become the national counter-terrorism co-ordinator and chief of the national police, was one. Another was Inge Bryan, who started out in the agency's technology team, later led the nuclear proliferation team and eventually rose to the top ranks of the police force before becoming head of the cyber risk team at Deloitte. Unlike college students, who moulded themselves to the existing organisational culture, these outside hires had their own ideas and weren't afraid to question entrenched practices.

When it came to computers, the AIVD was hopelessly naive and behind the times. In 2000 it had sixteen PCs, all of which used the search engine AltaVista to access open sources. They also had one computer given to them by the CIA that they didn't trust. Some employees wanted to throw it out immediately, but in the end they left only useless information on the machine until eventually they did get rid of it.

It was clear the AIVD needed to ramp up its computer skills. After considerable internal deliberation – and on the advice of Inge Bryan – the agency finally decided to employ hacker and internet expert Roland Vergeer. Vergeer changed the mindset, steering the agency away from a top-down, directorate-based approach towards one that was demand-driven and asked what kinds of information it theoretically ought to have.

Consequently, starting from about 2000, the AIVD's tactics changed. It began 'scraping' the internet: saving data from websites, online forms, open-web forums – basically everything it could get its hands on. This information was organised by topic. The agency was also starting to create virtual identities, inventing people with specific cultural backgrounds and online histories. For instance, a middle-aged Kurdish woman. If someone like this suddenly materialised on a web forum with no references to her name, it would look suspicious, so she needed an online past. Dozens of made-up people with bogus histories were thus ready to be deployed whenever operations required an online infiltrator.

The AIVD also got involved in data mining, combining telephone directory, wiretapping, chatroom, chamber of commerce and national land registry records. All kinds of connections could be teased out this way. As well as listening in on actual calls, agency personnel were also marrying that data with other data. So, while the general public was worried about the Millennium bug wreaking havoc with computers, the AIVD was already experiencing the value of metadata. By around the year 2000, despite a hesitant start, the Netherlands was among the digital frontrunners of the global intelligence community, alongside Israel, China, Russia, the US and the UK.

*

This transformation was still ongoing when the CIA and Mossad approached the Netherlands with their request to 'generate access' to Natanz. It made sense to ask the Dutch. The AIVD had a reputation for being small but capable and to all appearances relatively neutral – like the Switzerland of the surveillance world. Basically, the Netherlands wasn't that powerful a player. These qualities made it a preferred base of operations for the UK, too, which had multiple safe houses there.

What also helped was that the Dutch agency could more easily work under the radar. In Iran, Americans and Israelis stuck out. Furthermore, the AIVD enjoyed the latitude to act on its own initiative and was prized by the intelligence community for its inventiveness.

Iran had been targeted by the AIVD many times before. As far back as 2000, agency employees had breached the Iranian defence organisation's email systems out of Holland. This yielded useful information about the country's nuclear plans. It also explains why Western intelligence – most notably the CIA and Mossad – was so well informed about what was going on in Natanz. For example, that Iran was using IR-1 centrifuges, which were based on the stolen Dutch design for Pakistan's P1 centrifuges, and that this equipment used Siemens hardware. While Iran was still constructing the eight-foot walls of the complex and burying it under a layer of earth seventy-five feet deep, computer specialists from the US and Israel had already started crafting their computer bug. They had no intention of awaiting the outcome of diplomatic wrangling between the Iranians and the International Atomic Energy Agency (IAEA) – they wanted the capability to intervene instantly as and when they deemed it necessary.

The 2003 interception of MV *BBC China* was a stroke of luck precisely because it had aboard thousands of components for the same ultracentrifuge technology being used in Iran. It provided the US with the ideal material to test-drive its computer bug. While this helped to set things in motion, there was still one other obstacle to overcome: access to the facility itself. Not only was

Natanz hermetically sealed off from the outside world, its most sensitive networks were intentionally kept offline. What they needed was a mole.

Recruiting for a job like this is tricky. You need time, persuasiveness and in some cases cash. You also need false identities and fake companies. Putting all that together can take years. Little wonder, then, that in 2004 the CIA and Mossad were already turning to the AIVD. This marked the beginning of preparations for what would be the deployment of the world's first cyberweapon. Two years later, US President George Bush gave the official green light for Operation Olympic Games, and thus for the launch of Stuxnet.

Little of what transpired after that is publicly known. It's a fact that the Stuxnet virus struck at Natanz and that the AIVD played some kind of role, that it set up two front companies and recruited moles to infiltrate the facility. One front dead-ended because the recruit wasn't allowed in, but the other, an Iranian engineer posing as a mechanic, succeeded. The AIVD-recruited engineer managed to enter Natanz on this pretext on multiple occasions, the first sometime before the summer of 2007, and to collect information from the plant's internal network. Several updates of the Stuxnet virus were subsequently needed before it could be launched as planned. The engineer went back every few weeks or months to gather more information, and in the end to attempt to inject Stuxnet into the underground plant's computers. He claimed that he'd succeeded. One source, describing this dangerous operation, told me the Iranian engineer was 'the principal means of getting the virus inside Natanz'. Western intelligence sources also say the operation resulted in deaths. When the reports began filtering out about problems with the Natanz centrifuges, it came as no surprise to the AIVD. The launch of the world's first offensive cyberweapon had, after all, been made possible by the AIVD and 'their' engineer.

This is what had been happening when, in the summer of 2011, an Iranian infiltrated DigiNotar in the Netherlands. It wasn't a coincidence. After the Stuxnet attack, Iran retaliated. More than that, it became one the countries most active on the internet, successfully mounting attacks on a slew of Western targets. On US banks, where

Iranian hackers launched a series of distributed denial-of-service (DDoS) attacks that left Americans unable to access their money. It broke into the controls of a small dam in New York. It carried out cyberattacks on the United Nations. Also at universities, in the Netherlands and elsewhere. By unleashing a sabotage virus on Iran, the West had fired the opening shot of a digital arms race.

*

The second development that's crucial to understanding what happened at DigiNotar has to do with the AIVD itself.

The fact that I've been able to reconstruct this story at all is the fruit of many years spent cultivating the trust of intelligence sources. Years of frustration, in which I'd be making progress one day only to have sources go silent or refuse to meet the next. And of incomprehension, because very few people really grasp how agencies work and why they're so secretive. Even my colleagues.

I remember one conversation I had with *de Volkskrant* editor Philippe Remarque when at long last I'd managed to secure confirmation that Dutch far-right politician Geert Wilders was under investigation by the AIVD. It turned out they'd been running an inquiry on his ties within the Israeli Embassy.

Elated, I went to share my findings with Remarque. 'OK,' he cautiously replied, 'so what did the investigation turn up?'

'I'd love to know, but my sources won't say.'

'Can we take a look at the report?' he asked.

No, I explained again, that wouldn't be possible. There was almost no chance the AIVD itself would ever hand over documents. His face fell.

Of course I wanted more evidence and more information. But getting one source to talk was complicated enough, never mind two. And none would be willing to sneak out documents; even to try would be crazy. Everything they do is monitored.

At the side entrance of the AIVD's headquarters in Zoetermeer, employees have to stop for an iris scan. Smartphones aren't allowed inside. Too risky. There are also random checks. From time to time an alarm goes off and someone's belongings – bag, coat, shoes – are turned inside out. That happens to everyone on average five times a year.

The agency works with two computer systems, one for internal and another for external use. Technical experts have multiple systems. To search online, employees use anonymous browsers. To turn on computers, they need a pass card and password. All files are compartmentalised, which means you can't access anything without the proper authorisation. And searching for documents is pointless, because the really sensitive ones don't show up in the results.

What happens to people who copy files? Look at Edward Snowden. In 2015, the American whistleblower agreed to an interview with me and Dutch television reporter Eelco Bosch van Rosenthal and cameraman Joris Hentenaar. The whole endeavour required lots of stealth and secrecy and had to be arranged for us by a go-between. That Snowden agreed at all was remarkable, as he rarely talks to journalists in person. Following his instructions, we chose a hotel, arriving in Moscow a few days early to prepare, and gave our contact the room number. An hour before the appointed time, Snowden phoned the room to ask if he needed a keycard for the lift. We went down to the lobby to meet him, Eelco stationed at the front entrance, me keeping watch at the rear. Then, to our astonishment, the lift doors slid open to reveal Edward Snowden in disguise.

As we led the way back through the corridors to our room, he barely spoke. He seemed nervous. It's not hard to fathom why. Both the US and Europe are chasing Snowden to this day, so the slightest misstep could be fatal. Once inside the room, Snowden shed his disguise and visibly relaxed. The interview lasted four hours. When the time was up, he took off his glasses, rearranged his hair, pulled on a cap and vanished once more down the long hallways of the hotel – back to his self-imposed exile in Russia.

And that's what makes getting intelligence sources to talk so complicated. Even if they agree to meet, they have a whole bag of tricks to keep from directly leaking information – like speaking about a situation in terms of hypotheticals, or never calling agencies by name. Instead, they refer to 'Zoetermeer' – the city where the AIVD is based – and 'Frederikkazerne' or plain 'Frederik' for the old military barracks in The Hague that's home to the MIVD. Or just plain 'A.' and 'M.' Another strategy is to avoid being specific. Rather than 'yes' or 'no', it's 'could be' or 'that might be worth looking into'.

*

This explains why it took years to figure out what cards the AIVD was holding when the crisis erupted at DigiNotar. Not until the whole affair was ancient history were sources willing to open up, and then cautiously.

First of all, the Dutch agency and its American ally the CIA were jointly running an Iranian informant. He'd come into Dutch hands by a stroke of luck. Apparently, the man had committed a punishable offence in Iran and, fearful of being arrested, literally walked into a Dutch or US embassy in a Middle Eastern country one day to ask for help. He needed to get out of Iran immediately.

My own intelligence sources stressed this man was a highly placed official who knew a great deal about the Iranian Revolutionary Guard (IRG), Iran's elite military corps. The IRG was in charge of the country's nuclear plans and security services, and membership of its top ranks was reserved for a very select few. The man was also very knowledgeable about Iranian hacking groups. The AIVD gave him a code name, like all its informants. Since they were using place names at the time, his was a well-known Dutch coastal town.

From the moment they decided to use him as an informant the AIVD began co-ordinating with the CIA. During the man's lengthy interrogations, a younger operative from the AIVD was joined by an older CIA agent, a certain H. who was stationed in Holland.

For the AIVD, the main reason for working together, aside from the strategic benefit – the AIVD shared intelligence with the CIA hoping they'd return the favour – was financial. The US had fewer qualms about paying sources, and paid them more, whereas the Dutch believed that 'buying' information detracted from its reliability.

The CIA thus paid the Iranian several thousand euros a month. In time, he was relocated to another Western country for his own safety. That country consented to the Dutch–US operation on its soil under the condition that its intelligence bureau would also get the interrogation transcripts.

The AIVD was therefore holding a trump card even before DigiNotar was hacked. But that wasn't all. As we have seen, the agency had been keeping an eye on Iran for a while. In fact, it was already rooting around in Iran's electronic government systems as far back as 2000, when Iran had just connected to the World Wide Web.

But after 2005, Iran began turning inwards. It built its own, more insular version of the internet, both to keep out prying eyes and to shield it from foreign influences. Stuxnet rapidly accelerated this transition. The country also started scaling down its use of satellite connections. This was bad news for the MIVD, which had been intercepting satellite communications from its own station in Burum in Friesland.

These changes in Iran were less of a concern to the AIVD, which relied more on real people – informants and hackers – to remotely infiltrate computer systems. Tapping the Iranian internet, which was something only the Dutch could do, was a fairly pointless undertaking, as there was almost no way of predicting which Iranian internet traffic would wind up routed to the Netherlands. Moreover, it was complicated and costly.

Instead, the AIVD invested in hacking operations, which were both more targeted and less expensive. Concentrating mainly on foreign-focused intelligence services run by the IRG, it managed to penetrate Iranian hacking groups' computer and email systems on a regular basis.

When DigiNotar was hacked the AIVD thus had two irons in the fire: its own intelligence plus an Iranian informant who was knowledgeable about hacking groups. But it still took some time for the agency to connect all the dots. 'It was a major crisis,' someone inside the AIVD recalled.

As for relations between the AIVD and MIVD, the situation only fuelled resentment. The military agency didn't have access to the civilian agency's intelligence, and the latter refused to share it. It was quite clear the two Dutch agencies had no wish to work together.

Based on its own information, the AIVD was able to work out where inside Iran's internet the perpetrator had been operating. In fact, Iran has two kinds of internet: one is the strictly regulated web for the general public, the other is a looser 'scientific' domain reserved for government use. The AIVD could see that the hacker had used Iran's 'scientific' internet. Not only that, it could pinpoint which specific branch of government he was in. As a source later told me, 'We knew without a doubt that DigiNotar was the work of Iranian intelligence.'

That's not to say the AIVD thought anyone besides the twenty-year-old identified by Dutch police was involved in the cyberattack. Or that he was actually working for Iranian intelligence. Rather, in its bid to make strides on the internet, Iran had marshalled all kinds of hackers and criminal hacking rings. When the AIVD zeroed in on its suspect, it saw he was part of a social network that also had links to the Iranian government.

This explains why W. – the AIVD liaison – didn't want Dutch police sending Iran a request for information: he feared it would ruin the agency's unique access. Neither did the AIVD want police investigators playing digital detective on the agency's turf. When it comes to intelligence, agencies prefer to stay in control of an operation rather than disrupt it, because it could yield future useful information. Which is precisely the reason W. called this an 'absolute no go'.

The Foreign Affairs Ministry had its own reasons for not wanting to reveal the young Iranian's identity. Since the Netherlands didn't have an extradition treaty with Iran, there was no chance the Iranian government would hand him over. Conversely, publishing his name could get the young man into trouble should Iran decided a public 'punishment' was needed to maintain a pretence that he'd acted alone.

What happened at DigiNotar was noteworthy in many respects. It illustrated the vulnerability of the internet and of a government that doesn't understand it. It showed that agencies can exploit such vulnerabilities for their own profit. And it made clear that Western agencies, and notably the AIVD, are at the forefront of this digital arms race. There are those at the AIVD who say DigiNotar may well have been Iran's payback for the Stuxnet virus. Clearly there's a connection, but I'm sceptical. After all, Iran was using the access to spy on Iranians, in Iran.

DigiNotar also raised another question that continued to bother me. How was it possible that one kid with a laptop, operating on his own, could instigate such chaos?

4

Red Alert

José Robbe is leaving the Rijndam rehabilitation centre when she sees a man and a woman walking towards her. Robbe has been a nurse at the centre for several years. Each day she cycles the six miles from her home in the suburban town of Barendrecht to the centre in downtown Rotterdam, about a forty-five-minute commute. She's standing by her bicycle, keys in hand, when the man and woman approach. It's a Tuesday afternoon, 20 March 2012.

'Are you Mrs Robbe?'

She nods.

The woman, who's wearing jeans and a black windcheater, explains that she's with the police. 'I'd like to talk to you for a minute. It's about your son, Edwin. We're arresting him.' Robbe stares, frozen. The woman asks if she'll accompany them. Warily, Robbe agrees. Leaving her bike where it is, she follows the two officers.

At the police car, the cop asks Robbe for her house keys. They tell her they intend to surprise her son at home and arrest him on the spot. As soon as Robbe slides into the backseat of the dark Volkswagen, the male policeman asks, 'Where's Edwin's room?' Hastily she explains that it's on the top floor and has no lock on the inside. This detail seems important to the officers. They nod. All the while, Robbe's mind is racing. *It must be that computer after all*, she thinks.

One of the officers tells her what's going to happen; that she shouldn't be afraid. There will be lots of cops. Those cops will be in her house for a while. She asks if Robbe wants to be there for her son's arrest. 'No,' Robbe replies grimly. *Of course not.* It feels as if she has just betrayed her son. To stand by and watch would only make it worse. The police drop her off at a plaza by the local supermarket a few blocks from her house. As soon as they pull up, a woman with curly blonde hair wearing jeans and an identical black windcheater comes over. It's chilly outside, and she has the sleeves pulled down over her hands. Her manner is friendly. She asks for the keys to the front door of Robbe's house. Robbe has no choice, but still she feels terrible as the officers drive away towards her house, and her son, up there on the top floor – to arrest her eldest child, just a troubled seventeen-year-old boy.

In front of the duplex on Menuethof in Barendrecht, seven police officers stand awaiting the signal. Two more cops are positioned along the side fence. Across the street, a policeman in a nondescript Volkswagen records how the seven uniformed figures slip quietly into the house. How, a little while later, three re-emerge escorting Edwin between them. He offers no resistance. Next door, from a bedroom window, a neighbour films it, too.

Edwin is brought to a detention centre in Houten, near Utrecht. Once he's gone, José Robbe finally re-enters her house. She sits on the living-room sofa, feeling numb. Only an hour before she'd been about to hop on her bike, suspecting nothing. Now, her son's being booked at the police station and she's watching as cops rummage through cabinets, file up and down the stairs and bag up flash drives, CD-ROMs and telephones in her home.

*

It's several years after this incident that I visit José and her husband Ruud Robbe in their terraced house in Rotterdam, where they tell me about Edwin. He's not there. Glancing at the bookcase, I notice one book conspicuously sticking out: *Tonio*, a memoir by A. F. T. van der Heijden about the loss of his son.

I had tracked Edwin down through a source, got his telephone number and finally reached him after repeated attempts. At first he didn't respond to the WhatsApp messages I sent. When he finally did reply, it was from a different number. What I wanted to know was why he had attacked the Netherlands' biggest telecom company and plunged it into chaos. I wanted to know how he'd learned to do what he did. And what happened to him after his arrest.

Our chats were erratic. One day he'd be effusive and engaging, then he'd become remote. Sometimes days would pass before he answered a message. It would turn out he was in Asia. We also talked on Skype, once. I wanted to meet. He did, too, he said.

But we never would. Edwin was cremated a few months before this, my second visit to his parents. As we talk, grief over the loss of their adopted son rears up suddenly several times. Ruud, his father, was the last person to see Edwin alive, and it still weighs heavily on him.

*

Edwin was less than a year old when he was taken from his biological mother. She was a single mum, mentally impaired and unable to care for an infant. For months, she didn't even touch him. José and Ruud fostered Edwin. José worked in health care, Ruud was a chemical engineer at a company that processed ores for pigment. Being childless, they wanted to give baby Edwin a loving home.

But he was a troubled child. 'I always thought his anxiety started when he was still very little. He just couldn't bond with other people,' recalls José. He often complained of stomach aches. There were countless visits to the doctor and to hospital. Each time there'd be medical tests. It was suggested he had a gluten allergy. 'Honestly,

I think it was psychological,' says José. 'Edwin had a lot of anxiety, but the doctors focused on physical causes.'

Edwin wasn't like other kids. His foster parents saw it and so did his teachers. One time, at a parents' evening, a mentor asked, 'What's actually wrong with him? He has almost no friends.' He was a solitary child. His younger brother, also adopted, was more expressive and sociable. On the rare occasions when Edwin had friends over, it was always his brother they wound up playing with. Whenever he was around other people, Edwin became tense, clammed up and withdrew.

He almost never did any sport or played outside. Instead, he preferred to sit at the computer in his upstairs room. And José and Ruud let him do this, relieved that at least he had this one hobby. For their part, they knew nothing about computers. They used a computer to send the odd email or look for holidays, but that was about it.

After graduating from a vocational high school, in 2010 Edwin enrolled in an ICT course at Albeda College in Rotterdam. He wanted to do something with computers. His parents let him buy a PC that he put together himself at a computer megastore. It had a big memory card and loads of processing power. He set it up in his bedroom. Looking back, José thinks 'that may have been our biggest mistake'.

Edwin was obsessed with his new toy and only came downstairs for meals. Occasionally, his parents caught glimpses of what he was doing. Mostly, he played games, especially the kind in which people are violently killed. Like building amusement parks and then throwing people off the rides. Also lots of shoot-em-ups. 'He took classes in ethics at school,' says Ruud, 'so we thought it would be all right in the end.'

In the autumn of 2010, the Robbes received a letter from their internet provider, KPN, informing them that their internet access had been blocked. KPN said it had observed 'malicious activity' on the family's IP address.

When asked about it, Edwin brushed it off as nonsense. To José, he answered in jargon, saying somebody had cracked his 'WPA2 key' and exploited their internet connection. Baffled, José let it go. It was hard enough trying to get through to her son at the best of times.

KPN, however, did not let it go. The company's abuse team didn't buy Edwin's explanation and carried out its own investigation. This revealed that Edwin had used a rented server to mount an attack on bakabt.com, a website offering movie and program downloads. When confronted with the evidence, Edwin's justification was that he didn't like the site's administrators.

Edwin had bombarded the website with so many data packets that it crashed. This is what's known as a DDoS attack. It works a lot like a traffic jam: a road can only handle a maximum number of cars; if there are more than that, traffic gets blocked up and comes to a standstill. It's the same with the internet, only the road is digital and the traffic goes to websites.

This kind of attack is a crime. 'Edwin is very active on the internet, as are some of his friends. In some instances they're described as a hacking ring,' someone at KPN wrote to Ruud in an email. 'We wonder if he understands what kind of consequences his actions can have. We urge you to talk to him about this.' Ruud did, and wrote back: 'I've had a long discussion with him. He is a sensitive kid and is gradually coming to see that what he did is a serious offence.' Ruud and Edwin had agreed the computer would be off limits for three months and that he'd get it cleaned by a professional. 'I don't know anything about computers,' Ruud concluded his email. 'Do you have any suggestions on who could help me clean up his computer?' KPN never replied.

Edwin's parents could tell that something was brewing. He was on edge and hardly ever left his upstairs room. As soon as the computer ban was lifted, he was back on his PC for as long as twelve hours a day. He seemed indifferent but refused to explain what was wrong. School wasn't going well either. His course was heavy on classroom and group work, which didn't suit him at all. He preferred to do things on his own. He was dismissive of his teachers. 'I know more about computers than all of them put together,' he told his parents one evening. Also, the stomach aches had returned, and he was taking an anti-anxiety drug, oxazepam, to help him relax and sleep.

With his parents' consent, in the summer of 2011 Edwin transferred to an ICT course at Zadkine College in Rotterdam, where students were given more freedom and could work independently on projects. It didn't help. Edwin grew increasingly despondent. He lay around in bed and ordered tranquillisers such as diazepam and chemical and natural oils online. A doctor his parents consulted recommended letting him rest whenever he felt tired.

José and Ruud didn't know precisely how Edwin was spending his time. Occasionally he mentioned someone he knew in England or Australia, so they assumed he'd made friends online. 'At least he's finally socialising,' they said. Still, he seemed joyless. They told each other he needed space, that surely there were some things that gave him pleasure, and that he had a knack for computers. But on days he never left his screen, it was hard not to despair. More than once they wondered, 'Should we pull the plug?'

*

If computers were merely tools for his parents, for Edwin they were a gateway to adventure, to understanding and most of all to recognition. They let him do whatever he wanted. If he felt like gaming, he'd boot up Windows. But more often he chose Linux, his go-to operating system. From there he opened different virtual devices so that he could adopt multiple personas. On forums he met like-minded kids his age from all over the world who spent entire days at their computers and made the kinds of social connections online that they couldn't in the real world. Quiet and reclusive kids, mostly. Cloaked in made-up identities, they chatted about computers, girls and going out, and devised tricks to infiltrate private computer networks.

Online, Edwin was either xS or YUI – the latter a nod to the Japanese singer Yui, of whom he was a big fan. As YUI, he was different. Bolder, more self-assured. Online, quiet Edwin with the shy smile came alive. On chat channels he met an Australian, 'Dwaan', and an American, 'Sabu', in the course of 2011. The three talked about hacking and his new friends showed Edwin places they had managed to break in.

Sabu, as it happens, was a big shot in the digital world. He was the leader of LulzSec – a mash-up of 'lulz', for 'lol', and 'security' – a collective whose six members attacked a range of organisations and hacked the websites of big companies in 2011 to expose their shoddy security. Though teasing in some cases, in others their antics had serious consequences. Such as when the group stole data belonging to more than 70,000 US contestants on the popular TV show *The X Factor* in retaliation for an insult to the black rapper Common. Also targeted by LulzSec were the Sony PlayStation Network and the website of the CIA.

Several investigation agencies were hunting for Sabu but, like Edwin, he took care to cover his tracks. All the kids went by aliases on chat channels, some of which also required passwords to get in. Plus, they never logged on directly from their home connections, but, rather, through a secure VPN. Edwin connected to a VPN server first, then went online anonymously. It took some discipline. Forgetting to use VPN just once would instantly make his IP address in Barendrecht visible for anyone to see.

In time, Edwin found his way to chat channels where the serious hackers converged. Winning their trust was a first and crucial step, because police were also lurking, trying to infiltrate using fake identities. At sixteen, Edwin was orbiting LulzSec as well as a looser collective called Anonymous. Though not a member himself, he hung out on their chat channels. These were exciting times in the hacking world. Members of Anonymous had been targeting a succession of organisations and declaring their solidarity with WikiLeaks, which was publishing hundreds of thousands of US diplomatic communications. When Julian Assange's whistleblower website was blocked by the payment services PayPal, Mastercard and VISA, cutting off lots of donations to WikiLeaks, Anonymous struck back with a DDoS attack that took out the PayPal and Mastercard websites and inflicted an estimated $5.5 million in losses. One member would ultimately wind up doing eighteen months in prison in England.

Edwin's contacts abroad gave him a confidence boost. He spent hours chatting with people from all over the world about ways to hack websites. In Australia Dwaan tended to log on around noon, midnight his time, and the two would egg each other on. About going to DEF CON, for example, a famous hacker convention in Las Vegas.

Dwaan: 'Go to Defcon next year'
xS: 'Lol, why?'
xS: 'I'll go each year'
xS: 'From now on'
Dwaan: 'I wanna try to go'
Dwaan: 'Because in 2013'
Dwaan: 'It will be on like a week after I turn 18. And it's fucking epic'

From this exchange they moved on to drinking, partying, gaming and computers. Edwin often mocked 'normal' life and Western society. He denounced materialism and superficial concerns. 'All you need is water and food to survive, but everyone's just interested in material things,' he wrote.

But most of all they talked about hacking. Dwaan bragged about some of the places he'd been. To them, it was all a prank: getting in and out just to prove they could bypass a site's security. They never stole. That was something only the big guys did. All they wanted was to look. The same way bored kids, on discovering an unlocked door, might sneak inside a building. Slowly, even Edwin came out of his shell, eager to show off his skills and pull his own stunts.

What Edwin lacked in technical know-how he made up for with big talk and sense of logic. In December 2011, when he was seventeen, he had an online exchange with 'Phed', who showed him an 'exploit'. An exploit is a piece of code that takes advantage of vulnerabilities in a network's security to gain entry somewhere, like a key that opens old locks. Computer networks, especially at large organisations, rely on lots of different software. All software has one or two holes – some known, others still undiscovered. Whenever software makers discover such a vulnerability, they quickly take steps to create a patch and provide an update. Hackers, meanwhile, are snooping around for those very same weaknesses and working just as quickly to make a key – an exploit – to get inside.

That's precisely what Edwin did. Like a young hooligan out looking for open windows at night, he was trawling the internet and scanning networks to see who might be using software with a known hole. In this case, it was HP Data Protector. He searched sites manually using Google, entering 'Data Protector' as the search term alongside a specific web or IP address. In early December 2011 Edwin struck gold. He found a university in Norway that was using the software and hadn't installed the update containing the patch yet.

Edwin grabbed his exploit, executed it, and just like that he was inside NTNU. Looking around the university's network, he discovered he had six computer servers at his command. Excited, he told Dwaan of his conquest. Dwaan approved.

On a roll, Edwin next gained control over a 'super computer' at the University of Tromsø. He nosed around for a while but didn't take anything. Breaking in was exciting enough. All the same, once inside he pulled one more prank. He installed a 'backdoor'. This is a kind of program that's easy to find if you know where to Google. Edwin plucked one from another site. Now he could access the university's computer server again remotely whenever he wanted to.

Edwin pulled off his stunt without a hitch and earned himself hacker cred with his new friends. Dwaan responded to Edwin's feat with enthused fist pumps and exclamations of 'Looooooooolll' and 'OMG!' This only whetted Edwin's appetite. As he'd done in Norway, he went in search of new targets in other countries. His next victim was the University of Twente in the Netherlands, then a website in Iceland, and after that a university in Japan. He was unstoppable. As long as he took care to connect to a VPN server in Russia first, he left no tracks to follow.

Edwin wasn't like other guys who got sloppy and made mistakes; who forgot to turn on their VPN. Not Edwin. He was cautious. And so he didn't understand why his parents were worried – like the time his dad showed him an article about a young hacker who'd been arrested.

'That's just incredibly stupid,' Edwin snapped. 'Only stupid hackers let themselves get caught.' Still, he didn't let on what he was doing up in the upstairs room. He knew his parents would never approve.

That he was getting kudos online for his pranks seemed only right, however. A friend who used the screen name 'Droppy' asked if Edwin could oversee security for his website. Droppy was in the business of stolen credit cards. He wanted xS to keep an eye on his web set-up and check everything was working smoothly. Droppy would pay him from time to time. Edwin agreed to.

Another online friend with whom he chatted daily, 'Naomi' in Singapore, asked if YUI could harass her employer. She'd just been fired from her job at Singapore Press Holdings and wanted YUI to attack the company's website. No problem, YUI assured her, piece of cake.

There was also a setback. At the Norwegian university, Edwin discovered he could no longer log into 'his' servers. He'd been kicked out. 'I got detected,' he told his online friends, who had a brief laugh over the news before moving on to other topics. But Edwin wanted more. And in 2012, he found it.

It was while running another scan that Edwin noticed outdated software at KPN. Holland's biggest telecom was using HP Data Protector and hadn't installed the update yet. Here was an open window. Did he dare sneak in? Why not take a quick peek inside his own internet provider? After all, KPN was a big fish and would earn him massive credits. Edwin took the gamble. He entered a random KPN IP address, ran his exploit and then, using a detour through the Japanese university, slipped inside KPN's network.

He found himself in a far corner of the network, which is to say he was in, but still needed to open some doors. For instance, he couldn't send commands directly from his own computer to KPN. Neither did he have full rights across the whole network. He couldn't just walk around, because a firewall was blocking his way. But all this was child's play. By moving a program from his own PC onto the KPN computer, Edwin could bypass the wall. Now, he was free to do as he pleased.

Stupid KPN, he thought to himself. The whole place was riddled with holes. Scanning the rest of the network from the KPN machine he'd accessed, Edwin saw the obsolete software being used in hundreds of places. Almost every computer server in the telecom provider's vast network had a window open. The kid from Barendrecht strolled around unimpeded, and what he saw astonished him. He could control 514 computer servers. He could even access the core router, the backbone of KPN's entire network. He could see the data of 2.1 million KPN customers. He could block hundreds of thousands of people from connecting to the national emergency line. He could redirect internet traffic so that people who wanted to visit, say, a news site, would wind up somewhere completely different. Edwin could do whatever he wanted and KPN wouldn't know a thing.

Excitedly he told Dwaan of his conquest. At first, Dwaan refused to believe him, so to prove he'd gained command of KPN Edwin logged onto the chat channel from the KPN network. 'WTF!' Dwaan responded. When Edwin explained how he'd got in, Dwaan wanted to see for himself. A few minutes later, he was inside, too. Edwin tried to talk him down, but Dwaan was already running amok. What if I let the KPN computers communicate with each other and with us, he suggested. Edwin didn't like the idea, but Dwaan wasn't listening. He installed a bot so the computers would do precisely what he wanted.

Edwin was thrilled with his newfound status. He dropped out of his ICT course. At home, the tension eased. Relieved, his mother emailed a friend that 'Edwin has been feeling better. He's been exempted from attending classes this year and now he's doing a high school English course from home.'

Meanwhile, up in his room, Edwin was expanding his latest coup. 'I'm hacking my ISP,' he announced to 'Combasca', a Korean student. Combasca didn't believe him and demanded evidence. Again, Edwin entered the chat channel from the KPN network. He urged Combasca, 'U should become a hacker too.'

*

As Edwin gained plaudits online, a group of men and one woman sat in a high-rise off the A12 motorway outside The Hague staring at each other in dismay. Dozens of people had set up shop in a vacant office one floor up from the Fresh FM recording studio. They'd installed desks, laptops and network cables. To someone who didn't know what was going on, it would have been a curious sight: people rushing up to the top floor early each morning and not re-emerging until past midnight. Delivery services dropping off dinner in the evenings. And lots of secretive talk about something they called 'Project Victor'.

Some eighty to a hundred workers had been holed up like this on the building's top floor for days, many of them engineers and technicians from KPN and researchers from Fox-IT. Ronald Prins, boss of the big tech company, was there, too. It had all started with a message from someone called Combasca in South Korea. Combasca said he'd been chatting with a guy calling himself YUI who claimed to have hacked KPN. And he had evidence. After letting YUI boast about what he'd done, Combasca turned around and contacted KPN. Combasca snitched. His message wound its way through Twitter and the company's web care department, finally ending up at a security administrator. He rebooted a couple of computer servers hoping that would fix whatever was wrong.

It didn't. The server problems continued. By now, a good two weeks after the initial notification, there was genuine panic. Clearly, somebody was inside KPN's network. It could be a loner, or it could be a foreign state. Nobody knew. Nor could KPN or Fox-IT get a handle on the extent of the damage. They had to tread lightly, examining computers while keeping systems running so as not to disrupt service to millions of customers.

To begin with, they inspected the external layers. But the deeper they went, the more they found. On scanning internet traffic, it became apparent that hundreds of points in the KPN network were connecting to locations outside. Window and doors were gaping open all over the place. On 20 January 2012, KPN raised its alert level to orange. Its business operations were in grave danger.

A week later, on 27 January, there was another, even bigger discovery. The hacker had also broken into the core router, basically KPN's command centre. He had effectively taken control of the whole network and could do whatever he wanted: snoop on internet traffic, turn off TVs, take out the national emergency hotline. The alert level was raised again, this time to red. With the survival of the country's most important telecom provider in the balance, KPN notified the NCSC – successor to Aart Jochem's GovCERT – and the national police's High Tech Crime Unit. The next morning, one of KPN's board members filed a police report for computer invasion.

Much as at DigiNotar after it turned out the entire organisation had been breached and hackers could issue their own certificates, the situation triggered widespread alarm. Once again, the fragility of a network on which millions of people relied had been laid bare. Yet again, the cause was simple mistakes and negligence. Nobody at KPN had bothered to install the HP Data Protector patch which had been available since June 2011, more than six months before. More shocking still was the discovery that the external firewall had been disabled. Due to a faulty configuration it stood open for months, allowing anyone to stroll right in.

The crisis at KPN exposed a systemic failure. For one thing, the company's CEO, Eelco Blok, also served on the national Cyber Security Council, a body explicitly tasked with advising the government on crisis situations. But Blok never told the Council his own network had been hacked. Not until KPN filed its report weeks later did Blok's fellow Council members learn what had been going on. In addition, Aart Jochem's NCSC still had no mandate, so he couldn't act in any meaningful way. In the worst case, the government could grab the wheel as it had at DigiNotar. But although there was considerable panic, things weren't as bad as that yet. So far, there was no evidence that foreign hackers had taken control of the company or had malicious intent.

Further complicating matters was the fact that KPN's commercial interests were directly at odds with law enforcement's investigative task. The head of KPN's Network Operations Centre refused to switch off computer servers or allow a full scan of the network. That would cost money and manpower and could disrupt service to customers. But for the police investigation, it was vital.

It remained unclear what the impact would be if KPN really had been hacked by a foreign power. Would the national government still be able to do its job? How would it affect the AIVD and the MIVD, which relied on the KPN network for part of their communication? Nobody knew. Not for weeks.

Following the hacker's trail of digital breadcrumbs, the police team, Fox-IT and KPN finally identified the computer server through which he'd entered the network. But after that the puzzle became trickier, because the hacker was shielding himself using VPN connections. The police team flew to South Korea to talk to Combasca, and later to Japan, where a university network had been breached by the same individual. But they learned very little. Once again, police efforts were frustrated by physical limits: the attacker hid behind servers in myriad countries from Ukraine to England and from the Czech Republic to the United States. Time and time again they had to stop, send a mutual legal assistance request and wait for another copy of yet another computer server to arrive.

Meanwhile, the clock was ticking. If the hacker suddenly withdrew and erased his tracks, collecting evidence would become all but impossible. Luckily for the investigators, however, he did keep coming back – even after a KPN press release announced the hack on 8 February 2012. Far from vanishing, the hacker actually logged onto a chat channel via a hacked KPN server, this time, using the handle 'KPN'.

That's what finally put investigators on his trail. They could see the hacker was using a Russian VPN server whose IP address showed up more than once in KPN's network. Frustratingly, though, this information didn't really help the team, because VPN servers mask a user's identity. Still, it wasn't a complete dead end. There was one last thing they could try: to follow traffic from the VPN server to an individual computer in KPN's network.

That computer turned out to host a website, ndsmovies.com, on which a KPN customer shared downloaded movies. On that site's server, the investigators also found hacking files. What's more, they were precisely the kind of files used to exploit the holes in the HP Data Protector software that enabled the hacker to get inside.

The email address of the ndsmovies.com administrator was teqnology@live.com. When they looked it up, the investigators uncovered another lead: the same email address had been used earlier in correspondence with KPN about a blocked IP address. In 2010, an IP address belonging to teqnology@live.com had been blocked temporarily on account of 'malicious activities'. That IP address was linked to a house on Menuethof in Barendrecht.

Here, finally, was a big arrow pointing at the perpetrator. Even so, to have a case against him the investigators needed more. They needed a direct link from the hacker to KPN. Best of all would be if they could catch him live in the act – at his computer, inside KPN. By this time, the investigation had spun out for months and the problems at KPN still persisted. Pressure was mounting. Even though the telecom giant continued to maintain no customer data had been stolen, some of the media were reporting differently. 'KPN customer passwords made public,' headlined Dutch news site NU.nl. According to the NOS broadcasting organisation, 'Hack triggers highest alert at KPN.'

The last straw was when someone anonymously published a list containing hundreds of hacked KPN email addresses. After earlier claiming there had been no leaks, now the provider was forced to take drastic action. It froze email services for its two million customers, who were unable to access their inboxes for days. KPN's intervention severely disrupted communications for businesses, too, leaving them unable to deliver goods, place orders or send invoices.

Under relentless pressure, the investigators at this point decided to do something they shouldn't. They knew the hacker was renting a virtual server in Russia and that a copy of that server wouldn't reach Holland for weeks. What's more, it wouldn't contain all the data they needed. Because of the way copies are made, it wouldn't include data from the server's working memory. So, they decided to break into the Moscow server remotely, from the Netherlands. And there, in the working memory, they found exactly what they were after: chat logs – and one exchange in particular, between two kids about the hack at KPN.

Swordfish: '8 o'clock on NOS News on 1'
Swordfish: 'KPN confirms it'
xS: 'Yeah, whatever'
xS: 'I really gotta truecript my shit now'
Swordfish: 'I'm pretty safe if they come'

This seemingly trivial exchange provided two key pieces of information. First, that the attacker was in Holland and, second, that he was encrypting his computer using a program called TrueCrypt, popular with hackers for shielding documents from outside view. It also told police that if they wanted to catch him, they had to do so before he turned off his computer. Otherwise, all his data would be lost.

Slowly but surely, the police were closing in. In part, they had the attacker's own enthusiasm to thank for that. It seemed he just couldn't get enough of prowling around the KPN network. The next time he went to scan it for holes from the same Russian VPN server, KPN blocked the Russian IP address. That's when the hacker made a fatal mistake. He skipped the VPN altogether and entered a hacked KPN computer server directly from his home connection. With that, he exposed his home address.

Meanwhile, police also had a wiretap on the hacker's home in Barendrecht to gather some last bits of evidence, though they were encountering some snags there as well. For a start, all the internet data collected by the Fox-IT tapping software they were using, called Replay, couldn't be rendered into usable information. Even worse, one day their entire internet feed simply vanished, leaving the police staring at a blank screen. Their tap in Barendrecht was active, but no data was coming in. The problem, police discovered after calling

RED ALERT

around at KPN, was that KPN had accidentally blocked the suspect's internet connection.

A little more than two months after receiving the Korean Combasca's message, the police finally had enough evidence to pull Edwin from his computer. Two agents were sent to intercept his mother and get her house keys. Then they sneaked up to the upstairs room where Edwin sat, unsuspecting, taking the internet by storm as xS. Suddenly, uniformed men burst into the room. 'Police! Get your hands off the computer! You're coming with us!'

*

José Robbe puts a plate of biscuits in front of me and pours coffee. Ruud, Edwin's father, sits beside me. As we talk, he pulls a handkerchief from the pocket of his jeans a couple of times, pushing aside his glasses to dry his eyes.

Following his arrest in Barendrecht, Edwin was detained for forty-two days, found guilty of hacking and given a suspended prison sentence of 240 days plus community service. He didn't want to do community service, however, so did the time instead.

Afterwards, Edwin was even more withdrawn from his surroundings. He self-medicated with sedatives and experimented with a variety of drugs. His dad would come home to find the family room strewn with leaves and plants that Edwin was using to cook up some psychedelic brew. Once, he even secretly slipped LSD into his father's wine, sending him on an hours-long trip during which Ruud watched his bedroom ceiling dissolve into a lightshow. He was still hallucinating so badly the next morning that he had to call in sick to work. When the drugs finally wore off, Edwin couldn't understand why his dad was so upset. He'd merely wanted to give him an enriching experience.

Edwin was also delusional by this point and took exception to everything. To his parents, the situation seemed hopeless. Even professionals at the rehabilitation clinic De Bouman in Rotterdam where he was admitted sent him packing after a week, saying his behaviour made him impossible. Edwin asked Ruud if he could move

73

back home, but his dad didn't feel up to the task of taking in his now twenty-two-year-old son.

As Edwin stood on his doorstep, Ruud turned him away with a heavy heart. 'Come on,' Edwin pleaded.

But Ruud was at the end of his tether. 'We can't,' he said. 'I'm sorry.' Edwin left with a backpack. His parents had no idea where he'd go.

After several weeks with no news, Ruud tried to get in touch through WhatsApp and email. Edwin responded to only one of the messages, emailing back, 'Sure, everything's fine. I'm in Pyongyang, North Korea.' Edwin had a thing for Asia, particularly Japan and North and South Korea. Not for a second did Ruud believe his son was really in Pyongyang.

Attached to the message was a photograph. It showed Edwin dressed all in black, with eye-catching chains on his jacket. Standing next to him was a Korean soldier. With his slight build, squinting into the camera, Edwin looked vaguely Asian himself. He had posed in front of a picture of Pyongyang and the North Korean leader Kim Jong-un, probably a tourist attraction in South Korea. Edwin closed his email with, 'They monitor things like WhatsApp and phones. But at least they have computers.'

It was one of his very last messages. Ruud bows his head. 'Should I have let him come back home?' he wonders. 'Should I have given him *one* more chance?' And then, regretfully: 'I'd reached my limit. I just couldn't do it.'

I hadn't been planning to interview Edwin's parents. I'd wanted to hear the story from Edwin himself, but that didn't work out. The one time we Skyped, he'd been in a hotel room in South Korea. Eight minutes into our call he signed off with a smile and a peace sign. After that we chatted sporadically over WhatsApp. His final messages were laced with despair. 'I don't like it here,' he wrote, 'They've got guns' and 'I want to get out of here ASAP.' He stopped responding to my questions about KPN.

A few days later I was contacted by a source. 'Did you hear about Edwin?' He'd been found dead in a hotel bathtub, not far from Seoul's international airport. The door of his room, number 801, had been barricaded from the inside with furniture and pillows.

I waited quite a while before getting in touch with his parents. Although I didn't want to bother them for my story, if they knew a journalist had talked to their son only days before his death, they might have questions for me, too.

José Robbe agreed to my request to meet. At their home, she and Ruud pull out pictures of Edwin and tell me about his complicated youth. I can tell it pains them. They ask about my last conversation with him, about which Ruud observes, 'That was just before he died.'

Almost inevitably, our conversation comes around to the KPN hack. I explain that I'm fascinated by how a seventeen-year-old kid could almost topple the country's leading telecom provider and access the data of millions of its customers. According to his parents, Edwin's arrest and incarceration were a tipping point; after that, it was all downhill. His suicide is a scar they'll always carry with them. And questions linger. Was Edwin really as much to blame as the judicial authorities made out? Wasn't it KPN, after all, which left all those windows open? And if it's that easy to break in somewhere, isn't there a much bigger societal problem we ought to address?

It certainly doesn't help that they have only a hazy grasp of what Edwin actually did. The technical jargon authorities used in the case against Edwin meant nothing to them. According to the public prosecutor, it constituted 'one of the most serious hacks in the Netherlands' history'. Edwin's work was 'ingenious' and the 'impact on KPN and thus on society at large, immense'. By KPN's own reckoning, it suffered '3 million euros in damage'. The prosecutor praised the company for its openness, saying, 'It is quite rare, in light of the major commercial interests and reputational risk, for a company such as KPN to release this much sensitive information.' After the hack, KPN took measures to ramp up security in its systems. Although Edwin immediately pleaded guilty to all charges in court and co-operated with the judicial inquiry, the public prosecutor was scathing in his condemnation. Edwin's actions, he charged, had been 'malicious and deliberate' and caused 'imminent danger to life'.

Omitted from the court records is the fact that the investigation team hacked Edwin's VPN server in Moscow. This detail was 'whitewashed' by the Criminal Intelligence Unit (CIE), a police division that collects information about serious crimes and can protect the identity of sources. Since there was no need to name the source, no one noticed – not even Edwin's lawyer.

The court in part went along with the public prosecution's arguments, deploring the way Edwin had utilised 'his talents for negative ends'. Yet it also found extenuating circumstances. 'The defendant's relative social aptitude and the burden of his failure at school and in the social sphere,' the judge wrote, 'played a role in his seeking refuge on the internet and transgressive behaviour there.' Child protection services recommended giving him community service, but in the end Edwin chose to serve a prison term instead.

'We really had no idea what he was up to,' Ruud says. It brought home to him just how vastly different the risks of the digital world are from those of the real world. 'If you want to do a story about it,' José suddenly offers, 'we'll co-operate. Also to warn other parents. It never even occurred to us that he could cause something like this.'

'I'm more anxious about computers now,' Ruud admits. When he fills in his tax returns and can't get the site to work, he gets stressed out. 'Sometimes I'm afraid someone might be using my identity. I'm forced to depend on technologies I can't understand, and that worries me.'

So, that's the problem: the internet has ushered in new risks – risks we can hardly grasp. It wouldn't be long before the full import of this would truly sink in.

Part II

The Consequences

5

Bombing SIM Cards

She's tall, blonde and she's flying to Spain. That's all I know as I wait at the big red-and-white-chequered meeting point in Schiphol Airport's arrivals hall at half past six one evening. I'd received an email from this woman about a strange incident in England, and we arranged to meet. Suddenly, she's standing in front of me. 'You're Huib,' she says. 'Right?'

As soon as we're seated inside Café Rembrandt on Schiphol Plaza, she starts to talk. She wants to remain anonymous, so I'll call her Robin. A few years ago, Robin, a Dutch national, was living in England. She'd been searching for a job and looking online when she came across an advertisement for translation work for Appen, a company in Australia. They needed freelance translators from different countries, including Dutch speakers, to improve their speech-to-text software.

Robin went to the website and filled out an online application. A representative named Alan contacted her, saying she had to take a test first. If she passed, she'd be guaranteed to receive work and get paid through PayPal on a per project basis. The test consisted of listening to short audio fragments and transcribing word for word what she heard.

Robin passed the test and thereafter received another email from Alan. 'You should now see the following project available,' he wrote. She logged on, read the instructions and went to a project titled 'Dutch free speech transcription'. A list of clips appeared on her screen. When she clicked on one of them, she heard Dutch voices. Her job was to write down verbatim what she heard in the recordings, each of which was ten to twenty, sometimes thirty, seconds long. Other freelancers might be working on the same projects simultaneously.

What she heard in the recordings was taxi drivers talking, but the clips were too short for her to make out the context. Some of them concerned private conversations, such as one between a man and woman who were discussing a holiday to Turkey. She translated the calls but didn't give them much thought. Several weeks passed like this. She signed up for a whole string of projects and became increasingly proficient, translating thousands of recordings. PayPal payments followed like clockwork.

As time passed, Robin began to form an image of the people she heard. Oddly, the calls sounded quite recent. They mentioned current political affairs and news from previous weeks. What also caught her attention was that many were young people of Turkish or Moroccan descent. Most were taxi drivers. She heard them call the dispatch centre or one another. Also, the more recordings she translated, the more apparent it was that these people were all based around Amsterdam and The Hague.

Robin started to wonder how this was possible. How had an Australian company got hold of these phone calls? Occasionally, she had to transcribe what was obviously a chat exchange, consisting of brief messages read out by a computerised voice. It puzzled her. Were these people even aware that she was listening in on their conversations?

*

Robin's email came right at a time that I was spinning my wheels as an investigative journalist. I understood what attracts agencies to the internet. Without ever having to step foot across a border, they can spy inside other countries. And thanks to fake identities and VPN servers, they can't be seen. The only trouble is that it's hard to explain what the real consequences of those actions are. So far, most of the pieces I'd written were abstract and theoretical.

The taboo on eavesdropping was long gone, that much was clear. Since 2012, the American NSA had infiltrated more than 50,000 computers around the world. It had its own hacking unit called Tailored Access Operations which specialised in cracking routers and implanting software on organisations' computer networks. As well as providing continuous access, this enabled the NSA to divert data or even shut down whole networks. That tactic was gaining popularity, according to leaked NSA files, and within a few years the number of infected computer networks would run into the millions.

Technology created still more possibilities. Filtering data from fibre-optic cables was far more practical than installing shotgun microphones at sites. According to one of its own presentations ('Current Volumes and Limits'), around 2012 the NSA was saving more than 312 billion internet records and 135 billion telephony records a month. That amounts to 19 billion phone calls a month, or more than 600 million a day.

In the Netherlands, the AIVD intelligence and security service was vacuuming up whole web forums, in the process taking data about people who weren't targets at all. And if agencies were doing it, so too were companies and public authorities, for whom technology opened up new investigative methods that would once have been unthinkable. The Dutch tax administration was guzzling so much parking, payment and vehicle registration data that employees could practically track motorists in real time. Dutch law enforcement was combining all manner of data in a bid to predict crime. And their online research had been automated by iColumbo, a software program, so that now police just typed in a search term – an email address, vehicle registration or username – and it did all the work for them.

The newspaper articles I was writing sought to explain *why* these issues touch all of us, but it felt like the message wasn't getting across. In part, this was because the consequences had long been hypothetical. Take the KPN hack. The only reason seventeen-year-old Edwin drew so much attention was because he had access to millions of customer records, which he *could* have exploited (but didn't). When the Netherlands rolled out electronic medical records it was considered risky because of the *potential* for privacy violations (but there have been none we know of). Facebook's acquisition of WhatsApp made it *possible* for Facebook to grab data from WhatsApp (not that we'd be aware of it). And Dutch intelligence agencies' collection of metadata was contentious because it *might* be illegal (though even that's unclear). All things considered, it's not surprising that many people dismiss the threats.

My struggle was amplified by research in which the *NRC Handelsblad* noted a growing 'Snowden fatigue'. According to a survey by the paper's then editor-in-chief Peter Vandermeersch, readers were sick of stories about the NSA whistleblower who'd walked off with hundreds of thousands of secret documents. Vandermeersch, who zealously sent the editorial team daily lists of the top twenty-five best-read stories, often with points for improvement appended, had plotted long-term trends and concluded that the vast majority of readers skipped anything naming 'Snowden' in the headline.

The reason for this was twofold. Snowden was to some extent a media hype and, like all media hypes, interest waned over time. But there was also a more fundamental problem. Even now, it's not obvious to many people *why* articles about phone tapping and computer hacking matter, and in the end they just tune out.

It was time for a next step; to delve even deeper. What are the real implications for society when public authorities and spy agencies can grab ever more data? That's when I received an email from a woman who wanted to 'share an experience'. Sometimes, journalism is just a matter of luck.

*

Robin orders a Diet Coke and resumes her story. For months, she processed the phone calls of dozens of unsuspecting people. Then one day she heard something that really spooked her. It was a guy in a car leaving a voicemail about a business deal. 'It was my ex-boyfriend's voice, there was no question.' At first she thought she was going mad, but the next recording absolutely confirmed it. It was the same man talking to a woman and calling her by the same pet name he'd called Robin. 'It wasn't just any endearment, I can assure you. I nearly fell off my chair.'

Robin phoned her ex to find out if he knew about the project. 'I was that naive, apparently.' Her ex was upset. And he didn't believe her – not until she gave him details of the calls she'd just overheard; conversations he'd had only a couple of weeks before. He couldn't understand it. He'd never consented to have his calls recorded and couldn't imagine that Vodafone, his provider, would send his private calls to some company in Australia.

After this, Robin stopped taking the translation jobs. It felt wrong. She'd heard thousands, if not tens of thousands, of private phone conversations between people who had no clue someone else was listening in. How was that even possible? She couldn't bring herself to ask Appen, whom she didn't trust anymore. She tried to do her own research but never got very far. In the end, she let it go. For years. She didn't forget it, though, and when stories about NSA spying hit the news, she knew she couldn't ignore it any longer.

It was seeing me on a Dutch TV talk show that made Robin decide to reach out. In the airport café, I ask her to give me every detail she can think of to corroborate that she did in fact work for and get paid by Appen. She shows me emails and bank statements. She gives me her ex's phone number. When I call him, he confirms everything she's said. Even now, years after the fact, he remembers it with absolute clarity. Yet, to this day, he has no idea why anyone would want to eavesdrop on *him*.

Just to be clear, these are two well-educated people with good jobs. They're not conspiracy theorists. They're sensible. Articulate. They have no reason to blow the incident out of proportion; they haven't a grievance against Appen. More than anything, they're perplexed. They want to share what happened because it made a lasting impression. In the months after our meeting at Schiphol, Robin and I stay in regular contact. She sends me different bits of evidence, such as her registration with Appen, translation jobs she did for them and new projects she's offered. I can verify it and I can use everything, she tells me, on the condition that she and her ex remain anonymous.

*

As a journalist, my first step after receiving a tip is normally to ask my source a tonne of questions and tackle the information. What's already known? Who can tell me more about it? How and where can I verify a report? But modern technology has changed the way journalists investigate. These days, a story hinges on accurately interpreting *how* the technology works.

When the NSA story initially broke, I tried to find out where foreign agencies were surveilling in Holland. A logical spot would be the AMS-IX – that spaghetti junction of the internet in Amsterdam. Everyone I talked to had a different theory. 'You need to look just outside the data centres – that's the best place for wiretapping,' suggested one. Another said, 'I'd definitely check the cabinets where the cables are hooked up. That's where you want to be.'

One person informed me that besides being the perfect place from which to eavesdrop, the AMS-IX had also switched early on to hardware made by Glimmerglass, a US-based company. Could that be a lead? While browsing the Spy Files (leaked espionage documents) on WikiLeaks, I ran across a folder about Glimmerglass. It said their equipment was also popular with US intelligence. *Bingo!* I thought. Until someone else pointed out that having Glimmerglass hardware isn't significant in itself: what matters is *how* it's installed and who has access to it. Which took me right back to square one.

Another example: one story I wrote concerned a leak in the Android operating system discovered by researchers at Vrije Universiteit in Amsterdam. Millions of people use devices that run on Android, many more than use Apple's iOS. At the university's Amsterdam campus, one of the researchers showed me how he'd broken in. If he could access someone's internet browser, he could retrieve their Google login. Because Google uses the same logins for all kinds of applications – including Android phones – he could then install an app on his victim's phone via their browser, invisibly activate the app and so gain control over his victim's phone. After that, he could do whatever he wanted: turn on the camera, replace legitimate apps with malicious variants, intercept text messages, install malware and in the process even modify a person's e-identification, mobile banking, PayPal account and more.

After my story went to press it was criticised by experts. How easy was it really for hackers to exploit this leak, they asked, if it required researchers to jump through all sorts of technical hoops? Even if it wasn't too complicated for them, that needn't hold true for hackers. Moreover, was this technically a *leak*? Wasn't it more of a weakness arising from Google's own preference for using the same login to access all its services? A spokesperson at Google countered that if a hacker gets their hands on your username and password, you're already screwed. Which is true. In other words, it's a question of definitions. What's clearly a leak to some may not be to others.

Things get even more complicated when spy agencies get their hands on this technology. A notorious story published by Bloomberg in 2018 claimed China was spying on at least thirty big American corporations using computer chips the size of a grain of rice. Allegedly, the microchips were hidden inside the motherboards of computer servers. The Bloomberg article, which was based on anonymous sources, was titled 'The Big Hack'.

The story was reported as a terrific espionage scandal, but in the weeks following its publication major corporations like Apple and Amazon issued vehement denials. Experts had searched every nook and cranny of their motherboards and had not found a concealed chip. UK and US authorities refuted the Bloomberg piece as well.

When Snowden's NSA files went public, it caused a spate of espionage reports, each wilder than the next. Media in Norway, Spain and France, for instance, said that the US was wiretapping phone traffic on a large scale. But was it? Did the data leaked by Snowden afford any basis for such a conclusion? The NSA presentation – title: 'Boundless Informant' – on which journalists based their reporting provided no definitive answers. Though there were graphs detailing the type of communications intercepted in each country and the technologies used, nowhere was it stated *who* was doing the intercepting, and *where* exactly, and *what* kind of communication it was.

Months later, it transpired that it wasn't the US but, rather, European countries themselves that had been listening in on phone calls and relaying them to the NSA. Many media had misconstrued the situation, and even Holland's Interior Minister Ronald Plasterk, who was in charge of the AIVD and had access to salient facts, got the wrong end of the stick. He told a major national news programme that the US had probably intercepted calls made by 1.8 million ordinary Dutch citizens. What really happened was that the MIVD had tapped 1.8 million telephone calls in Somalia, and the Netherlands handed that data to the NSA.

*

Sometimes it takes years for all the pieces of a puzzle to fall into place. As it turns out, those 1.8 million telephone calls tapped by the MIVD concealed a much bigger story.

On the face of it, the situation seemed straightforward. The MIVD uses a cluster of white dishes in the Friesian village of Burum, in the north-eastern Netherlands, to intercept satellite communications. In 2012 the Netherlands took part in an anti-piracy mission off the coast of Somalia. As the Middle East and North Africa both lie within range of the MIVD's dishes in Burum, they could also intercept Somali phone traffic. This is what's known as SIGINT, short for signals intelligence. In plain English: gathering information from signals.

The MIVD acknowledged it had been intercepting cellular data, that the data concerned Somalia *and* that it had shared the intercepts with the NSA. But it hadn't used the dishes in Burum. In one NSA document, I read how, at the time of the Dutch-led mission off the coast of Somalia, the MIVD decided it wanted to intercept Somali phone calls from offshore. According to the classified American presentation, the MIVD had 'informed NSA that it was secretly placing a [...] SIGINT team on the Dutch vessel HNLMS. *Rotterdam*'. There was only one problem. The MIVD didn't have the specialised surveillance equipment and software needed. So, it asked the NSA if it could borrow them.

NSA agreed, but wanted something in return: 'NSA does not have access to Somali [...] communications,' the document said. In exchange for NSA provision of 'capability', the MIVD would share intelligence it collected from its Dutch ship with the US. That's how spy agencies co-operate: I scratch your back and you scratch mine.

The Dutch intelligence came in very useful for the NSA's own covert operations in Somalia, where it was deploying unmanned aircraft armed with explosives to take down the terrorist organisation Al-Shabaab. 'Targeted killings' was the term they used. In fact, these were summary executions. Without any form of due process, the US sent drones to fire missiles at suspected terrorists. The Dutch government's line was that lethal attacks of this kind were illegal outside declared war zones. In other words, the Netherlands did not officially support these actions.

To conduct covert strikes, the NSA chiefly relied on computer and cellular data – that is, on SIGINT. This was the case particularly in Somalia, where the closest US air base was some 700 miles to the north, in Djibouti. Yet, according to documents published by the American online news site *The Intercept*, in 2011 and 2012 American surveillance didn't even meet the minimum requirements for reliability. Among those requirements is that surveillance drones have to track a suspect before a strike to verify they have the right target. Due to a shortage of drones and the long flight distances from the base in Djibouti and back, however, that wasn't happening.

To make up for this gap in reliable intelligence the US turned to a program called Armada Sweep, described as a 'ship-based collection system'. And that's where the MIVD came in.

The NSA's powerful computers processed the intercepted calls they received and used network analyses to identify who was in contact with whom. It was based on these analyses, an American source told *The Intercept*, that US intelligence agencies selected their targets. By linking a SIM card or an IMEI number (a mobile phone's unique identifier) to a specific individual they could map where a phone had been and thus zero in on suspected terrorists.

When the right moment presented itself, they launched the strike. To *The Intercept*, the same source described how 'Once the bomb lands or a night raid happens, you know that phone is there. But we don't know who's behind it, who's holding it.' Basically, they were bombing SIM cards. In Yemen and Somalia more than half of targets were selected on the basis of metadata. According to a US drone pilot, this could be confirmed 'because you'd go back to the mission reports and it will say "this mission was triggered by SIGINT"'.

On Sunday 26 January 2014, the US carried out one of those missions. On CNN, a scheduled newscast was interrupted when the anchor announced: 'This just in to CNN. We're getting details of a US military mission that targeted a militant group [...] in southern Somalia.' The target was a high-ranking individual within the terrorist group Al-Shabaab. Over the phone, CNN correspondent Barbara Starr reported that the US military had 'good reason to go after him'.

*

'I was in southern Somalia also, that Sunday the 26th of January,' the Somali herdsman says. My fellow *Volkskrant* journalist Maud Effting and I are in a stuffy room in downtown Amsterdam, sitting across from a screen.

Other stories had distracted me from Somalia and MIVD surveillance there for a while. Then a source phoned. He told me two Somali men had been injured in a US drone strike and that they'd been put in touch with Dutch lawyers.

I was keen to talk to the Somali men myself. But for me to visit Somalia was practically impossible: it was an unofficial war zone and would cost *de Volkskrant* thousands for insurance and security. Arranging a video call was also problematic. The two men had to travel south to the country's capital at Mogadishu, a hazardous trip that took days and required a security escort. The only option we had was to bring them to a safe house in the capital where they could tell their story through an interpreter over Skype.

The first man we interview is a Somali herder named Omar Mohammad Ali. On that particular Sunday, says Omar, he had taken his herd of forty sheep and goats to a large plain around the southern village of Haaway. Accompanying him were his two daughters, Saharo (nine) and Nimo (eight). The girls were especially fond of the goats.

Omar was near the road from Haaway to the city of Barawa when he suddenly heard cars approaching. 'Pickups,' he says. 'There were many, at least five or six, and they were driving very fast. In the cars were men with weapons. I'd seen them there before.'

They were members of Al-Shabaab. Omar crouched behind a tree ten yards off the road. Al-Shabaab was known for terrorising the local population, for abducting young men and stealing money and cattle. 'Go and hide,' Omar shouted to his daughters. The girls ran off towards some trees. They weren't even halfway there before Omar got to his feet, intending to follow them.

Then, out of nowhere, came several deafening blasts. *Tchuk. Tchuk.*

The ground shook. Just as Omar was about to raise his head, there was another bang.

'Daddy!' Nimo screamed. 'Daddy!'

Omar had been hit. 'It felt like a stone went through my leg,' he says. 'And something was wrong with my head. I couldn't see a thing.' There was smoke everywhere. And great clouds of sand. Then it went dark.

Sitting next to Omar is his friend and fellow local herder, Nuur Osman Gurey. He picks up the story. After the blasts, Nuur saw black smoke and tall flames. He ran towards them. There were several off-road vehicles on fire and he found Omar unconscious on the ground. He had shrapnel in his head and a big gash in his leg. There was blood everywhere. Not far away lay sheep, goats and cows – all dead.

Then, among the fallen cattle, he saw the bodies of Omar's daughters. Nimo had been hit in the abdomen but was still alive. Saharo was dead. Nuur picked up the corpse and carried it several miles to her mother, running all the way. Meanwhile, other members of the clan had rushed to the scene to tend the wounded. Omar remained unconscious through it all. It wasn't until much later that he awoke in a hospital bed in nearby Merca. That's where his wife told him that both his daughters had been killed by the airstrike. Nimo died of internal bleeding.

Omar's leg was in bad shape. The doctors wanted to amputate it, but that would mean him giving up his livelihood. He vehemently refused for several days. But then, when the leg turned black, he gave in. With no money to pay for a prosthetic, Omar went home on crutches.

In the West, little is known about the fate of casualties like Omar the herdsman. Media can't investigate in Somalia because it's too dangerous. Instead, they have to rely on what American military sources tell them. Inasmuch as those sources – like the CNN's – are willing to share anything at all about clandestine missions in Somalia, it never concerns civilian casualties. Counter-terrorism is also about spin, after all. You shine a light on the successes, not the collateral damage.

Omar is the human story behind the intelligence deal between the Dutch MIVD and American NSA. His tragic account illuminates the ramifications of a blind faith in technology. When the Americans fired that missile, what intel were they using? According to US sources, the target of the attack – Al-Shabaab leader Ahmed Abdi Godane – was not killed. It's not even clear if he was anywhere near the area at all. The situation raises some thorny questions. Is the Netherlands culpable for what the US does with Dutch intelligence? Or, to take it even further, does the Netherlands share the blame for the death of Omar's daughters?

Spy agencies don't like to talk. When we ask the MIVD to comment, they get irritated. Two agency analysts are clearly annoyed that we've got hold of documents about surveillance in Somalia. In their opinion, that information is a state secret and we shouldn't have it. For us, it's important to get a reaction, not least to prevent us from inadvertently publishing details that might disrupt legitimate operations.

But the MIVD analysts refuse to tell us anything. Not even which information they think is too sensitive or may jeopardise human lives. Based on their reasoning, to disclose even that much would be to reveal new state secrets. We're left at this awkward impasse until finally a Defence spokesperson comes up with a solution: we journalists will wait outside the room while the analysts tell the spokesperson which information is disruptive to legitimate operations, and then *he* will tell us. But even this ploy doesn't ease the strain, because we won't promise to censor information. Not wanting to take any chances, the next day MIVD spokespersons threaten us with an injunction to block publication. In the end, though, they back off.

Whether or not Dutch intelligence played a role in the airstrike that injured Omar and killed his daughters will never be known: spy agencies don't tell each other if and how they use intelligence. The Americans are no less secretive about their methods than the Dutch – not only to guard their procedures, but because they believe it's the safest way to work. Leaking intelligence or methods could endanger lives and aid adversaries. State interests always win out over those of any one individual.

Nevertheless, in late 2013 the Dutch House of Representatives passed a motion seeking 'to impose an explicit condition on the sharing of intelligence, prohibiting its use for illegal targeted killings'. This would prevent the use of Dutch intelligence for attacks of the kind Omar suffered, and the Dutch Minister of Defence, Jeanine Hennis, committed to implementing the motion. There was only one problem: the Dutch government has no control over what the US does with information. The NSA is free to use intelligence however it pleases, and Hennis, as the minister in charge of the MIVD, was perfectly aware of that. Even if the NSA were to promise never to use Dutch intel for targeted killings, there's no way to verify whether it kept the pledge, since the NSA never grants outsiders access to its systems. No more than the Dutch MIVD and AIVD would ever allow the US into their systems. In other words, the Dutch Defence Minister's commitment was meaningless.

For the administration, however, it was the only way to keep some semblance of control over the Dutch intelligence agencies. In subsequent years the regulatory authority would apply more rigorous oversight to the sharing of information with foreign partners. The agencies would also be required to draw up so-called 'weighing reports' to assess countries' adherence to human rights treaties before any information was exchanged.

Omar was the unfortunate witness to a retaliatory action by American spy agencies. At the same time, his tragic fate was a consequence of advancing technology. Ever since the terrorist attacks on 11 September 2001, the US has been conducting a global war on terror, for which drones have become indispensable.

I have seen first-hand how this works. On US air force bases in Nevada and New Mexico there are air-conditioned trailers in which American pilots sit staring at monitors. Using joysticks, they fly planes thousands of miles away in countries like Pakistan, Afghanistan, Yemen and Somalia. Though these planes can't be seen from the ground, the pilots flying them remotely from those trailers back in the States *can* see what's happening in the streets below. In fact, a drone camera is so sharp it can pick out a ball in a children's football match.

The pilots sit here for eight to ten hours at a stretch flying a single drone in pairs. One keeps it in the air while the other operates a sensor guiding the missile to its intended mark. Through their headphones, they hear directives from an intelligence analyst to 'go to city X', 'keep tracking that person' or 'disengage now'. The pilots don't know the analysts, who are mostly CIA, or where they're located. At the press of a button, they can launch a Hellfire missile that hits the ground in fifteen seconds flat at a speed of almost 1,000 miles per hour. At the end of their shifts, they emerge from their climate-controlled trailers into the searing desert heat. They grab a Coke with co-workers, pick up their kids from school, watch Netflix at home.

It's no wonder the US loves drones. Without risk to American lives, these unmanned aircraft can eliminate terrorists anywhere in the world. During his term in office, President Barack Obama dramatically ramped up the number of drone strikes, praising this type of assassination as 'more precise' and 'more effective' than what the American military could accomplish with mere boots on the ground.

But there's also a downside. The CIA and the US military, which carry out the strikes, don't report civilian casualties. One drone pilot has told of his experience when tasked with monitoring a compound in Afghanistan. After watching the building for a few hours, he received the order to fire. Presumably, there was a high-ranking Taliban leader inside the compound. The pilot aimed his sensor at a corner of the house and released the missile. Just before it hit the ground, he saw something move. It looked like a figure running around the house. Then the missile struck, and when the smoke cleared there was nothing left. The house was destroyed. 'Did that look like a child to you?' he asked the analyst watching the same scene at some other remote location. 'Per the review, it's a dog,' the analyst replied. The drone pilot was positive it had been a child. In the six years he worked there, his squadron would kill 1,626 people.

According to recent figures from the Bureau of Investigative Journalism, an independent organisation that has been keeping count of civilian deaths through estimates and eyewitness accounts, there have been 6,786 confirmed strikes by unmanned aerial vehicles since 2004. Approximately 10,000 people have been killed, including between 800 and 1,700 civilians and at least 253 children.

Often, it's not even clear if a target has been brought down at all. As in the strike Omar witnessed. Intelligence data suggested that Al-Shabaab leader Ahmed Abdi Godane was in one of those pickup trucks. Back in the US, a pilot pressed a button. Godane wasn't killed. Two innocent little girls were.

*

Robin and I have now been in touch for two and a half years. My search has been arduous. The Australia-based Appen is pretty much unknown in Holland. Through LinkedIn I manage to find a few other Dutch nationals who'd worked for them in the past, but they're hesitant about meeting with a journalist. Even though they no longer work for the company, they signed confidentiality agreements and therefore can't tell me much.

I decide to try a different tack. If I can't find anyone who knows or is willing to talk about Appen, maybe experts can venture a guess as to why private telephone calls in the Netherlands were recorded for Robin in England to transcribe. The first person I talk to is speech-to-text expert Ralph Biesbrouck, who works with similar software. He tells me he'd never be able to get his hands on raw data files of the kind Robin described. 'I can only speculate about why Appen can.' What he does know is that spy agencies are taking a keen interest in tools that convert speech into text.

Their interest makes sense. Although technological capability to intercept phone calls has been steadily growing, listening to them is just as time-consuming as ever. Text also has the advantage that you can easily run automated searches for key terms.

I'll give an example. During the time Dutch armed forces were deployed in the Afghan province of Uruzgan (2006–10), the MIVD recruited thirty speakers of Farsi there. To ensure that these people, who included asylum seekers, would treat information confidentially and fully commit to the agency, it also gave them and their families residence permits to live in the Netherlands. These recruits would prove a trump card.

Around the same time, the NSA – an agency with a budget as big as that of the entire Dutch Ministry of Defence – had a shortage of good Farsi translators. The Netherlands played its trump card. Just send your intercepts to the Netherlands, said the MIVD; we can translate them for you. And so it happened that engineers laid a secure transatlantic cable connection to Holland and for a time the MIVD enjoyed exclusive access to America's powerful intelligence apparatus.

Machines translate faster than interpreters, however, and the intelligence community has long been working to automate the process. When I share Robin's story with intelligence expert Constant

Hijzen, he also immediately suspects intelligence involvement. 'Data processing is a problem for larger agencies. It's logical they'd want to develop software to mine their data faster.' But Appen isn't a spy agency, I counter. True, Hijzen replies, 'But UK and US agencies routinely work with industry.'

I also call two people at big telecom companies who know the rules around wiretapping. Permitted to talk only on condition of anonymity, they both say customer calls and data are under no circumstances allowed to be made available to external parties, with the *sole exception* of law enforcement and security agencies. Each can think of only one scenario to explain how Appen obtained the phone call made by Robin's ex: an agency must have been tapping Vodafone calls and sending the recordings to Appen to build speech-to-text software.

The last person I ask is René Pluijmers. He's a telecom expert with the Dutch National Forensic Research Agency and is often consulted in legal cases. According to Pluijmers, digital evidence is growing increasingly important in courtrooms, but judges tend to lack the background and knowledge to grasp technological complexities. He offers an example. Following a shooting, police arrested a man identified by witnesses as the gunman. In his own defence, the man said he'd been on the phone to a friend at the time the incident occurred. A lie, said the police, because their investigation showed his phone hadn't connected to the nearest cell tower. Ergo, he hadn't been on the phone.

The man's lawyer engaged Pluijmers to give a second opinion. 'I saw his phone could have connected to a different tower. Both signals were equally strong. So, the police had been careless in their calculation.' Thanks in part to Pluijmers's research, the suspect was acquitted. 'But for that, he'd certainly have been convicted. That's a shocking discovery.'

When I set out all the details Robin gave me, he also immediately suspects an intelligence agency, and more specifically intelligence in the UK. 'The British GCHQ taps dozens of fibre-optic cables and has experience with speech recognition software going back to 1981,' Pluijmers explains. 'Plus, they have a major stake in automating identification of call content and metadata. They might send Appen tapped calls to improve its software.' That makes sense. And by choosing an Australian company rather than a British one, outwardly there's less cause for suspicion.

I decide to call Vodafone, Robin's ex-boyfriend's provider. Their spokesperson is adamant: 'Vodafone Netherlands does not and never has worked with the Appen company.' Appen, for its part, denies ever co-operating with 'telecom companies', but won't say if the same applies to investigation agencies: 'We can't give details of the work we do for our clients.' Appen only gathers data with the assent of 'participants', I'm told. 'Everything is done with their consent.' Yet Robin's ex never consented to sharing his phone calls.

As happens so often, questions remain. The experts are unanimous, but their suspicions can't be proved. This is as close as I'll come to an answer: if it really was the work of British spies, I'll probably never have confirmation.

All the same, this information has yielded one new insight. Technology is making it easier to eavesdrop on communication all around the globe. Britain's Government Communications Headquarters, GCHQ, is among the best and most powerful spy agencies in the world. Even more data passes through its systems than at the NSA. In 2011 alone, GCHQ logged an astounding total of fifty billion internet metadata *per day*. Plus another 600 million telephone metadata daily, equating to almost 100 million phone calls.

GCHQ has permanent taps on twenty key fibre-optic cables in three locations. When data packets leave the Netherlands, the odds are high that they'll pass through the UK agency's filter. The internet can't be constrained by borders or by parliamentary motions. Foreign agencies may be barred from intercepting private communications in the Netherlands, but if Vodafone routes voicemail messages and telephone calls through a data centre in England, no one can stop GCHQ from listening in. In fact, if the UK agency wants Vodafone to hand over Dutch call data, all it has to do is ask. The Netherlands has no law against it.

Digitisation has caused us to lose control of our personal information. Should we be worried? Events in Belgium suggest we should.

6

A Many-Headed Hydra

Still slightly tipsy, I ring up my boss from aboard the high-speed train from Belgium, on my way home. 'It's a wrap,' I announce. 'We've got the final piece of the puzzle.' I'd been sitting in a Brussels pub for hours, downing endless rounds of La Chouffe with a Belgian source. With every pint he grew chattier, until finally the story about the spying at Belgacom spilled out.

The Belgacom hack is the Watergate of the surveillance world. Briefly, British and American intelligence agencies were caught red-handed in the very heart of Europe. I covered the case for more than four years and wrote two in-depth reconstructions. New questions just kept cropping up. How exactly did the British and American spies manage to break in? What did the Belgian authorities do when they realised their UK and US allies had attacked their tiny country? And why Belgacom? What was it that made this particular Belgian telecom company so critical?

Never before had I seen the consequences of digitisation at such close range. For years UK and US agencies had access to Belgium's biggest telecom provider and therefore to all of its customers as well. Worldwide, Belgacom provided telephony and data services to 1,100 companies, including 500 mobile operators like T-Mobile and KPN. The spies could see it all: even phone traffic from NATO, the European Commission and the European Parliament.

More than anything, it was the ingenuity of the hack that astounded even experts. So elegant, so difficult to find, so good, that eyewitnesses still call it the most astonishing thing they've ever seen. The assault weapon was years in the making, cobbled together by the American NSA and British GCHQ's best technical specialists. Teams from both agencies spent long hours mapping out their attack, leaving nothing to chance. It was a mission that could not fail. And it didn't. Because when British and American cyberspies crept inside Belgacom in late 2010, nobody noticed.

Unfortunately for them, there was one thing they couldn't have foreseen: that NSA contractor Edward Snowden would put every detail of the state secret operation onto a flash drive and release the files to journalists. That's how Scottish investigative journalist Ryan Gallagher got them in the autumn of 2013. At the time the NSA leak hit the news, the unassuming thirtysomething was writing about national security and privacy for UK and US media. He was fast earning worldwide acclaim and had joined with Glenn Greenwald – the journalist to whom Snowden leaked the NSA files – to write for his investigative platform *The Intercept*. That put Ryan Gallagher among a handful of international journalists with access to the hundreds of thousands of classified documents.

I first met Ryan in Brazil while visiting Greenwald. Straight away, Belgacom captured our mutual interest: not only was it the digital breach of the century, but there was hard evidence to prove it. The Snowden files contained fantastic details, such as descriptions of how the UK went about selecting system administrators at Belgacom through whom to smuggle their advanced offensive weapon inside the company. But we both knew we needed more. We needed sources who were willing to talk, who could contextualise the technical details and explain their significance.

There was no way I could reconstruct an intelligence operation crafted by the world's most powerful agencies on my own. With a little luck I might be able to find a Dutch source who knew something about Belgacom. Finding a Belgian source would be trickier, let alone a British one or an American. That could easily take years. It was the same for Ryan. He had the files, but would have difficulty finding a source in Holland or Belgium. So, we shook hands and agreed to work together.

When intelligence agencies want to control who can access information, they classify it. They have three categories: confidential, secret and top secret. The UK and US add even higher classifications. The UK has what's called the STRAP system, with levels 1, 2 and 3. STRAP 3 is the most sensitive and constitutes intelligence from tapping systems or locations. The Belgacom operation was classified STRAP 2, the second highest security level. Anyone who leaks STRAP 2 documents can look forward to a long prison sentence.

Ryan and I sent each other updates through extra-secure email. Later, Belgian journalist Nikolas Vanhecke of *De Standaard* came on board and we organised short chat sessions to keep each other informed. When sharing documents, we took ridiculous precautions. Ryan would send a document over an encrypted chat channel. That document would be secured with a long password. Then he'd send an enciphered email with a clue on where to find the password – say, 'chapter 3, paragraph 3, line 1.' Finally, over a different encrypted channel, he'd send the title of the book concerned. The only possible way someone else could open that document was to tap all of our communication channels and to crack the encryption. As a final precaution, the password-protected document was available for one week only; thereafter it was gone for good.

The three of us published our first story, 'The Inside Story of How British Spies Hacked Belgium's Largest Telco', in *The Intercept* a little over a year later, in 2014. At the time, we thought it was the definitive account of what had happened at Belgacom. But discussion surrounding the espionage scandal kept flaring up as new details – and new questions – continued to emerge. Why did Belgacom keep changing its answer to the question of what had taken place? Why did the Belgian government persist in playing dumb? And why did sources keep revisiting the case of their own accord? When we reconnected three years later, Ryan's experiences chimed with my own. We agreed to dive back in once more.

*

Impossible to miss, the two glass towers rise ostentatiously just outside Brussels-North railway station. These are the headquarters of what was Belgacom, a proud corporation with 13,000 employees and profits exceeding €500 million.

But in early July 2013, the overriding feeling among executives up on the twenty-fifth floor – where an air bridge connects the two gleaming towers – was one of anxiety. For a while now there had been issues with an internal mail server. Emails among staff were either taking ages to arrive or they never arrived at all. A Microsoft update only exacerbated the problems, but when Belgacom asked the software giant for help, it couldn't find anything wrong.

Ivo Cools, the telecom company's chief technology officer, rang Ronald Prins and asked the Fox-IT director to come and investigate at Belgacom's head office in Brussels. 'Sure,' he said, 'if you don't mind me wearing shorts.' Prins and his family were on a weekend holiday in the Belgian town of Spa and he hadn't packed a suit. 'Not a problem,' assured Cools.

Prins dispatched his top specialists to Brussels where they set up in an office next to the boardroom. Prins himself made many trips to the glass towers on Koning Albert II-laan to discuss the latest with Cools and Belgacom CEO Didier Bellens, dashing into town in his grey Maserati.

Those discussions became increasingly grim. Unlike Microsoft, the Fox-IT team did see an anomaly in the mail server. They found what appeared to be a Windows file, but wasn't. Working carefully, they scanned the systems in search of more traces of a possible intruder.

For Cools and Bellens the search was taking too long. They wanted to clean up the infected systems and move on. It's too expensive, there's no point, they complained, against which Prins argued that good research takes time. The more complicated the research, the potentially bigger the problem. To stop now would in itself be risky, the Dutchman warned the two directors: just look at what happened with Vodafone in Greece.

What happened in Greece was a scandal. During the 2004 Olympic Games, as it later transpired, the phones of more than a hundred Greeks, including the country's prime minister and other politicians, had been bugged by someone invisibly modifying legal tapping software at Vodafone Greece. The modification came to light after a software update resulted in problems with Vodafone's text messaging service. Vodafone investigated the problem, discovered the infiltration and immediately erased all the traces. As a result, Greek investigators had no way of tracking down the perpetrators.

Not long after this a network manager at Vodafone took his own life. Greek police believe that the man's suicide was linked to the wiretapping scandal and the pressure he was under, although this has not been proven. Ultimately, the 'Greek Watergate', as it came to be known, turned out to be the work of the American NSA. For its failure to protect customer data and then impeding an investigation, the Greek privacy watchdog slapped Vodafone with a €76 million fine.

Cools and Bellens agreed unhappily to let Fox-IT continue its painstaking detective work. Inside Belgacom's systems they found small files that would alert the owner if opened to signal they'd been discovered, known as booby traps. The more the researchers explored, the more mysterious it all seemed. But after two weeks at least one thing was certain: this level of complexity could only be the work of a foreign state. Only the most highly skilled specialists could infiltrate this deep, masquerade as Microsoft, plant booby traps and remain hidden the whole time.

Belgacom immediately informed all the necessary organisations, and in mid-July 2013 federal police, cyber experts and Belgian security agencies descended on Koning Albert II-laan. Dutch and Belgian specialists meticulously studied the manipulated software that was so cleverly crafted it left researchers speechless. 'It was all *so* ingenious,' a Belgian police investigator said. Frank Groenewegen of Fox-IT called it 'by far the best I'd ever seen'.

An important difference between the hacks at DigiNotar and KPN was that here investigators were up against a supremely professional opponent. The weapon deployed at Belgacom was a kind of modular malware that snaked its way like a many-headed hydra through the company's 26,000 IT systems, adapting to each new environment and depositing eggs along the way. It was capable of installing itself on computers that weren't switched on or online, where it would lie in wait until they were booted up again to send documents and other data from those computers unseen. It could also make screenshots, copy passwords and restore deleted components. Most malware has a couple of unique features; this malware could apparently do it all.

A few days later the target came into view. The area where the 'hydra' had been most active was around BICS, one of Belgacom's highest-grossing divisions. BICS was a data connectivity hub for telecom providers and had a vast global network serving and linking hundreds of companies. What the AMS-IX internet interchange was for the internet, BICS was for telephony.

BICS was a major data carrier for telecoms in Africa and the Middle East. It also provided data roaming services for phone companies. That's when you make a call abroad and your phone connects to a different carrier from your normal domestic one. With some 1.2 billion cellular subscribers calling, messaging and texting over the BICS network, anyone who could gain access to BICS effectively had access to the world.

Researchers could see the hydra had been stealing information at BICS. It was sending nuggets of data to IP addresses all over the world, divided across multiple packets so as not to be noticeable in the daily sea of data flowing in and out of Belgacom.

The team figured they were finally in business, but when they examined the files all they saw was nonsensical strings of letters and numbers. So cleverly were the packets encrypted that there was no way of getting inside. Tracing them to their destinations was no help either, because those were just leased computer servers in India, Romania, Indonesia and the Netherlands.

*

What was it that so attracted UK and US spies to Belgacom? And why were the two countries working so closely together?

To answer this we have to go back to a secret conference held in 2009. On 1–5 June, top surveillance specialists from British, Canadian and American agencies met in an unknown location for the SDC, short for SIGINT Development Conference. Along with counterparts in Australia in New Zealand, these agencies form an alliance known as the 'Five Eyes'. This alliance has its origins in the Second World War, when England and the United States wanted to exchange information about decoded German and Japanese communications.

In time, they expanded to sharing satellite communications. But here they ran into a problem: because satellite coverage is geographically limited, a ground station in the US can't intercept satellite traffic as far away as, say, the Middle East. The solution was to bring in more allies, which the US did, resulting in the creation of the Five Eyes. Together, these five countries had wide enough coverage to eavesdrop on the entire world. The alliance continues to this day and constitutes the world's most powerful intelligence organisation. Once a year the allies convene to talk about the latest eavesdropping techniques. The year 2009 was a pivotal one, because the Five Eyes were finding it increasingly difficult to do their spying. Existing techniques were no longer delivering, so something had to change.

What was the problem?

To begin with, the internet was growing in all directions. More and more countries were connecting to the worldwide superhighway. With the proliferation of internet connections it was also becoming harder to predict over which path data packets would travel.

Normally, that's whichever route is fastest and cheapest. But the more routes there are available, the less predictable it is which one traffic will choose.

A second development was that telecom providers had started encrypting data packets and using VPNs to transmit their customers' communications from A to B. This encryption made it impossible for intelligence agencies to open and read intercepted data packets. To do that, telecom providers had to give them the key.

The June 2009 conference was about these developments. Agencies wanted to intercept and open data packets. What would enable them to do so?

The Five Eyes weren't the only ones wrestling with this problem. Other agencies were encountering similar obstacles. Dutch sources suspect Israel dealt with it by mobilising a secret arsenal of sorts. They'd noticed that from the 1990s onwards a remarkably large number of former Israeli Unit 8200 intelligence personnel were starting up high-tech companies to supply surveillance software. Were they simply capitalising on their acquired know-how or carving out the perfect position from which to spy? Many of these companies were based in other countries, since not everyone is keen to do business with Israeli firms.

These companies grew to be global market leaders in the supply of surveillance software. Even the American NSA uses spyware from Israel. The Netherlands is also a consumer of Israeli products. The MIVD, for instance, uses surveillance software made by NICE Systems, while law enforcement uses Cellebrite, and the police phone-tapping unit used Comverse (until 2018). The Ministry of Security – following an obscure procedure – yet again selected an Israeli supplier for its tapping software in the summer of 2019; in this case Cyber Intelligence, which is a subsidiary of Dutch Defence supplier Elbit Systems. KPN relies on Verint. As does the American NSA.

Two Dutch intelligence sources claim the reason Israeli organisations have been so successful is that they can sell their products below market price thanks to Israeli government funding.

This has helped them win a succession of contracts. Once taken on by a client, the companies are ideally positioned to spy on information before it's encrypted and sent online. If and how often 'Israel' actually employs this espionage capability the Dutch sources can't say. Israel is an ally, after all, so the Netherlands doesn't examine its espionage activities that closely.

Coincidence or not, Israeli companies are also leaders in telecommunications billing solutions. Because customers often use carriers besides their own for services like wireless roaming or call completion through other networks, telecoms have to bill each other for those individual phone calls and text messages – legally, within seventy-two hours. Israeli firms MIND CTI and Amdocs supply software that handles this. The latter is or has been used by, among others KPN, Vodafone, the Dutch bank ABN Amro and nearly every telecom provider in the US.

For intelligence agencies, this billing data is a goldmine. It lists who's contacting whom and which numbers are important. That Israel occupies a prime spot in this arena was attested to by a controversial book by investigative journalist Gordon Thomas about the Israeli Mossad. He describes how Israel bugged Monica Lewinsky's telephone and eavesdropped while she had phone sex with then President Bill Clinton. The Israeli agency used those intercepted calls to pressure President Clinton to pull the plug on a counter-espionage operation against Mossad. Later, Lewinsky related under oath how Clinton told her a 'foreign embassy' had indeed been listening in on their intimate chats.

The Five Eyes can't deploy these weapons any more. But they have other options. Rather than waiting for information to cross the traffic network, the Americans want to grab it at the source, inside the computer networks of telecom providers and UN organisations. A specialist unit in the NSA takes care of this by either remotely infiltrating hardware or modifying equipment before delivery to an end user.

An internal NSA catalogue published by *Der Spiegel* illustrates how this works. Computer systems are built up in layers. Routers and firewalls are crucial links between those layers, sending internet flows in the right direction and guarding against attacks. Network routers are the traffic regulators. They direct internet traffic to specific destinations – just like your router connects your iPad, smartphone or PC at home. That makes routers a favourite target for spying.

The NSA can remotely break into routers such as those manufactured by the US-based Juniper and Chinese Huawei and leave 'implants' to gain permanent control over the device. Even if computers are rebooted or upgraded, the agency can continue spying undetected by the owner.

It's the same with firewalls. These stand between internal computer networks and the World Wide Web, rather like airport customs checkpoints to monitor who and what's allowed inside. The NSA targets hardware firewalls of all major brands, sometimes even before they're delivered. Designated personnel seize a shipment, unpack it, install additional components, tape the box back together and send it on its way. The result is that a firewall which was supposed to recognise and block hackers in the manner of a digital customs checkpoint instead throws open the barriers whenever the NSA drops by.

Specialists from the UK intelligence service GCHQ came to the secret conference with a plan. GCHQ had studied the global traffic network and discovered where its vulnerabilities lay: in telecom companies that handle communications for a multitude of organisations. Companies like Belgacom, and specifically BICS, the division that carried data for many telecom players around the world.

There was a further reason to target BICS in particular. Of the three largest telecoms offering worldwide data roaming services, only BICS was based outside the United States. US federal law already allowed the NSA to surveil roaming providers on American soil. Access to BICS would give the UK, the US and their intelligence allies a gateway to the rest of the world. The Five Eyes approved the British plan.

Now came the tricky part. How would they get inside? Belgacom was an important company with high-level security. Only with meticulous preparation and a great deal of patience would the British and the Americans – with the latter leading the offensive – be able to pull off their mission.

Step one was to canvas the target. How was Belgacom's network put together? Where were its vulnerabilities? GCHQ turned to its extensive network of wiretaps. By default, it already filtered internet data from telecom system administrators, who have key information about their networks. Within this data pool, they went fishing for Belgacom IP addresses and came up with three suitable candidates.

Next, they looked up information on all three administrators. Their email addresses, LinkedIn profiles, the operating systems they used and websites they visited. The British agency also used cookies – the small files advertisers put on computers to track browsing behaviour – to follow the three targets' online habits. GCHQ stored cookies, too, from which it extracted the information it wanted. The chosen targets happened to be two Belgians and a Venezuelan.

This preparatory phase took a full two years, by which time the UK knew everything about the three targets, including when they were online and who they were in contact with. It was time for GCHQ to attack. Whereas hackers often send phishing emails in the hope that recipients will be tempted to click on an attachment, intelligence agencies use more sophisticated methods. In this case, they built exact replicas of the targets' LinkedIn pages. When the Belgians and the Venezuelan went to the LinkedIn site, they were instantly and imperceptibly redirected to the identical fake page. Now GCHQ could enter each target's computer and access the Belgacom network and BICS infrastructure.

When they knew enough about the network, they released their weapon – a virus that could worm its way through Belgacom to BICS. Once inside, it received commands. For instance: search for and send back all data on phone number X in the UK. Regin, as this virus was called, was co-engineered by the UK and the US and was incredibly effective. No other agency in the world had anything that could match it.

In 2011, this many-headed hydra burrowed its way deep inside the very heart of BICS. It would be two years before anyone noticed something was wrong.

*

Belgian Prime Minister Elio Di Rupo was furious. Sitting in an emergency meeting with his head of military security, police investigators and the ministers of Justice and Public Enterprises in late August 2013, he'd just learned that his country's biggest and majority state-owned telecom company had been hacked by a foreign state.

It was the first time Belgium had faced this new threat and the prime minister wanted to make his position clear from the outset. It was an unprecedented violation of his country's national integrity; Belgium 'strongly condemns this intrusion', he stormed in a public statement. 'If this hypothesis is confirmed and it is indeed cyber espionage' his administration would take 'appropriate action'. Solving the breach became a national priority, and the federal prosecutor who normally handled terrorism enquiries was put on the case. According to Di Rupo, the state's interests were at stake.

Researchers had by this time been marvelling over the hydra inside BICS for weeks. They could see it was moving around and doing something, but not exactly what. They thought it might be sending signals to the attacker. But who was that? Most malware contains some clue as to the perpetrator, such as where stolen files are sent, or traces of the time zone where the code was written, or possibly some reference to a country. The researchers could find none of these things. The data packets were all going to leased servers of the sort used in India for online gaming, and then onward from there. Belgian police filed an information request to find out who was leasing the servers, but it would be months before they got an answer. In some cases, it could take years.

Then, just as Belgacom, Fox-IT and the teams of specialists were getting ready to clean up the company's systems, something strange happened. All at once, the hydra retracted. 'I think the attackers knew they'd been discovered,' one of the researchers said. 'They pushed a button to destroy the malware.' In the blink of an eye the virus erased its tracks and deleted portions of itself. Though they could see it happening right before their eyes, there was nothing the team could do to stop it. The clean-up operation had to be suspended.

Two weeks later, hundreds of Belgacom staff, computer experts from the MIVD and police and judicial investigators gathered for a second attempt to clean the systems. Following the hydra's trail through the network, they reset or removed computers, routers and firewalls. Afterwards, Belgacom felt satisfied, believing that the attacker had been booted out of its network and hoping to quickly close the door on this nerve-wracking period.

Fox-IT still had some sensors running inside the company, though, and a few days after the clean-up they picked up some odd activity: two external data packets had got inside the Belgacom network – packets that didn't belong there. It was the hydra once again. Even more distressing to the Dutch team was when they saw it pass through a critical router made by Cisco, a US company.

Cisco routers of the kind used at big telecoms can run into the hundreds of thousands of dollars. Anybody who could hack them would have complete command over the network. So, how had this happened? Had the routers at BICS been infected even before the breach? Or were the UK and US able to hack them? Either scenario would be big news. Belgacom decided to ask the manufacturer for help. Cisco agreed to send experts, but it didn't want anyone snooping on their work. The software was secret and too sensitive, they said, so if they came in, Fox-IT had to go.

Belgacom gave in to Cisco's demands, but not everyone approved. 'Evidently, Belgacom doesn't want an independent investigation,' one of the original researchers remarked disapprovingly. Others could understand Cisco's logic. Only the firm knew how its routers worked, and if they were found to be infected and that information got out, Cisco would have a massive problem on its hands.

The Dutch team was made to sign confidentiality statements and sent packing. When they left, the hydra was still active, so when Belgacom immediately thereafter announced its systems were clean they were understandably startled. According to a company press release issued in mid-September, 'there is no indication that BICS' telecommunications network [...] has been impacted by this intrusion'.

The British documents Ryan Gallagher and I obtained through Edward Snowden a year after the hack was discovered stated in black and white that the UK's GCHQ had access to the core of BICS. British spies wrote that they'd gained access 'deep into the network' and that '[t]his work has been very successful'. The hack accomplished its objective: through BICS, the UK and the US had obtained a gateway to hundreds of other telecom companies.

Even more astonishing was when Geert Standaert, Belgacom's vice president, told an EU parliamentary hearing that nothing was wrong. He characterised the years of UK spying as having impacted 'only on the internal IT systems' at Belgacom. 'As to the reason behind this attack,' he said, 'we can't really draw any conclusions from the facts at the moment.' EU parliamentarian Sophie in 't Veld was stunned by Belgacom's portrayal of the affair. 'It was absurd. Everyone sensed that Belgacom's representatives weren't telling the whole truth,' she told the Belgian press.

When UK and US media subsequently published documents describing the breach in minute detail, the Belgian administration did an abrupt about-face as well. Prime Minister Di Rupo, initially furious, in public softened his tone. 'It would almost be surprising if Brussels, as the EU capital and seat of countless civilian and military international institutions, were to escape cyber-espionage,' he told the Belgian parliament in late November. In 2016, Belgian Telecom Services Minister Alexander De Croo would even suggest Belgium might have invited British spying. 'It might very well be that the Belgian intelligence services said, "Yes, please go ahead, why not?"' Later, De Croo refused to explain the comment.

*

Why did Belgacom act as though nothing had happened? And why did the administration's fury dissolve when UK and US spies were revealed as being behind the breach?

It didn't make any sense. That is, not until Ryan and I attempted a second reconstruction of the events. This time around, we found a story about Belgium's criminal investigation into British spying and about how the Belgian police team had been skilfully thwarted at every turn. For each step forward, the team took two steps back. Every time they thought they were closing in on the perpetrators, another door slammed shut.

For instance, they'd get the names, addresses and bank details of people leasing the computer servers in India, Romania, Indonesia and the Netherlands, to which the hydra sent its stolen files. They traced them to Germany and Denmark. When Belgium asked Germany for more information, the address of that suspect turned out to be a theatre. Hence, a dead end.

A next option was to sift through the payment data. Some servers had been leased with credit cards issued in England. On closer inspection, however, police found they were prepaid cards purchased anonymously. Investigators also found some IP addresses that could be traced back to Great Britain, but when they asked the UK's Home Office for more information, the answer was a resolute no. 'We have decided to refuse this help. The United Kingdom believes that this could jeopardise our sovereignty, security and public order.'

Out of pure desperation the police team finally turned to Europol – the agency that helps EU member states combat terrorism and serious crime, and which has a special Cyber Crime Centre dedicated to 'the law enforcement response to cybercrime in the EU'. But Europol declined, too, stating it 'would not carry out investigations into other European Union member states'. Coincidentally or not, Europol's director at the time was Rob Wainwright, a man who had once worked for MI5.

Every lead was a dead end. The team knew the UK spy agency was behind the breach but had no way of proving it. GCHQ used 'intermediary machines' and 'covert infrastructure' to execute such attacks, Ryan and I read in their top-secret documents. All hacking activities, GCHQ wrote, 'must be UK deniable'. No wonder the Belgians weren't getting anywhere. '[W]e were fighting against two big cyberarmies from the UK and the US,' said a Belgian police investigator. 'We knew we could never win this.'

Even the Snowden files which described the operation in full detail were off limits to the police team. They'd wanted to visit the NSA whistleblower in Moscow to verify what the documents said, but the Belgian prosecutor put his foot down. It could antagonise the US.

Herein lies the explanation for Belgium's flip-flopping: the Belgians needed the UK and the US more than those two needed Belgium. This is further illustrated by the investigations following the Brussels bombings on 22 March 2016. Thirty-five people died as a result of the attacks that morning at an airport and underground station, and 270 were injured. The bombers were part of a terrorist cell that also struck in Paris in 2015 and which had long had Belgium in its grip.

Belgium can't do counter-terrorism without the intelligence capability of larger countries like France, Britain and the United States. After the attacks in Paris, Belgium turned to the NSA to help it track down one of the suspects, Belgian-born Salah Abdeslam, by collecting bulk phone data at the funeral of another terrorist cell member. Amid all this violence, Belgacom was just a detail. 'The UK and the US are assisting us with counter-terrorism. The feeling was we couldn't allow the Belgacom inquiry to jeopardise that,' acknowledged one of the Belgian police investigators.

Belgacom, meanwhile, had its own motives, most notably to protect relations with customers and shareholders. That's not unusual with companies that fall victim to espionage. Thus, while Belgacom downplayed the damage in its public statements, internally it took strong measures, replacing infected infrastructure, scrambling to recruit ethical hackers and splitting the company up into separate networks in order to fend off future infiltration. The company estimated the total damage at more than €15 million, and the investments to prevent a repeat occurrence at another 46 million. Belgacom also changed its name: today, the sign on the tall glass towers spells Proximus. Any reminders of the UK hack were scrubbed away.

For years the UK had been able to tap potentially hundreds of millions of phones. Nobody could or would stop them. So high were the stakes that the Belgian government was willing to allow the UK and the US to take control of the country's most important telecom company. Belgacom was even willing to lie about it.

An IT expert who saw the UK spying at Belgacom in the summer of 2013 later said he was convinced the British agency was still inside. And that it's impossible to keep systems clean, because you can replace all the infected Cisco routers you want, but the new ones may be infected, too. 'If the British and Americans are after you,' he said, 'you don't stand a chance.'

That is the story of Belgacom. Such are the capabilities and power of the UK and the US that they can strike everywhere and at any time. Regin, the many-headed hydra that infected Belgacom, was later found on a personal staff member of German Chancellor Angela Merkel. The virus also crept inside companies in Pakistan, India, Turkey, Iran, Argentina, North Korea, the United Arab Emirates, Ireland, South Africa and Zimbabwe.

Both Belgacom and Omar – the big telecom company and a poor, insignificant herdsman – didn't stand a chance against the digital aggression perpetrated on them. Where could they direct their grievances? Or obtain justice?

Digitisation is changing the nature of liability. Omar never saw the murderer of his two daughters. Belgacom didn't know the spies who released a virus inside its company. Catch a spy in the act and you can deport them, but cyberspies are shielded by anonymity. They can take more risks and carry out sustained attacks with little fear of being caught. Other countries can't call them to account and they seldom wind up in the spotlight. They can attack, overpower and even crush individuals and organisations and they can get away with it.

And there's another reason to be concerned. What the UK and the US can do, other countries can, too. Each in its own way.

Part III

The Outlook

7

Too Close

Just beyond this black door with an antique silver handle, within arm's length of where I'm standing, lives the most wanted hacker in the world, a thirty-three-year-old man who's managed to elude the FBI for years. A man whom US President Barack Obama, as one of his last acts in office, placed on a sanctions list. The FBI has offered $3 million – the largest reward ever for a hacker – for the golden tip leading to his arrest.

It's the spring of 2017 and I'm on the fourteenth floor of a yellowish apartment block in Anapa, a Russian seaside resort for young families where the attractions include rundown amusement rides and men carrying around leashed monkeys. Parked in front of the apartment building, just outside the barrier, is a black Jeep Grand Cherokee, licence plate O400YO. According to the FBI investigation report, it's exactly the kind of car this shaven-headed 5ft 9 suspect would drive. A modest ride, considering his income. Estimates put this at hundreds of millions of dollars.

His name is Evgeniy Bogachev. His crime is breaking into more than a million computers to commit electronic bank robberies. His speciality is financial fraud: stealing bank data from computers and using it to empty accounts. One of his first victims was the major Dutch bank ABN Amro. Many thousands of other institutions followed, from a Massachusetts police department to hospitals, as well as hundreds of random individuals whom he extorted online using ransomware.

Bogachev isn't just a crafty hacker, he's an exceptionally savvy entrepreneur with his own criminal empire, who invests his stolen millions in property here in Anapa. His power and connections have made him an attractive partner for Russian security services, and his knowledge and skills have made him a valuable asset. According to the United States, he's a spy.

In the hallway to his apartment, it's quiet but for the ticking of a half-open utility box. Overhead, a cylindrical security camera trains a steady eye on me. There's a white doorbell with the number '223' written on it in marker. I ring it.

*

A couple of months ago I would never have imagined I'd wind up in Anapa. I'd been reading up on Russian espionage and how it was advancing on all fronts, especially in the cyberworld. There was one name that kept cropping up: Bogachev. Why was he so important to the Russians? As always with new information, I reached out to some sources. Some by phone, others face to face.

But my harvest was slim. I no longer had a good line on what was happening in the intelligence world and my access to the flow of NSA documents had dried up. Sources who'd once been able to clue me in didn't know about new operations. Periods like this are frustrating. The newspaper leaves me free to pursue my own research and expects good stories in return. But by the winter of 2016 nothing had presented itself, and I was starting to feel edgy.

The best sources in the digital world are those who have just left an agency. They know a good deal and feel less obliged to keep secrets. The drawback is that they're no longer in the loop on new operations, so their knowledge is limited. This puts me on a perpetual search for new sources.

What I needed, first of all, were names of intelligence personnel. Of course, those names are kept secret. I spent several weeks meeting up with old sources, trying to tease out new names. Ultimately, I managed to get three: mostly former colleagues of my existing contacts who worked in Dutch general or military intelligence – that is, the AIVD or MIVD.

Step two was tracking down their addresses. Most intelligence personnel stay away from social media and they certainly don't post pictures of their homes on Facebook. They're well aware of the risks. I did find a LinkedIn profile for one name, but there was no town or other clue to hint at his address. Helpfully, though, LinkedIn also shows you who else has looked at the profile you're viewing. In that list was one woman. Could she be his wife?

Scrolling through her profile, I saw that, like the man, she, too, lived in The Hague. Also, that her résumé said she'd lived abroad in exactly the same years as he had. I tried feeding the woman's name and city into the land registry database. *Bingo*. I had an address.

With another name, I again managed to track down a spouse and, through her, an address. On Facebook, she was friends with a bunch of apparently random people. When I looked at those people more closely and plotted their addresses on Google Maps, they all turned out to live next door to one another, forming a big circle. Neighbours, I guessed. Sure enough, when I went to check out the area, I found precisely the name I was after on one of the front doors.

Now you're standing on someone's doorstep. What do you say? The opening gambit makes all the difference. I don't work undercover, so I always say upfront that I'm a journalist. But do I wait until I've crossed the threshold, or should I announce my purpose over the intercom? For me, it depends. If the person's startled, it's better to cut to the chase. If they're unfazed and curious, I tend to have better luck if I can get inside before explaining why I'm there. Next dilemma: what time to knock on someone's door? People tend not to be home in the daytime, but in the evening my visit is bound to be inconvenient.

I remember one rainy evening when my *Volkskrant* colleague Tom Kreling and I went to visit the late Gerard Bouman at his house. Bouman was the head of the AIVD and later of the Dutch national police. Tom and I were writing a story in which his name came up and we wanted to give him a chance to tell his side without a spokesperson's interference. This way, he'd be free to speak off the record. Had we gone through official channels, that path would be closed to us, as at least one other person would know we'd talked.

Bouman lived just outside Rotterdam. His house was set back from the road, fenced off, with an intercom at the front. From the street we couldn't tell if anyone was home. We tried the intercom but got no response. We waited a few minutes. Still nothing. We drove back to Amsterdam.

The next day we tried again. This time I thought I saw lights on in the house. We pressed the button. No answer. We walked up the road a bit, waited, turned back. We pressed the button again. At first, nothing. Then, static, followed by an obviously irritated, 'Yes?'

This was our one and only shot. We had to find an opening while at the same time making it clear we were journalists.

'Hello, Mr Bouman. I'm a journalist with—'

Beep, beep. He'd hung up. Dammit.

Back in the car, we texted him, explaining we wanted to give him a chance to comment and tell him what our story was about.

'Go to hell,' he texted back.

On the A4 back to Amsterdam a little later we got a call from the national police.

'Mr Bouman says you've been harassing him. Please stop stalking him.'

Later, Bouman's press officers also called the newspaper's editorial office to complain.

This is the risk of approaching people at home. It can annoy employers, too – certainly when the employer is the AIVD. After I'd sought out intelligence personnel at their homes a few times, I found myself summoned to the agency's headquarters in Zoetermeer, where I was accused of endangering staff. I disagreed. I hadn't parked my car in front of their houses, I'd made sure I wasn't being followed and I knew enough never to bring along my phone. 'And besides,' I argued, 'this is my only option as a journalist: to approach people in person, introduce myself and ask if they're willing to talk. If they're not, so be it.'

The AIVD wanted my word that I'd never again visit intelligence personnel at home. I refused to give it. Journalists have the right to ask questions, after all, just as anyone being questioned is entitled not to answer.

Of the three people I tracked down, in the end one was willing to keep in touch. We sent each other encrypted messages over Chatapp. Whenever there was a news story or something potentially interesting, I asked his opinion. A few months later, we arranged to meet for lunch.

I developed several contacts like him, and sometimes spent entire evenings texting back and forth with three or four of them. They were people who helped me understand the technology, but who also wrote incomprehensible things like 'I think because they use Sneier electronic software'. What mattered most is that they were knowledgeable about the intelligence world. With their input, I could gauge whether events were newsworthy and how much my sources knew.

Now I was sitting across from my new source in a hotel restaurant off the dual carriageway. I told him a little about myself, we agreed this was off the record and then we got down to business. I'd thought of a few operations beforehand that he might know about. Some of his answers were short: 'Nope, never heard of it.' About others he was more expansive: 'Sounds familiar, that's something you may want to look into.' The longer I stayed in touch with this source, the better I became at reading him. No two sources are ever really the same. With some, a curt nod tells you all you need to know; with others it's more like a cross-examination. Some get straight to the point, others dance around the subject. Some exaggerate, others are precise.

Sources can be motivated by an element of vanity, but more often they agree to meet out of a shared fascination with the mystique of the spy world. Such is the secrecy within agencies that even employees only ever know bits and pieces of what's happening. Sources tend to open up more if I hint from time to time that I'm already acquainted with particular operations. Maybe the idea that they're with an insider puts them at ease, as well as the fact that they're obviously not the only ones talking to journalists.

When our tuna club sandwiches arrived, we were on the topic of Russia. Russia had been an increasingly prominent focus of annual reports published by the Dutch security and intelligence agencies. If they were to be believed, the Russians were a grave menace, especially online. 'How come?' I asked. 'How do the Russians work and what do our agencies know about them?' I wanted to get a better handle on how Dutch intelligence measures up. My source told me about this one Russian hacker named Evgeniy Bogachev. He was notorious – the Pablo Escobar of the cyberworld. Then he added, 'Could be the Netherlands has something on him.'

Sometimes that one nugget is all I get, which means I need to find more people to verify it. Often, I can't. Dozens of these snippets of information and subtle leads come my way each year that end up going nowhere. This time, though, it was surprisingly easy. Everybody I asked about Bogachev knew him. His past was legendary. Four weeks was all it took to work out the story of the notorious Russian.

*

Bogachev's story also makes clear how the Netherlands came to be such a pivotal actor in the cyberworld. It was in 2007 that Dutch police and experts from Fox-IT first began to hunt Russian crooks.

These were still the early days, and Bogachev was as yet unknown to them.

That year, large amounts of money began disappearing from the accounts of Dutch ABN Amro bank customers. Curiously, all clues pointed back to the customers. The transactions had been executed using their own logins and their own passwords from their own IP addresses. To all appearances, they'd made the transfers themselves.

ABN Amro wasn't the only bank wrestling with cybercrime. As online transactions surged in the late nineties, so did the scams criminals cooked up to get their hands on this money. The Netherlands had been quick to embrace the internet, thanks to a combination of the country's small size, fast connections and government subsidisation of nationwide internet access. Online banking swiftly followed, putting the country at the forefront of the digitising world.

This attracted criminals. At another bank, ING, employees discovered a small black box taped to the underside of a desk. It being summer, and hot, the tape had come unstuck. The box turned out to a transmitter: criminals had worked out a way to take command of computer keyboards and, using ordinary baby monitors, could spy on bank staff. Whenever a bank employee got up from their desk, the thieves pounced and remotely transferred cash.

What happened at ABN Amro was that a ring of Romanian criminals had tweaked a chip in the card readers used in their bank branches. Whenever a customer inserted their bank card and made a transfer, unbeknown to them the device copied their card's magnetic strip. Once a week the Romanians dropped by, put their own smartcard in the reader, read out the chip containing new magnetic strip and PIN-code data and used that to clean out people's bank accounts. And it wasn't a one-off incident. Back in Romania, a factory was producing fake card readers on an industrial scale.

In 2007, the mystery was far more confounding. ABN Amro's systems showed nothing suspicious, but victims all maintained they hadn't withdrawn the money from their bank accounts. To work out what was going on, the bank decided to call in Ronald Prins. Maybe he could get to the bottom of it?

Demand for the tech-savvy Ronald Prins and his company Fox-IT was growing steadily around this time. The energetic Prins, a native of The Hague, was the embodiment of Holland's rapid digitisation. While he was studying e-cash at Amsterdam's national research institute for maths and computer science, the institute was pioneering early forms of the internet. He went on to carve out a reputation in the mid-nineties by cracking the coded Excel files of drug lords Johan V. and Etienne U., then installed the first police internet tap on Etienne U.'s accountant and, later, the AIVD's first internet tap on a suspected terrorist.

Prins wasn't the only person called in by ABN Amro. Law enforcement also took an interest in the case. Not long before, a new police unit had been created to specialise in digital investigations. This was the High Tech Crime Unit, headed by Martijn van de Beek. Van de Beek was ambitious, someone known for thinking on a big and broad scale. According to him, it was no use fighting cybercrime in the Netherlands alone. What was needed were international contacts. The ABN Amro case would prove Van de Beek right.

Technical experts had already been scratching their heads for months when, as a last resort, they thought to check account holders' own computers. And there they found it: all the machines were infected with the same bug, ZeuS, as its authors called it.

This computer virus, which became world famous among scammers and infamous among researchers, was nothing short of a masterpiece. Designed to steal data such as usernames, passwords and addresses, it infected computers when unwitting users clicked on an email attachment. Once inside, it performed the ingenious trick of perfectly recreating a bank's login page at the very instant a user went to log in to their account. In effect, it slid this extra window in front the bank's login page. While customers assumed they were entering their personal details on a bank's legitimate website, in actuality they were typing everything on the hackers' phoney page. Occasionally, those pages would also request additional details such as answers to security questions, telephone numbers or codes that banks send for verification purposes. With that information, the robbers cleaned out their victims' accounts.

Almost nothing could be done to counter this kind of crime, not only because ZeuS was exceptionally effective, but also because its creators hid behind anonymous internet browsers. Besides ABN Amro, they targeted other banks in Europe and the United States as well, leading to hundreds of millions of dollars in damages. Much of this online criminal traffic used Dutch data centres, but the perpetrators themselves were far away. For Martijn van de Beek, it was clear that to catch them on foreign soil, the Netherlands needed to get creative.

In the autumn of 2007, Van de Beek went to Russia. From Moscow, he boarded a Tupolev to Khabarovsk near the Chinese border, where the FSB – the Russian Federal Security Service – was hosting a conference.

After the FSB director opened the conference and Russian President Vladimir Putin gave a brief word of welcome, it was Van de Beek's turn to speak. He had already noted that the room was packed with delegates from security, intelligence and investigation agencies all over the world, including the CIA, FBI, Israeli Mossad and German and South African services. That wasn't remarkable in itself; despite political differences, national agencies still regularly gather to discuss topics on which constructive co-operation *is* possible. Chiefly, topics like terrorism and cybercrime.

Much of the Khabarovsk conference was about routine networking – the shaking of hands and handing out of business cards. But Van de Beek had something else up his sleeve: he'd hatched a bold plan through which he hoped to win the Russians' trust.

By this time, the head of the highly specialised National High Tech Crime Unit was well aware that the true cyber menace came from Russia. For the country's unemployed youth, the internet exerted a tremendous pull as a fast path to money and power. So, in his speech, Van de Beek did something counter-intuitive. First, he praised the capabilities of the Russian FSB. Then, he thanked them at length for their 'terrific' co-operation. Because, he emphasised, without the Russians, the Netherlands would have got nowhere in its battle against hackers.

Surveying the audience, Van de Beek saw surprise on the faces of dozens of delegates from all over the world. He could almost hear them thinking: are ties between the Netherlands and the FSB that good? His ruse had worked. During the break, several FSB officers approached Van de Beek to thank him for his fine speech and to exchange details. We want to do more to combat cybercrime, they said.

The connections Van de Beek made in Khabarovsk in 2007 inaugurated a productive partnership between Dutch police and the FSB. What also helped was that the Netherlands' police attaché in Moscow, Ludo Pals, knew the mores in Russia. Like brazenly parking your car across the pavement. Telling crude, darkly comic jokes. But most of all, it was the trouncing of their security special forces, Spetsnaz, in a shooting match that earned Pals the Russians' eternal respect.

The question now was whether the FSB would also be able to help the Netherlands track down the criminals who were defrauding a Dutch bank.

*

Ronald Prins and Martijn van de Beek both suspected the people behind ZeuS were Russian. The only trouble was, they hadn't yet got tangible proof. But they did have a plan. They knew the criminals chatted with one another using a program called ICQ. ICQ chat traffic went through web servers owned by the Dutch company Leaseweb, which at the time transmitted 27 per cent of all European data traffic. According to an internal police memo, 'An ultrafast internet connection, relatively inexpensive product and high degree of freedom and anonymity' was the main reason most customers chose Leaseweb. Including quite a few criminals.

ICQ traffic that went through Leaseweb's servers was not encrypted. That meant the police investigation team, led by Van de Beek, could try something they normally couldn't: tap all ICQ traffic coming through Leaseweb from Russia briefly to see what they could turn up. Just maybe, that data would contain some clues about the criminals who wrote ZeuS.

To intercept this data, the police needed special gear. For €600,000 they purchased the P10, a filtering system that could analyse internet traffic content using a method known as 'deep packet inspection'. In effect, this analyses data packets as they speed by, filtering for specific characteristics such as message sender, size and content type. However, since this method rapidly scans tens of thousands of people's private messages, it had already become controversial. In some countries, like China, it's used to filter out content the regime doesn't like.

By autumn 2008, the High Tech Crime Unit was ready. The next step was to ask foreign services for help unravelling the ICQ traffic. Such co-operation made sense because, with the ZeuS virus claiming victims around the world, it was a shared problem. What the Dutch police needed in particular were the ICQ numbers of known criminals. Ukraine's security service quickly responded to the Dutch request, followed by Germany and the UK. The FBI took two months and finally the Russian FSB sent a list of unique numbers three months later. All told, the Dutch police obtained 436 unique ICQ numbers. Van de Beek's speech had done its work.

Once the tapping order had been signed off by the team's lead prosecutor, Lodewijk van Zwieten, the operation could start. The P10 began vacuuming up data packets from Leaseweb in the Netherlands, and soon the first chat logs came in. Police investigators at the national headquarters in Driebergen watched in fascination, reading the messages as they arrived. Day in, day out, their computers were flooded with reams of criminal chatter. Superficially, it was hard to make sense of the jumble of vague screen names and brief chat logs. But gradually, as the team progressed, things started to gel. They could tell that one individual was definitely calling the shots. Everyone talked about him, he was on all kinds of forums and he told other people what to do. The police called him 'Umbro', one of his many screen names. Others were 'Lucky 12345', 'Monster' and 'Slavik'. The police also learned from his messages that he communicated in Russian, lived in the Seychelles, had a wife and a child, ran a restaurant and was the boss of a large criminal network. But most important of all that he was the author of ZeuS, the virus wreaking havoc at European and American banks. It had taken him three years to write, he said in the ICQ chats. What's more, the police discovered he was still updating and selling it.

For the first time, the network behind ZeuS was coming into view. And the Netherlands, with its major data centres, had been instrumental in making this happen. By tapping the ICQ traffic, foreign services were now wise to this criminal network, too. The success of the concerted operation galvanised interest in co-operation on additional fronts, with each country contributing its own specific expertise. The FSB supplied identity data on known Russian criminals, the Netherlands tapped communications and the FBI deftly infiltrated criminal chat forums and helped with investigations. It was clear at this point that Umbro was behind the attacks on ABN Amro and numerous other banks in Europe and the United States. Now, it was just a matter of uncovering his real identity and location.

*

No answer. Does the doorbell to apartment 223 even work? I can still feel the eagle eye of the camera on me. Unlike my first trip to Russia, when we interviewed Edward Snowden in Moscow, the atmosphere feels different now. Tense. When my interpreter and I approach Russians in the street and ask about Bogachev, they're evasive. 'Can't help you,' they say, and gesture as if to shoo us away. People here must recognise his name, if only because his ill-gotten millions are invested in local property. Clearly, though, they don't want to talk about him.

Earlier this morning, my interpreter and I went out to the marina, ten miles from the penthouse door where I'm now standing. Bogachev keeps one of his luxury yachts berthed there, I'd heard. It was quiet. There was a fence with security cameras to keep out nosy visitors. With my interpreter, I walked to a nearby pier to get a better look.

Fishermen sat gazing out across the water, squinting and motionless. A delivery truck was unloading Coca-Cola vending machines stamped 'SOTSJI 2014', leftovers from the Winter Olympics.

When we walked further up the pier, a man in sunglasses, a polo shirt and smart leather shoes began trailing us at about thirty yards. Presently, three more men and a woman came walking up behind him from different directions. The woman had a camera aimed at us and was taking photographs. They continued walking in an arc, faces turned towards us.

I felt myself getting nervous. Who were these people? Why were they circling me? Warily, we headed back down the pier towards the harbour. The four men and the woman continued to watch us as they approached us. Slowly, the circle closed and they came right up to us. My interpreter turned to the man in dark glasses and asked what he wanted. 'We could also just kill you right now,' the man answered, and smirked. Then all five just stood there, surrounding us, not saying a word. When we walked on, they followed until we were off the pier. Then they got into a big black SUV and drove off.

The signal was loud and clear: mess with Bogachev and you'll make some powerful enemies. Fine, I thought, but let's just try one last, quick shot. On the drive to his house, we passed an internet provider. Unlike the people in the street and on the pier, the staff inside politely answered our questions. Bogachev, it turned out, was a customer there. From a drawer, an employee drew a stack of papers including bills, one of which was in Bogachev's name. Attached to it was a copy of his passport. His address was printed on it.

As we crossed to his apartment building we passed one of the other residents. In Russian, the interpreter asked about the famous bald hacker. Sure, the man nodded, he'd seen a bald guy on the fourteenth floor before.

This really could be where Bogachev lives. I ring the doorbell again. Yet again, silence. I knock. My knuckles rap loudly against the wooden door, the sound echoing down the hall.

*

It didn't take the Dutch police long to figure out that 'Umbro' was Bogachev, thanks partly to their teamwork with the FSB. Relations were particularly good with one of its chiefs, Sergei Mikhailov, deputy head of the FSB's cybercrime department. He regularly visited the police headquarters in Driebergen for consultations, when he'd share information from Russian files compiled through old-fashioned detective work. The Dutch sometimes marvelled at the sheer amount of private data the FSB culled from criminals – as though it were a fly on the wall, eavesdropping inside their homes for years.

Members of the High Tech Crime Unit regarded Mikhailov as a skilled and keenly analytical specialist. He was also nice. They'd been working with him for years by this time, and he enjoyed the trip through Europe. So frequent were his visits to Holland that Mikhailov even knew the best way to eat a *stroopwafel*: lay it over a steaming cup of coffee until the treacle between the waffles melts.

During those visits, Mikhailov also shared information about Bogachev. Curiously, though, every time they felt sure he'd finally be arrested, the FSB came up with some excuse: the timing wasn't right, or he was out of town. All the while, Bogachev's imperium continued to expand. He sold his virus through online forums on the dark web – a part of the internet accessible only with a special browser that keeps users anonymous – supplying it in ready-made packages that enabled hackers to steal financial data and logins. Those packages went for thousands of dollars.

Like any good businessman, Bogachev knew the value of good customer relations. Buyers of his software also received technical support and regular updates. They could send in questions, and he responded quickly if they got stuck.

But in 2010, Bogachev changed tack. His newest version of ZeuS was made available only to an exclusive group of young Russians and Ukrainians whom he trusted absolutely. They called themselves the 'Business Club'. Each group member brought in specific expertise about software, or banking, or counterfeiting passports, or email distribution. Working together like a well-oiled machine, they targeted banks around the globe, draining private and corporate accounts. And other institutions, too, like hospitals in the US, where they hijacked accounts just as payrolls were being processed.

To cash their spoils, the Business Club needed bank accounts of their own. Lots of them. They solved this by recruiting money mules, paying people to open accounts using fake passports and then withdraw the money and transfer it to Bogachev and his crew.

Bogachev also continued growing his business. For one thing, he came up with a clever scheme to draft more money mules. Just as he'd broken into victims' computers to tweak their online banking pages, now he hacked job sites like CareerBuilder.com, editing them to show postings that weren't actually on the site. Such as: 'Administrative position, flexible working hours, starting salary 2,000 dollars a month.'

It was an easy gig. The new operatives got a few false passports with which to open bank accounts, and then thousands of dollars came rolling in. They were allowed to take a 10 per cent cut for themselves and transferred the rest into the Business Club's accounts. And dozens of money mules in myriad countries were all doing the same thing.

Then, in 2012, something changed. ZeuS was behaving differently. Besides financial data, suddenly the virus was also stealing very specific information about Turkish, Georgian and Ukrainian secret services. It scanned systems for documents with Georgian and Turkish agents' email addresses. It scoured computers for files containing keywords in Turkish like 'general security directorate' and 'contractor' or 'Russian soldiers' and 'Syria'. It was as though, once inside a computer, ZeuS split itself in two.

The Dutch team thought it was odd. Why would a hacker who'd spent years perfecting his virus to rake in mountains of cash go trawling for information about intelligence services? Moreover, where had he got the names of those foreign agents?

And he had hundreds of them. The search queries further coincided with important political situations, such as the Russian invasion of Crimea in 2014 and rising tensions with Turkey. As the Dutch investigators and FBI saw it, there could be only one explanation: Bogachev was working for Russian intelligence. Could that be why the FSB still had not arrested and extradited him?

At some point, the Russian agencies must have reached a crossroads. How would their domestic interests be best served? By taking down a big, smart hacker – or by enlisting him? That's a choice every powerful nation makes, whether it be Russia or the US, Israel or China. The Netherlands takes a harder line: we don't do deals with crooks. But the Russians have a history of collaborating with criminal actors and aren't afraid to get their hands dirty. If they do intelligence work on the side, hackers can go around stealing all they like.

Compounding this is the fact that the Russian FSB, like the American FBI, is a combined service that does both policing *and* surveillance, both investigations *and* covert operations. In the Netherlands, those roles are kept strictly separate. Police do investigation, the AIVD and MIVD gather intel. The police arrest, the AIVD looks at where the threats are and who's spying.

For that reason, the AIVD wasn't keen on the Russian visits to the Dutch police. Who said they were helping to chase down crooks and not to spy? To the AIVD it looked fishy. Here was a case of two worlds colliding: the police, who were pragmatists and welcomed Russian co-operation, and the AIVD, which viewed ties with Russia through the lens of politics and risks.

As a precautionary measure, rooms in which Dutch officers met with FSB agents were turned inside out afterwards, even to the point of dismantling modular ceilings. The National Police Services Agency's 'sweep team' checked for spy apparatus the Russians might have furtively left behind. Added to that, as of 2012 any police personnel who interacted with the FSB had to brief the AIVD both before and afterwards.

To police investigators who actually worked with the Russians, this reeked of paranoia. The FSB agents they knew were ordinary policemen, uninterested in intelligence or espionage. Like Mikhailov. He was a real cop who delighted in a good investigation. And what about the FBI? Weren't they secret police, too? Were they any more trustworthy than the FSB? If the Russians said 'yes', the police knew they really meant 'yes'. If they gave their word, they kept it. Unlike the Americans, who were more cunning.

One of the Dutch policemen had first-hand evidence of this. During a meeting with the FSB and FBI in Driebergen, a Russian colleague approached him. Pointing to one of the FBI agents, he warned, 'He's copying your data.' When the policeman went to check, he found the American had put his own flash drive into a police laptop and was brazenly stealing Dutch information.

But in the end this co-operation couldn't help bowing to political pressure. After the Russian annexation of Crimea in 2014 and the shooting down of Malaysia Airlines flight 17 – with mostly Dutch passengers on board – in the same year, diplomatic relations between Holland and Russia cooled. With the criminal investigation into the downed flight also being carried out at the police headquarters in Driebergen, it seemed tactless to meet with the FSB literally next door, so the police moved these visits to Amsterdam or Rotterdam.

That didn't put an end to the sharing of information, however. It was still possible to have reasonably productive discussions about criminals, even Russian ones, and Mikhailov still visited in order to supply information about certain individuals. In spite of the political friction, personal ties remained. On the night flight MH17 was shot down, one Dutch police investigator even received a text from an FSB agent offering his sympathy and condolences.

All the same, political tensions were driving a deepening wedge between the two countries. Delegations from the FBI and FSB twice came to the Netherlands to discuss broader co-operation – the first time in The Hague's Babylon Hotel and the second, in February 2016, at a private social club in the same city. Mikhailov talked to two FBI agents on the latter occasion, but after that relations became so chilly that the meetings ceased.

Bogachev, meanwhile, had become even more of a force to be reckoned with. Both the US and the Netherlands were convinced by now that he was spying for Russian services. When the FBI posted a $3 million reward for any tip leading to his arrest, the Dutch team couldn't resist baiting Mikhailov. Teasingly, they conjectured that he must know where Bogachev was hiding, and asked what he would do with the money after ratting on him. 'A luxury yacht, Sergei?' 'Or how about a country estate in Italy?'

*

Bogachev isn't answering the door. I take one last chance and knock.

Still nothing. Is he just out doing errands? Or is the world's most wanted hacker in hiding somewhere else?

For my last stop in Anapa, I drive by a villa on the edge of town that's registered to Bogachev's ex-lawyer's property company. Over the phone, this lawyer claimed he'd last seen Bogachev two years ago in Anapa, but had no idea where he was now. I want to visit him anyway, just to be sure.

His walled villa is perched high above the coast. Somewhere, dogs are barking non-stop. I press the doorbell and, after a couple of tries, a young man in joggers answers the door. I ask him if the lawyer is home. Politely, he says he doesn't know anyone by that name. When I mention Bogachev, his attitude shifts. With a curt 'No', the door is slammed shut.

From Anapa I take a taxi to Krasnodar Airport, about 100 miles away, and catch a flight home via Moscow. As we're taxiing towards the gate in Amsterdam, I get a sudden flurry of texts from my interpreter. 'Are you OK?' he writes, and, 'Please call me ASAP.'

When I phone back, he explains that he got a call from the hotel. Just after we'd left, a couple of plainclothes policemen came and asked to speak to the hotel staff. They had photographs of the two of us and demanded copies of our passports and details of our stay. When the staff asked what the police were after, they claimed, 'We're looking for them because they're terrorists.' Wanting to warn us, the hotel called my interpreter. I'm safely back in Holland, I assure him.

Towards the end of 2016, Mikhailov abruptly stopped returning calls from Driebergen. For weeks, no one could reach him. The police didn't know what to make of it – until they read in the Russian press that he'd been arrested. It happened at an FSB meeting. A bag was thrown theatrically over his head and he was dragged from the room. The official charge, according to the media, was high treason. Mikhailov had allegedly leaked information about Russian operations to Western agencies. It was the biggest scandal to hit the FSB's top ranks since the Soviet breakup in 1991.

The team in Driebergen was appalled. Some of those in the department were so affected they could barely sleep. Would Mikhailov still get to see his children? Had he been sent to a prison camp? Over the following months, new FSB agents visited the Netherlands a few times to get acquainted. These encounters were awkward. Trust had taken a hard knock on both sides, and although information was still shared, there was not the personal rapport there'd been with Mikhailov. Personal meetings with the FSB and the FBI tailed off in the years that followed. The Dutch police could only guess at the real reason behind Mikhailov's detainment.

That Russian authorities arrested another man alongside Mikhailov only deepened the mystery. That man was Ruslan Stoyanov, head of cybersecurity firm Kaspersky Labs' investigation unit. He, too, was charged with high treason.

If the police struggled to understand what had happened, the AIVD was less surprised. Hard as it was to parse developments in Russia, the agency had been observing the East since 2010. It knew that Russia, and also China, had discovered the potential of the internet, and that they were inventing their own ways of using it.

8

Conspiracy in Amsterdam

N. was no technology expert. Nonetheless, in 2013 she was put in charge of the Russia and China Team in the AIVD's Digital Espionage unit, or 'dispi' as insiders called it. N., raised a Catholic, was a career woman who'd worked her way up through the ranks. Starting out as a translator, she was promoted to desk jobs, sent out on assignment a few times – once to a country in the Middle East – and finally promoted to team leader. Her expertise was in counter-espionage – finding out how and where other countries were spying on the Netherlands – and in 2013 her task was to map out the digital threat coming from the East.

At fifty-three, N.'s leadership style was business-like: risk-averse, analytical, cautious and observant. She wasn't exactly someone you'd pour out your heart to, though those who managed to break through her armour got to know a more sociable side.

N. had been heading the Russia Team for about a year when the AIVD got a request from the United States. The FBI wanted to gain covert access, also known as 'surreptitious entry', to a target. It concerned a spy assignment in downtown Amsterdam. The operation would be carried out by the CIA in the Netherlands, but because of its technical complexity they hoped the AIVD could assist.

The request didn't come at the best time, coinciding with high-level discussions over the once so solid relationship between the US and the Netherlands. Edward Snowden had just revealed that the US was spying around the world on a massive scale, and in the Netherlands, politicians and intelligence services were demanding answers. Had the NSA been eavesdropping in the Netherlands, too? Which NSA documents specifically had been taken? And did any of them say anything about Dutch operations?

On 11 October 2013, Dutch Interior Minister Ronald Plasterk and the directors of Dutch intelligence hosted NSA chief Keith Alexander on what was meant to be a conciliatory visit. Holland was certainly not an NSA target, Alexander said. 'We don't collect on the Netherlands.' The reason was simple: whatever the Americans asked, the Dutch delivered. The AIVD and MIVD kept few secrets from the US. The way the relationship worked was that the Dutch shared, regardless of what they got in return. The CIA shared very little, mostly briefings and intelligence reports. The NSA were more forthcoming, and even shared raw data.

To gauge the leak's impact on Dutch operations, the AIVD and MIVD asked Alexander for a list of the stolen documents. Alexander assured them he understood their concern, apologised, and said his staff were working on it. 'We'll send an overview as soon as it's finished.' That was an empty promise: only bits and pieces of information, less detailed than the Dutch agencies had hoped for, would trickle in over the years that followed.

During his visit, Alexander announced that, in view of the leak, the NSA would henceforth be sharing less with allies. The Dutch agencies were astonished. Here the Americans had screwed up, letting hundreds of thousands of secret documents get out, and now the NSA boss wanted to punish *them*? What were they trying to pull? In fact, it was all too typical of the US–Dutch partnership, in which the Americans were unwilling to admit mistakes, convinced of their superiority.

It wasn't the first time this attitude had put them at loggerheads with the Netherlands. The AIVD and CIA had a long history of working closely to monitor arms shipments, in accordance with international agreements among Western governments to keep a lookout for countries attempting to secretly expand their weapons arsenals or develop nuclear capacity. This meant intelligence services kept one another updated about who was sending and receiving arms. But after 11 September 2001, things changed. When the US invaded Afghanistan following the attacks on the Twin Towers and the Pentagon, Pakistan was recategorised as an ally in the American 'War on Terror'. So when the AIVD asked the CIA for the final destination of nuclear materials in Pakistan, they got no reply: overnight, the US stopped providing data. After multiple attempts, lots of waiting and persistent nagging, the American agency sent a terse message: 'We don't report on allies.' Without warning, they had unilaterally decided to stop upholding a decades-long treaty because it was now in their interests to keep Pakistan sweet. The AIVD were livid, and the American CIA liaison was *persona non grata* for months.

Holland's military intelligence service also had clashes with its US counterparts. One was in the period during which the MIVD was active in Afghanistan, when the US called its headquarters in The Hague angrily accusing the MIVD of having accidentally exposed an American source. When senior officials at the MIVD looked into the matter, they discovered that it was not the Dutch but the Americans who had exposed the identity of their source. 'Oh, sorry,' came the reply.

The plain fact is that the US could do and ask more. It's big versus small. If they're unhappy, they let it be known loud and clear, especially if terrorism is involved. When it transpired that one of the terrorists behind the Brussels bombing had been at Schiphol Airport in Amsterdam, the Americans wasted no time. Without consulting

Dutch intelligence they went straight to Schiphol to tell American airlines how to ramp up their security. And when an Afghan man stabbed and injured two American citizens at Amsterdam's central railway station, US ambassador Pete Hoekstra was quick to criticise. Dutch intelligence should have shared 'more information faster', he told Dutch daily *De Telegraaf*. For the Netherlands, his interference felt 'like a teacher reprimanding a child'.

Which brings us back to N. In spite of these mutual aggravations and escalating tensions following the NSA leak, she was willing to lend a hand. For one thing, aiding a US operation opened up opportunities, because it would give the Netherlands access to new information. It was also a chance to learn from American technology, which could be slightly more advanced. And since the Americans didn't really have to worry about money, they could do more costly operations.

The target in this case was Kaspersky, a Russian cybersecurity firm that makes antivirus software. According to the CIA, the firm's best and brightest would be gathering in Amsterdam that October. Used by 400 million people worldwide, their software is supposed to protect computers from malware and hackers. The company has a solid reputation and its products are in high demand. Its tech experts do their own espionage research and in the process have also exposed US spy operations – operations such as the Stuxnet attack on Iran and an ultra-sophisticated successor in the Middle East. The problem, from the US point of view, was that Kaspersky was headquartered in Moscow. As digital hostilities between the two countries flared, the FBI grew more distrustful and wanted to know if Kaspersky posed a risk to American safety. Was Kaspersky part of the long arm of Russia? As head of the AIVD's Russia Team, N. wanted to know, too.

*

N. had a further reason for agreeing to the FBI's request. She was well versed in the detection of foreign spying and knew the hallmarks particularly of China, Iran and Russia. Yet, since the advent of the internet, espionage had changed. Recent developments had been fast and furious, and it was a struggle just to keep up. Another factor was the size of the AIVD, whose 1,300 employees numbered only a small handful of hackers. The NSA (50,000 employees) and GCHQ (6,000) were significantly larger, while China was daily deploying an army of over 100,000 hackers.

One of the new developments was long-term espionage. Spy agencies were infiltrating organisations using custom-made viruses like Regin at Belgacom and staying inside for years. 'Advanced persistent threat' is the term used for these extended espionage campaigns, or APT for short. N. kept mixing it up with ATP, the acronym of the international Association of Tennis Professionals. For N., the FBI's request presented an opportunity to learn. About Kaspersky, about Russian operations, and also about American techniques.

Inasmuch as spies did everything possible to obscure where they were operating from, combating this kind of espionage was tremendously complicated. Dedicated units within intelligence agencies specialised in these persistent spy operations, and all countries were doing it. Notorious in Western eyes were Iran, North Korea, Russia and especially China, which had been training a spectacularly large cyber espionage force since the beginning of the new millennium.

In 2013 it was beginning to dawn on the West what China was up to. That same year, the US cybersecurity firm Mandiant came out with an extensive report. It was the first time anyone had published so specifically about ongoing espionage by a group of hackers and documented a state hacking ring in such minute detail.

What Mandiant described was a white, twelve-storey tower block in a neighbourhood of restaurants and massage parlours on the outskirts of Shanghai. On the roof, a few small satellite dishes; inside, hundreds of Chinese military personnel. This was a secret division of the Chinese People's Liberation Army known as Unit 61398, and its hackers were systematically attacking scores of Western organisations.

Within this unit, everyone had their own job to do. One would make up email addresses, someone else composed phishing emails in

English and yet another did the actual hack. Facilitating them were teams of translators, systems administrators, engineers and support staff, as well as more than a thousand computer servers around the world through which they executed their attacks.

Over the course of seven years from 2006 to 2013, China broke into at least 141 companies, from Coca-Cola to defence firms. Once inside, they stole passwords first, then data. In some cases, they lingered in organisations for months, even years. The average length was 356 days; the longest, almost five years. The hackers vacuumed up whole companies, in one case stealing 6.5 terabytes of data over ten months – roughly the size of six big university libraries.

These attacks intersected with Chinese government interests. Say Coca-Cola was considering a takeover of a big Chinese soft drinks company. Unit 61398 would sneak inside the company and then its specialists could swipe the negotiation strategy and other company-sensitive information. More than anything, though, they coveted proprietary information from high-tech companies, military organisations, chemical plants and telecom providers. At the Lockheed Martin aerospace and defence corporation, for instance, the unit made off with the blueprint for the Joint Strike Fighter. That's how China managed to replicate the aircraft and build its own fleet years before any of the countries that were actually paying for the trillion-dollar JSF programme.

With the release of the Mandiant report, Unit 61398 became known to the world as APT1: the first identified state-sponsored espionage organisation. Officially, Mandiant published its methods to warn other companies and governments. They could then study its specifications – like IP addresses and forms of malware – and so take action to fend off the Chinese hackers.

But politics came into it, too. Publicising the minutiae of spy operations can work as a deterrent. Dutch sources I talked to suspected Mandiant was actually getting its information straight from American intelligence services, because they benefited if details of Chinese spying leaked out. The US administration eagerly grasped the opportunity to openly accuse China for the first time ever of a wave of cyberattacks targeting Western companies and governments. Where once governments would have hushed up this kind of information to prevent damaging diplomatic relations, the American exposure of enemy strategy marked a new step in digital battle tactics.

All the same, it didn't stop China, which was deploying tens of thousands of hackers on a daily basis. The methods they used were pretty crude. I got a demonstration of this from Yonathan Klijnsma, a researcher who was then studying new types of malware for Fox-IT in Delft.

Klijnsma was used to seeing unknown software at client firms. Most of the time it wasn't anything to be concerned about, but one day he entered the specs of an unfamiliar program in a public database and saw it had been documented in other places as well – in government departments and businesses in the United States, Myanmar, India, Canada and Germany. There was even a link to the Netherlands. Intrigued by this new software, Klijnsma began devoting his evenings and time between assignments to pinning down its authors. After months of research, he was able to expose their entire working method, offering a rare glimpse into how China's hackers work and ultimately steal information.

At eight o'clock in the morning, five young men enter a small office in Guangdong province in south-eastern China. They boot up their computers. One of the five opens Writer – China's answer to Word – and starts drafting a news item in English. He's had a good Chinese education, so his English is fluent. Now, he works for the Chinese government.

The item is about Rheinmetall, a German defence firm which just signed a deal with a Dutch supplier of parts for an armoured fighting vehicle called the Boxer. He puts together a short piece on the merger and sends it to a co-worker to check. In May 2012, this news item lands in the inboxes of employees at Rheinmetall. The Chinese are hoping at least one recipient will open it and click on the attached file. Sure enough, someone opens the document and thus unknowingly installs a small program called ShimRatReporter on their PC. This program analyses Rheinmetall's organisational network and sends useful information such as configuration settings and installed software back to the group in China. The victim, meanwhile, is oblivious.

Once inside, the Chinese group receives updates about the system and, sometime later, plants a virus in the company network. To escape detection, the virus hides behind common antivirus software like McAfee, Symantec and Norman, fooling the infected Rheinmetall employee into thinking his computer's running an update. In reality, a Chinese virus is sneaking into the network.

To transmit data from Rheinmetall to China, the virus communicates across websites masquerading as legitimate pages. The group uses domain names like mail.upgoogle.com and support. outlook-microsoft.com, as well as a page made to look like the *New York Times*. These websites serve as transmitters that let the malware 'talk' to its operators while camouflaging their true origin, and their spying.

The five Chinese hackers had this access to Rheinmetall for years, and through it to the technological know-how of its subsidiary in the Netherlands. Nobody there noticed they were the target of spying. Not until Klijnsma exposed the group's work and alerted Rheinmetall did they see the damage. And they weren't the only ones: other companies breached by these same five hackers included a manufacturer of solar cell technology in Canada. Over the course of three years, they hacked at least twenty-four organisations.

China has tens of thousands of hackers who log in daily and remotely rob entire companies. Their methods change all the time, and they're aggressive and thorough. Moreover, they don't have to fear getting caught. Not only are they rarely unmasked, they're protected by the Chinese government.

This was the situation back in 2013 when N. was approached by the CIA. Cyberspying was on a steep rise. China was cramming hackers into office blocks to steal Western treasures, while Great Britain and the United States were collecting bulk data from UN organisations and telecom providers like Belgacom. And Russia? They were playing their own game, of which the Dutch AIVD was picking up the first signals. How did Kaspersky fit in? Suspicious of the Russian company, the Americans decided to enlist their colleagues in Holland.

The Kaspersky researchers visiting Amsterdam were the company's brightest minds: the specialists who analysed malware, the nerds who hunted for links and dissected the most intricate viruses, exposing them just as Mandiant did Chinese spy unit 61398. That research was what kept Kaspersky customers safe, ensuring their antivirus software protected them against the latest espionage threats. Normally, this team of malware analysts worked across the world, but in October 2013 they were scheduled to hold a big team meeting in the Dutch capital to coincide with a major tech conference. They were booked into a hotel near the central railway station in Amsterdam.

For the CIA it was golden opportunity, because rarely were all these analysts physically present in one place. Some would also be attending the RSA Conference afterwards at the RAI convention centre, just south of the city centre, where in hall G107 – one of the smaller halls – the team's Romanian leader Costin Raiu would be debating a new and 'controversial' issue in information security, known as advanced persistent threats. Were APTs a serious menace? Or a security hype?

More important for the CIA was the three-day gathering that twelve people from Kaspersky would be holding on their own. Initially, the AIVD and CIA considered bugging their hotel conference room, but that plan was aborted as being too complicated.

N. talked it over with H. – the CIA's liaison to the AIVD in the Netherlands. With his narrow head, greying hair, glasses and oversized suit, the CIA operative looked more like a stuffy bureaucrat. The two came up with a plan. An AIVD observation team would trail the researchers when they left the hotel. Meanwhile, a second team would try to break into their hotel room, take their laptops and turn them over to the CIA.

From the very first day of their team meeting, the Kaspersky researchers smelled a rat. They kept running into the same people around the hotel, in the corridors and the restaurant. These people acted oddly. One of them even barged into a meeting. They broke up early that day. Sensing that they were being watched, the Kaspersky analysts clutched more tightly to the laptops they already guarded with their lives. One even decided to call up a Dutch contact.

*

Where the AIVD by this time had a full-fledged cyber espionage department and was actively recruiting hackers, on the digital front its military counterpart the MIVD lagged hopelessly behind. It still relied on dishes like those at the satellite station in Burum to pluck information from the air.

Unlike the AIVD, the MIVD was mostly concerned with radio and satellite communications. In the past, that meant diplomatic cables between embassies and their home countries, but these days it was communication among the Taliban in Afghanistan or jihadist fighters in Mali. Traditional intelligence-gathering methods were perfectly effective for that kind of interception. In fact, at the time the United States invaded Afghanistan, the Taliban was still using old-fashioned walkie-talkies and field radios. The MIVD was able to intercept those high-frequency radio transmissions from an antenna field in the village of Eibergen, near the Dutch–German border, and so obtain useful intelligence.

Another speciality the MIVD had was eavesdropping from submarines. Dutch Walrus-class submarines regularly plied foreign coastlines to gather intelligence and map ports and aerial defence systems in countries like Iran. These activities were crucial as neither the UK nor the US had submarines operable at such shallow depths. But submarine deployment was also time-consuming and expensive, and hence an ongoing bone of contention among senior Dutch defence officials. Even a 'minor' spy mission to Iran could easily be six months in the making, including the trip of several weeks.

By the summer of 2011, more and more communication was digital. And, unlike the MIVD, other agencies that once did radio interception – like the NSA, GCHQ and Israel's Unit 8200 – had all switched to digital techniques. In the month that the navy's

Pieter Bindt became the MIVD's new director, its staff newsletter was peppered with warnings about the new digital threats: 'Never Underestimate a Cyberspy!' And about social media: 'Did you know that when you link your "smartphone" to your account on a social networking site, like Facebook, it shows your exact location from moment to moment?' The MIVD's top security tip was: 'Discretion is a must when it comes to personal data on the internet.'

Well aware that the MIVD was trailing behind in digital developments, its demanding new boss wanted to catch up fast. Already for some time there'd been political plans to combine AIVD and MIVD surveillance capabilities into one big new spy unit. This project, called Symbolon, kept snagging in mutual aggravations, but Bindt wanted to iron out the kinks. As he saw it, this was a chance for the MIVD to benefit from the AIVD's digital expertise. Writing to the agency's employees as their new director, he noted, 'One partner we'll be focusing on in particular is the AIVD. The world is big and turbulent, while our two services are relatively small. One plus one should equal at least three.'

Headquartered in the fourteen-storey Frederikkazerne building at the edge of The Hague, the MIVD's offices are, like the AIVD's premises in Zoetermeer, an impenetrable fortress. Employees first have to clear a barrier manned by military guards. At the entrance are three turnstiles which require a pass card and five-digit PIN to open. Smartphones aren't allowed in the building and have to be stashed in a locker in front of the entry gates. Once inside, employees take the lift to their floor, using their pass card and PIN once again to enter. Advance authorisation is needed to access any given floor.

Confidentiality is also taken very seriously. Case in point: when Jaap van Tuyll, a retired employee, wanted to publish a book about the MIVD, he received a summons from the agency's director. Van Tuyll had been a valued cryptanalyst whose job was to decipher intercepted messages; say, from foreign embassies. After working at the MIVD for about thirty years, by this time Van Tuyll had been out of the service for twelve years. His book drew on his time there, but mainly talked about decoding methods. He hadn't written a word about secret operations.

Even so, the MIVD wasn't taking any chances. Granted, Van Tuyll had been gone for a dozen years, but – they reasoned – his knowledge was still valuable. In a personal meeting with the agency's chief, the former staffer was given two options. Either he published his book and the MIVD would file for an injunction, or he let the MIVD publish the book itself. Van Tuyll chose the latter. He got to present his book at the AIVD office in Zoetermeer, but didn't get a copy to take home afterwards. The MIVD had decided to classify it as state secret, which meant it wasn't allowed to leave the building. Van Tuyll couldn't even put the book he himself had written in his own bookcase at home.

Two years into Bindt's tenure, the anticipated co-operation with the AIVD was making little progress. Partly this was to do with the AIVD's director, Rob Bertholee, who assumed his job in the same year that Bindt joined the MIVD. Stern and straitlaced, Bertholee prioritised the agency's efforts on tracking suspected jihadists over other tasks, like cyber espionage and charting long-term trends. He was a career army officer who stayed steadfastly loyal to his political commanders. Tall and wiry, he was also an avid runner who played it very safe by never taking the same route twice. That he barely protested cuts to AIVD funding and, moreover, was content to put up with the domineering and rather large ego of his political superior Ronald Plasterk did not win him any points with agency staff. His rigid personality didn't help, either, as it made him unapproachable to his colleagues.

In a way, Bindt at the MIVD was Bertholee's polar opposite: trained in the navy, a risk-taker, unafraid of conflict. The cigar-smoking rear admiral had a formidable temper yet was also approachable, and was known as a smart officer who took the long view. Born in the mid-fifties, both Bindt and Bertholee belonged to the same generation, yet their temperaments consistently clashed. After years of bickering, a go-between was enlisted in the person of Paula Wiegers, a former AIVD officer and later top official for the ministries of Education and General Affairs, to galvanise the two agencies to work together and unite them in the brand-new Joint Sigint Cyber Unit.

Just what an uphill battle this would be was clear as soon as a few dozen MIVD employees were installed in the AIVD office to staff the new unit there. Before letting them into the building, the AIVD made them submit to an in-depth security screening. To the military personnel, who already had security clearance, it was a smack in the face. But the AIVD was not to be swayed, and the MIVD was left seething.

It wasn't until 2014, more than three years after Bindt's appointment, that the new joint AIVD–MIVD unit finally, albeit half-heartedly, got off the ground. Both agencies had delegated specialists: the AIVD, hackers, and the MIVD, high-frequency radio and satellite interception experts. All told, the new spy unit consisted of some 350 people. About a hundred of them made up a 'digital business unit', responsible for cyber operations, which was further subdivided into several teams focused on activities like wiretapping or running sources. There was a separate team devoted to computer network exploitation, or CNE. There were also AIVD hackers authorised to carry out offensive operations, their job being to break into and infiltrate enemy networks. As the new unit went to work, it became apparent that one of the two partners had got a head start. The AIVD's hacking team was already working on a top-secret operation deep inside Russia.

*

How the Dutch–US operation to gain covert access to Kaspersky ended is unknown. According to AIVD sources, the agency managed to lift at least one laptop from a hotel safe, which it brought to a room where a CIA tech team was waiting. They watched enviously as the Americans pulled passwords and encryption keys from the memory in the blink of an eye and then copied the whole laptop onto a flash drive. After that, the Dutch agents returned the laptop to the safe. Mission more or less accomplished.

Years later, Kaspersky said this story was unlikely. Hadn't the team been suspicious from the very first day they arrived? What's more, the researchers took extreme care with their laptops and it was

Kaspersky policy never to leave them in hotel safes. Then there'd been that researcher who got suspicious and called a Dutch contact. That person had in turn notified the AIVD. Allegedly, he was told it was a misunderstanding. If the researcher thought he'd been followed from Amsterdam's central station, it hadn't been by any AIVD observation team.

Over the course of two years I talked to five sources about this spy operation at an Amsterdam hotel. Several questions remained unanswered. Why was the FBI so keen to get inside the laptops of these particular Kaspersky employees? What kind of company intelligence did they hope to glean?

I wrestled long with the question of whether or not to include this story, with all its loose ends, in this book. The fact is, the FBI's interest in Kaspersky is bound up with the online war being waged between Russia and the United States – a war in which Holland's AIVD has chosen to side with the US. It's notable that these agencies already had their sights on Kaspersky back in 2013, given that it didn't turn into a public issue until some years later, in 2017, when the US Department of Homeland Security banned all Kaspersky products from government departments over allegations of engagement with the Russian FSB. But without knowing all the facts, to what extent could I shed light on the story's true significance?

Doubts like these are part and parcel of writing about secret services. You can't expect to have all your questions answered all the time. Sources may be too scared to tell you more, or they may not know more, or you just can't dig any deeper. Do you go ahead and publish what you've got? Or do you hold off a little longer until maybe you can fill in the gaps? That's the trade-off every time.

It's the same journalistic dilemma I find myself facing in late 2016 when a reliable source says the AIVD found Russian malware on the networks of the Eastern Scheldt Storm Surge Barrier – the colossal 5.6-mile floodgate protecting the Netherlands from the North Sea. As part of the country's most critical infrastructure, this is potentially big news. But my source is too nervous to share details.

A year later I get vague corroboration from another source: 'Yeah, I've heard that, too.' With two sources confirming the story independently of each other, at this point I could say it's good to go. Only, it feels too thin. How did the AIVD discover this malware? How long had it been there? What kind of malware was it? How sure are they that it's Russian?

Nine months pass. I find another person who was involved. If the story's true, this person *must* know about it. He adamantly denies having ever heard anything of the kind. When I double-check with my first source, he sticks firmly to what he said but won't or can't give me details just now. Neither will several other people who might know more. I can't publish.

Another example: I'd learned that the AIVD and CIA had jointly attempted to recruit an Iranian technology whizz studying at a Dutch university. But it all came to nothing, because he had no interest in working for intelligence.

It's a good story. What's more, I get another confirmation, plus the student's name and a description of what he looks like. Not wanting to put him at risk, I send an encrypted message saying I'd like to hear his side of this story, as I'm interested in the AIVD's and CIA's techniques. What did they offer him? And how did they find him in the first place?

No reply. Nor to the two more detailed emails I send after that, stressing I won't reveal his identity. So, now what? The story's legitimate, I'm certain of it. I get that he doesn't want to be drawn in. And I don't want to publish his name, his college or his background. Only, without that information, there's not much of a piece left. I opt not to publish.

I put the story about the spy job in an Amsterdam hotel aside for a long time. I tried to find new sources and dig up more information. At first, without much success. Until, one day, someone happened to tell me about another AIVD mission. A covert operation that seemed to be related to that job in the hotel. It looked like maybe the AIVD wasn't finished with Kaspersky yet.

First, though, back to 2013. It had been a tough year for the AIVD. The fight against Islamic terror had taken a toll. Between the Islamic State in Syria and Al-Qaeda in Africa and the Middle East, all the bloodshed was demoralising the whole country. That year, the AIVD reported almost nothing about Russian cyberspying, and didn't mention it once in its 2013 annual report. The following year? Thirty-seven times. Clearly, 2013 marked an inflection point.

That's not to say the AIVD hadn't seen what was happening. That Russian cyber criminals' know-how and infrastructure was paving the way for Russian security services. The country's fast and cheap internet was a magnet for the nation's unemployed youth, and Russian crooks were using online forums to sell hacking tools. Price of hacking a Facebook account: $200. Price of hacking a Gmail account: $117. Price of a tool to plant malware on a Windows PC: $600.

Russian spy services were well aware of the potential to exploit this knowledge for their own devices. That's why the AIVD wasn't thrilled when Sergei Mikhailov – the Russian FSB cyber unit's second-in-command – kept dropping by the Dutch national police headquarters in Driebergen. As far as the AIVD could see, the Russians hadn't the least intention of rounding up online crooks; on the contrary, they wanted to draft and deploy them. It was obvious the Russians weren't to be trusted, least of all the FSB, with its combined law enforcement and intelligence powers.

Take the breach of American search engine Yahoo in 2014, where hackers made off with the passwords, email addresses, telephone numbers and settings of an astounding 500 million users, constituting the biggest data theft in history. Who was responsible? Supposedly, a twenty-three-year-old Kazakhstani man in Canada. But the real orders, the FBI discovered, came from Russia – from a pair of high-ranking intelligence officers in the FSB's cyber investigation department. Immediate colleagues, as it happened, of Dutch police contact Sergei Mikhailov. Like Mikhailov, these two FSB officers worked closely with foreign investigation services, ostensibly to help them root out cyber criminals. In fact, they themselves supervised the hackers who raided Yahoo, and the FSB used the stolen email credentials to spy on White House employees, on military personnel, on CEOs in a host of Eastern European countries, and on Russians, too – including journalists, government staffers and activists. 'The involvement and direction of FSB officers with law enforcement responsibilities make this conduct that much more egregious,' observed US Acting Assistant Attorney General Mary McCord.

Mikhailov did wind up convicted in the end, albeit in Russia. Found guilty of high treason, he was sentenced to twenty-two years in prison for selling information to the FBI.

And this brings us to another reason why Russian espionage wasn't really on anyone's radar in 2013. The Russians have long played their own impenetrable game and know how to leverage criminal networks. One of the first countries to really grasp how the internet could be exploited for espionage, it had already infiltrated both the US Department of Defense and NASA as far back as 1998.

That the Russians nonetheless went undetected for so long is a testament to their capabilities. Compared to the preferred Chinese method of storming defences and bombarding companies, the Russian approach is more sophisticated. They're savvier, more disciplined and better at covering their tracks. They're incredibly skilled at raiding infected systems. And they'll stay inside, patiently ferreting out the most sensitive information, for as long as it takes.

In 2014, around the time the Ukraine crisis broke out and Russia annexed the Crimean peninsula, Belgium discovered a virus inside its Ministry of Foreign Affairs. It was a piece of professional spyware that had been copying diplomatic messages, including a confidential diplomatic report on Ukraine. All clues pointed to Russia. But no one could unravel *which* Russian hackers were behind the attack.

Another reason Russian spying went undetected had to do with the West itself, which was more focused on threats from China and Iran than Russia. In 2014, the MIVD's 'Russia Desk' was staffed by just six people. Five years later it had grown tenfold. And the AIVD's Russia Team consisted of about five people. Capacity for operations was limited.

Added to that, political ties between the Netherlands and Russia were still quite good in 2013, which was even declared a 'Year of

Friendship' to celebrate relations between the two countries. President Vladimir Putin travelled to Amsterdam to attend the opening of a satellite branch of the Hermitage Museum, and King Willem-Alexander and Queen Máxima paid him a return visit in Moscow.

During the Winter Olympics in Sochi in the spring of 2014, the Dutch king and queen met Russian President Putin again, this time at the boisterous Holland Heineken House. A photo of a grinning King Willem-Alexander sharing a pint with President Putin attracted worldwide attention. Later, Prime Minister Mark Rutte assured Dutch national media that it was 'fine' if the king wanted to drink a toast with Putin. Contacts were good, after all, and Rutte was 'unreservedly positive' about the friendship between the Kremlin and the Dutch Royal House.

Behind the scenes, however, the tide was already reversing. Putin's army was on the brink of invading Ukraine. Relations between Russia and the West were cooling rapidly. Russian hacking groups were escalating their attacks at an unprecedented rate. And the AIVD was keeping a close eye on Russia's intentions and behaviours.

Then, by a stroke of 'luck', one of the AIVD's investigations stumbled right onto a trail of Russian espionage. Following the trail back to its source, agency hackers found themselves inside a university building in Moscow. What they discovered there went beyond anything they could have imagined.

9

Caught on Red Square

'Why do you want to know? Why are people talking about this?' Upset, a source I've been in contact with for years hangs up. I've never heard him so angry before. It's a Saturday afternoon. The editorial department at the *Volkskrant* office is deserted, apart from a cleaner who walks up and down between the desks emptying wastepaper baskets. A co-worker and I are on weekend duty. Our job is to keep an eye on the domestic news.

A scoop on the Dutch tech website Tweakers catches my attention. Apparently, Chinese hackers have breached ASML. Based in Veldhoven, to the south, ASML is the market-leading manufacturer of machines that make chips for devices like mobiles and computers. Customers include Intel and Samsung. It's a competitive industry and ASML is locked in a perpetual arms race with other manufacturers to be the best. In this case, that means making ever smaller chips with ever more computing power. By spending billions on research and thanks to some very expensive and unique technology, the Dutch company has so far managed to stay one step ahead.

That Chinese government hackers have breached this multi-billion-dollar company could have tremendous ramifications. ASML supplies many of its chip-making machines to customers in Asia. If China steals ASML's technology, soon it could be making and marketing chip machines itself. It raises all kinds of questions: how did China break inside ASML? How long have they been in the company? How serious is the damage? And how was the spying discovered?

I call four sources over an encrypted connection in the hope of learning more. But they're cagey and uninformative, and my one good source is clearly annoyed. He's angry that other people are talking about it, and that the hack has been made public at all. That attention will only hurt ASML and hamper investigations into the hack.

His fury surprises me. I've heard this argument before from intelligence services – they don't talk about foreign spying so as to keep adversaries in the dark – but this source doesn't work for intelligence. Why is he so furious?

Something strange is going on. In the last five years there's been a dramatic rise in spying by means of the internet. Public authorities on all sides warn of the dangers, rumours circulate about companies that have been affected and it's a hot topic at conferences. But it's difficult to come by concrete evidence, because everyone's lips are sealed.

Even when a company is hacked, as in the case of ASML now, I come up against a brick wall. ASML downplays the spying. 'We never respond to queries about specific security cases,' the chipmaker initially tells me, only to offer partial confirmation a few days later: 'As it appears now, only a small amount of data was accessed.'

When a company discovers it's being spied on, it calls in security experts. These experts analyse the spying, root out the hackers and restore the systems. First, though, they have to sign confidentiality agreements. Whatever they happen to encounter inside that company, the experts can't say a word about it afterwards.

If it's serious, specialists from security and intelligence agencies will want to take a look as well. They certainly won't talk about it. Their work is secret, and in their eyes that secrecy serves national security. After all, if foreign powers know their spying has been detected, they can simply change tack. Keeping silent is in everybody's interests.

I run into the same problem when writing about Chinese spies at the defence firm Rheinmetall's subsidiary in Ede. The company won't comment. Nor will Yonathan Klijnsma – the researcher who analysed the Chinese spying – say whether China had access to Rheinmetall. When I ask other sources about it, they're equally tight-lipped.

Only one contact offers me the barest confirmation. Excited at this possible opening, I try probing deeper. How long were the Chinese inside? What did they take? No reply.

When *de Volkskrant* runs my piece 'China Hacks Dutch-German Defense Company', it causes a stir. It gets picked up by other media and the Dutch Defence Minister is called to account by parliament. *Finally*, I think: it's about time we had a real political discussion about spying. Eagerly, I await Minister Jeanine Hennis's response to the parliamentary questions. Will she say what China stole? Will she bring up other spy incidents?

A few weeks later, the conservative-liberal Defence chief submits her answers to the Dutch House of Representatives. First question: 'Is it true that confidential data was stolen from the Dutch–German firm Rheinmetall Defence during a cyberattack by Chinese hackers?' Answer: 'It is not up to the Ministry of Defence to disprove or confirm such reports.'

Which puts us right back where we started. With denials. Generalisations. Still, it makes you wonder: though the Dutch government routinely warns of the hazards cyber espionage poses to national security, whenever spying actually occurs, it claims the information is too classified or company-sensitive to say anything more.

Imagine, for a moment, that there's a spike in violent hold-ups targeting jewellers. Criminal groups are going around breaking into shops and stealing expensive merchandise. There would be a public outcry: politicians calling for law enforcement to crack down, anxious proprietors banding together to demand police protection. Civilians might also feel unsafe. If the government then responded by neither confirming nor denying that robberies were taking place, it would be strange to say the least. So why is it an acceptable response when the thefts are digital? The damage to society is no less real or great. If China raids high-tech know-how from ASML, the consequences are utterly devastating.

'People have always spied,' a slightly older intelligence source counters when I express my amazement. 'But this isn't about discovering just one spy like in the old days,' I remind him. 'This is about systematic attacks.' Flip through the AIVD's annual report from 2014 and you'll see that 'many hundreds' of organisations were the targets of digital espionage attacks. What's more, 'The AIVD believes that the attacks it has actually observed represent only the tip of the iceberg, with the total number many times higher.'

Starting from 2015, the American NSA was burrowed deep inside a global payment services company and could see who was transferring money to whom at hundreds of banks. China had sneaked past the security of Marriott hotels and was stealing the data of millions of guests. Russian hackers were harassing the German parliament and French television channel TV5 Monde, masquerading as Islamic State and sending death threats to US servicemen's wives.

Technology has paved the way for large-scale espionage and influencing. The threat and the magnitude bear no comparison to the spy networks of twenty years ago. We're not talking about one-off incidents, but a rupturing of the social fabric. Companies can fail, political processes can be influenced and citizens can be manipulated.

Tentatively, my source nods, saying he understands why this bothers me. 'The thing is, if agencies talk about it they'll lose their intelligence edge.' And therein lies the paradox: our vulnerability is increasing, and talking about it increases our vulnerability.

Not only that, the nature of espionage is also changing. It's no longer limited to *exploring* and *exploiting* enemy computer systems. In some cases, the objective is to *destroy* computer networks, as Israel and the United States, aided by the Netherlands, did with Stuxnet. The term for this is 'computer network attack'. It's what Israel did when it used computers to take out Syria's aerial defence system just before dropping bombs from overhead. It's what Iran did when it planted a destructive virus inside the Saudi state-owned oil company Saudi Aramco and broke 30,000 computers. It's what Russia did when it launched an online attack that cut power to parts of Ukraine.

American journalist Kim Zetter characterises this evolution from exploitation to destruction as the difference between the films *Ocean's Eleven* and *Die Hard*. In *Ocean's Eleven*, eleven skilled professionals come up with a cunning plan to rob casinos in Las Vegas. In *Die Hard*, twelve terrorists attack a target using brute force and don't hesitate to inflict casualties along the way. The digital world is mirroring the plot of *Die Hard*, transforming bit by bit into a battlefield on which businesses are destroyed and real casualties occur.

How do intelligence agencies figure into this digital arms race, and what are they doing about it? Can they protect democracy, whatever the cost?

*

It was the spring of 2014. Along Europe's eastern borders, trouble was brewing. Russian troops had just forcibly annexed the Ukrainian peninsula of Crimea and there was still heavy fighting in eastern Ukraine. The Russians were also throwing their virtual weight around. Russian hacking rings were harrying Western governments and Russian troll accounts were hijacking discussions on social media. That's when the AIVD made its discovery. By sheer coincidence, the agency stumbled onto a trail of Russian espionage.

The AIVD gathered up these digital breadcrumbs and turned them over to its hacking team – a group of five staffers whose sole job was to force their way inside enemy computers systems. Routers and firewalls were their preferred entry ports, these being so utterly vulnerable that there's always a way in. One of the five got to work on this new information. This was a man with extraordinary hacking credentials: Holland's secret weapon. He managed to tunnel his way deep into Russia, eventually ending up in a university building on Moscow's Red Square. He broke into the building's computer network and there he left behind a small file; an implant.

Breaking into networks requires extreme precision. You don't want to make too much noise. Professional hackers therefore start by planting a minuscule file to do the initial canvassing for them. It checks out the network, counts the number of connected PCs and sends back that information, in this case to Holland. The AIVD hacker didn't actually know at this stage where he was. He and the rest of the team thought it was probably a student hall of residence.

This was a reasonable enough assumption. Although the AIVD and other Western agencies were seeing more and more signs of Russian espionage, they still had no clear picture of how the Russians operated. It's incredibly complicated to retrace a hacker's exact steps when all you have to go on is a virus inside an organisation. Sometimes the malware offers tiny clues such as the language in which the first few lines of code are written. Or the tactics used to get inside the network or to siphon off information may betray something about the hacker's origins. Like their counterparts in the UK, Russian agencies take great care to cover their tracks, using servers in different countries to shield their identity and contracting hackers to execute attacks on their behalf.

That's why the AIVD at first assumed it was in a hall of residence where Russian students did the occasional job for Russian services. As soon as the AIVD hacker had a sense of the network and felt it was safe, he left another implant. He hid it somewhere inside the computer network, possibly in the memory of a PC. Slightly larger than the first, this second file could process more commands. Basically, it was a spy post behind enemy lines. Agencies maintain thousands of these kinds of outposts all over the world. They can send and receive commands like 'report all network activity once a day' or 'alert me anytime a classified document passes by'.

Leaving implants is not without risk. Spy posts can be discovered. Some agencies therefore prefer to access computer networks manually each time – say, using stolen passwords – and then leave. That way, no traces of their visit remain.

Looking at the Russian computer network, the AIVD hacker could tell there was a security camera hooked up to it. He tried the default password first. Failing that, he could have fished around for it in connected PCs. Having gained access to the camera, he could see it was mounted in a curved hallway and pointed at a door. Everyone who walked through that doorway into the room beyond was captured on camera.

The AIVD hackers rigged the camera to take screenshots. These small files were parked somewhere in the network and sent to the AIVD one by one. Not too many at once, so as to avoid drawing attention. Then, a couple of weeks into this 'observation', the team made an astounding discovery.

By analysing images from the security camera and tracking the group's behaviour, they were able to piece together an increasingly detailed picture of where they were. It was a room in a largish university complex. The group's make-up varied, but there were usually about ten people. The first clocked in at around six in the morning and most worked until four in the afternoon, but a few stayed later into the evening. Among the people they saw entering the room were high-ranking Russian intelligence officials and known hackers. Further clues to the group's identity were culled from their working methods and the viruses they used. Putting all these puzzle pieces together, it finally dawned on the AIVD team that what they'd stumbled on to wasn't just a bunch of college tech-heads. This was the notorious Russian spy ring APT29, better known as 'Cozy Bear'.

It was an electrifying discovery. The AIVD team was normally a reserved bunch, used to pulling off tricky operations, but this time they were stoked. Cheers could be heard going up behind the agency's tinted and shuttered windows. Cozy Bear was a much-talked-about group that specialised in persistent spy operations and known for hacking international organisations and governments. Numerous security firms were already dissecting their behaviour and malware the group used. Its victims, they found, belonged to a few very specific sectors: military, diplomatic, telecom and energy.

Just how actively Cozy Bear was attacking ministries and companies was revealed earlier in 2014 when Kaspersky analysed one of the group's computer servers. It counted 84 hits in Georgia, 61 in Russia, 34 in the United States, 14 in Great Britain, 8 in India and 4 in Ukraine. Cozy Bear used dozens of such servers, continually switching between them. Much as experts and agencies tried to keep the group in their sights, nobody knew where Cozy Bear hid out or the identity of any of its members, let alone whether they were indeed taking orders from the Kremlin.

Having penetrated the network, the AIVD started to gather first impressions. They had to proceed with extreme caution, since any misstep could alert the Russians to the Dutch presence. AIVD boss Rob Bertholee had been told of the agency's unique access but was unsure whether to apprise his MIVD counterpart Pieter Bindt. Officially, the AIVD hacking team fell under the Joint Sigint Cyber Unit in which the two agencies now worked together. But, as usual, Bertholee hesitated about sharing information. Distrustful as he was, it took him weeks to tell Bindt the AIVD was inside Cozy Bear's computer network.

While the AIVD was snooping on Cozy Bear in Russia, an alarming report arrived at the Russian Interfax press agency on the afternoon of 17 July 2014. A passenger aircraft en route from Amsterdam to Kuala Lumpur had been shot down over eastern Ukraine. At 3.18 p.m. the jetliner vanished from the radar and crashed. Soon, amateur shots began circulating online showing black smoke pluming from a field outside the Ukrainian village of Hrabove, and then of the first pieces of smouldering wreckage and scattered bodies of passengers. It quickly became clear that none of those 298 passengers – 196 of whom were Dutch – had survived.

At the AIVD headquarters in Zoetermeer, the tragedy caused chaos. That evening, intelligence workers rushed back to the office in a mad scramble to gather information. But with the ongoing threat of jihadism and recent budgetary cuts, the AIVD found itself short-staffed. Valuable Russian-speaking analysts had been laid off, leaving the agency without contacts in Kiev. With no time to lose, a retired employee was drummed up and dispatched to Ukraine to start filling in the gaps.

Although the Malaysia Airlines flight 17 disaster overshadowed the AIVD's access to Cozy Bear, its hacking team was still inside the Russian spy group. It's unclear if they also saw any useful information about flight MH17. Another Russian spy group – APT28, aka Fancy Bear – did later get involved in the information war surrounding the crash. Far from discouraging its spying abroad, however, Russia actually stepped up its espionage activities after the incident. And the AIVD hacking team in Holland saw it happen. Within months of infiltrating the Cozy Bear network, they watched as the Russians opened fire on the United States.

*

The first time I got a snippet of information about the AIVD operation in Moscow, I didn't fully grasp the real significance. I was sitting on a terrace with a source, asking about current developments.

This was in the summer of 2017. By then it was well known that Russia had staged a cyber offensive to influence the outcome of the American presidential elections. Their interference had helped Republican candidate Donald Trump into the White House. From computers in Russia, they besieged American citizens, voting systems and the Democratic Party. And they didn't even need to step foot in the United States; with one click they could cross the digital superhighway from Moscow to Washington.

To do this, the Russians had mobilised an arsenal of cyber-weaponry. On social media, they fanned the flames of social discord. Hundreds of mostly young Russians put in twelve-hour shifts in an office building in St Petersburg, their jobs consisting of posting messages, pictures and videos. Sometimes they incited trouble, other times they merely stirred it. Just how cleverly they went about this work was illustrated by an article in the *New York Times*.

In a town in Louisiana, inhabitants woke up one morning in 2014 to disturbing text messages. 'Toxic fume hazard warning in this area until 1:30 PM. Take Shelter. Check Local Media.' People who looked on Twitter saw just how serious it was. Hundreds of accounts were reporting an explosion at a nearby chemical plant. 'A powerful explosion heard from miles away,' tweeted one 'Jon Merrit'. Someone else tweeted a photo of an inferno and another posted a video of the explosion itself. Local and national journalists received accounts of the blast, too. They were tagged in posts. News of the disaster spread like wildfire, even making national headlines, as a screenshot someone posted of the story on CNN's homepage showed. On YouTube, a video appeared of a man watching Arab TV, followed by masked ISIS members claiming responsibility. Even Wikipedia had already created a page about the catastrophe, and local and regional media were also reporting it on social channels.

But it was all fake. Over the course of a few hours, dozens of phoney accounts churned out hundreds of tweets, pictures and staged videos as part of a disinformation campaign orchestrated from a troll factory in St Petersburg. The news triggered panic, with frightened residents calling emergency services and officials at the chemical plant. And that's precisely what the young Russians had been told to do: create unrest and sow discord.

Something similar happened after flight MH17 was shot down. The two days immediately following the crash remain the troll factory's busiest ever, in which they clocked more than 100,000 messages. As an investigation by Dutch weekly news magazine *De Groene Amsterdammer* showed, clear attempts at influencing opinion started the morning right after the disaster, when trolls launched three hashtags in Russian – #Kievshotboeingdown, #KievProvocation and #Kievtellthetruth – laying the blame for the crash on Ukraine.

Russian trolls deployed the same method during the 2016 US presidential elections, firing fake ads and incendiary texts into the campaign. Over two years, Russian accounts posted 80,000 messages on Facebook intended to push American voters towards Trump, who was less hostile to Russia than any of the other presidential hopefuls. Forty per cent of Americans saw these messages. At the same time,

Russian hackers were also attacking voting systems in twenty states. In Illinois, they took data on 90,000 voters, and they also hit a local election office in Arizona, a government website in Tennessee and a tech company in Florida.

But the heaviest assault was on the Democratic Party, when the two Russian cyberspy groups Cozy Bear and Fancy Bear invaded the Democratic National Committee's computer network. The hackers watched and they searched for information that could incriminate Democratic presidential nominee Hillary Clinton. Fancy Bear in the end stole almost 20,000 emails – later published on WikiLeaks – that were damaging both to party officials and to Clinton herself. Russia's interference literally stunned Americans; even US agencies were powerless to stem the online aggression. According to some American media, it was a 'cyber Pearl Harbor'.

The Russian meddling reverberated long after the elections. Did Donald Trump or anyone in his inner circle know the Russians were advancing his bid for the presidency? Had there been any meetings between the Russians and Trump confidants? Dutch journalist Eelco Bosch van Rosenthal and I set out to find some answers. We'd worked together before to interview Edward Snowden in Moscow, and now we teamed up again, pairing his good contacts in the United States with mine in the world of intelligence.

For a long time, neither of our connections bore any fruit. We suspected there had been a meeting in the Netherlands between a Russian spy and someone close to Trump, but the evidence was flimsy; no more than a few vague rumours and inconclusive confirmations. In the summer of 2017, I'd decided to try my luck with another source who, yet again, refused to bite. Our conversation drifted to other topics. Then, at the mention of cyberspying, he casually noted that the Netherlands had seen something of the American Democratic Party hack.

My thoughts immediately leaped to the multitude of Dutch data centres and the Amsterdam Internet Exchange. It stood to reason that Russian hackers would conduct attacks via the Netherlands, whether intentionally or simply because they happened to choose a VPN server located here. Dutch intelligence agencies could have tapped that VPN server and so discovered what the Russians were up to. But my source wouldn't say any more.

When I mentioned my hunch to others, however, most were disbelieving. Nobody else seemed to have heard this rumour. Was my information right? Or had I jumped to the wrong conclusion?

At the same time, Eelco was working on his American sources. Weeks turned into months. Still I remained convinced that the Netherlands *must* have seen something because of the likelihood that the Russian hacks went through Dutch data centres. That hunch was cemented when I stumbled upon another startling story.

It concerned an otherwise unremarkable server at the web hosting company Leaseweb. In 2011, the FBI had asked Dutch police if they could tap a web server at a data centre just outside the city of Haarlem, in the Waarderpolder business park, up the road from an IKEA store. According to the FBI, it contained important data about a drug cartel. The Dutch High Tech Crime Unit sent a specialist to the business park, put a tap on the server so it would send data back to police headquarters in Driebergen and from there transmitted the encrypted communications to the FBI.

This went on for a year and a half. A new request was filed every four weeks, as legally required, and the tap was duly extended. Getting the data to the FBI was child's play for the High Tech Crime Unit, but they had only an inkling of the operation's significance. They knew this server was a 'BES server', used to store BlackBerry messages. When they eventually disconnected the tap at Leaseweb, someone close to the police learned this particular BlackBerry server had been leased to the Mexican Sinaloa Cartel, the world's most notorious drug syndicate. It was left up to Leaseweb whether or not to shut the server down, though the Americans advised letting it run a bit longer because, as one of the provider's employees was told, 'Otherwise some people in Mexico will die.'

Not until the operation wrapped up did its true significance become clear. Early in 2014, two FBI agents visited the Public Prosecution Service Rotterdam. In a presentation, they explained to senior police officers why they'd been so keen to tap that specific BES server in the data centre outside Haarlem.

The FBI had got hold of an IT specialist, a man in his late twenties, who was in charge of communication inside the Sinaloa Cartel. He used BlackBerries, a type of telephone long popular with criminals on account of their much-touted security. Text messages and calls are encrypted and the encryption keys can be saved to a private computer server. If police can't see the server, there's nothing they can do.

The FBI got this IT man in its sights and managed to lure him into a hotel room in New York City. They offered him a choice: either co-operate with the FBI and get a reduced sentence or spend a long time in jail. He opted for the former and started working undercover for the agency. That gave the FBI the opening it needed. Thanks to their new mole, the agency knew where the BES server was located and got the encryption keys to decrypt the Sinaloa Cartel's communications.

There was only one other problem: the BES server was in Canada. Under Canada's strict privacy laws, you couldn't just tap a server and send all the content to the FBI. The cartel's IT man would have to move the machine to a different country. The US was out, since not only might that draw attention, but American laws on tapping were fairly rigid, too. Before placing a tap domestically, the FBI would have had to spell out what it expected to find. Instead, the FBI turned to the AIVD. Because the US and Holland already worked together closely and Dutch rules around tapping requests were less exacting – merely the suspicion of an indictable offence is enough – the FBI got its recruit to relocate the server to a data centre run by Leaseweb, in that business park just outside Haarlem.

After that, they asked their Dutch partners to put a tap on the machine and send them everything. Listening to the decrypted phone calls, FBI investigators soon picked out one voice in particular. It was, they suspected, the cartel's boss – Joaquín Guzmán Loera, better known as 'El Chapo' – the most wanted drug criminal in the world. In the calls, he could be heard instructing his henchmen. American and Mexican federal investigators had been hunting El Chapo since the 1980s, and putting him permanently behind bars had become an obsession. Somehow, every time they locked him up, he flew the coop. Once, via a mile-long, thirty-foot-deep tunnel his cohorts dug under the shower of his prison cell. The tunnel had been fitted with lamps and lined with rail tracks over which a cart whisked El Chapo back to freedom.

The FBI compared the voice they heard to a recorded interview El Chapo gave in hiding to the American actor Sean Penn. It matched. According to a source, 'It was the first time in at least five years that the Americans heard El Chapo speak.' Over time, hundreds of the drug lord's telephone calls flowed through the Dutch data centre, and with the AIVD's assistance the FBI was able to piece together his daily routines. After a while, the eavesdropping operation became so streamlined that whenever El Chapo dialled an accomplice, within a day the FBI had received, decrypted and listened to the data sent from Holland.

Something similar must have happened after Russians hacked the American Democratic Party headquarters. As far as I could see, this was the only possible conclusion. The AIVD or MIVD must have got a tip or just happened to stumble across a server in the Netherlands that was being used by Russian hackers. But no matter whom Eelco and I asked about it, no one had ever heard of anything like that happening. And so the mystery deepened.

*

Back in the university building on Red Square, the Russian hackers continued their work, never suspecting the Dutch spy post in their midst. Some months later, the AIVD was still watching inside that network when they noticed that Cozy Bear gearing up for an attack. The Russian hackers were writing emails, composed in perfect English, and sending them to addresses ending in @state.gov. The addresses belonged to US State Department staff.

Phishing emails are often the first stage of an attack. After identifying their quarry, hackers send an email as bait. If a target clicks on the attachment, it installs some initial malware, which steals things like login credentials. That's what the Russian hackers did. It worked, and soon they were in the unclassified part of the American State Department's computer network.

When the AIVD realised what was happening, they warned their American colleagues via the NSA liaison at the US Embassy in The Hague, who in turn alerted the NSA, the CIA and the FBI. But when the agencies' technical experts went to work to root out the Russians, the Russians simply attacked from somewhere else.

This was digital warfare on an unprecedented scale. While the Russian hackers kept trying to drill deeper into the State Department, its defenders – teams at the FBI and NSA – fought back with the help of Dutch intelligence. The fighting lasted twenty-four hours. The Russians were terribly aggressive, but they never realised that the AIVD was right there, watching their every move. These Dutch spies enabled the NSA and FBI to block the enemy at every turn. So crucial was this information that the NSA opened a direct feed from AIVD headquarters to guarantee the fastest possible transmission of Dutch intelligence.

What the Russians were attempting to do was communicate with 'command and control servers' – computers they controlled – to send commands to their malware in the State Department network. But while the Russians were trying to connect to these servers, Dutch spies were sending their IP addresses to the Americans. By blocking all State Department traffic to each of those IP addresses in turn, the Americans could cut off every new Russian attempt. They then countered by opening more command and control servers. According to sources quoted by CNN afterwards, it was the 'worst cyberattack ever' on the US government. The State Department's email system had to be shut down for several days to restore security.

Although the Americans managed to boot the Russians out of the State Department in the end, by then the hackers had already exploited their access to email someone inside the White House. Given the sender's address, that person assumed he'd received a message from the State Department and clicked on the link. The link opened a website on which the White House staffer entered his credentials, and so the Russians got it.

This let the Russians infiltrate the White House servers, including a computer that stored President Barack Obama's emails. Though they couldn't crack his personal BlackBerry containing state secrets, sources later told the *New York Times* that they did access email exchanges with embassies and diplomats, as well as agendas and notes on policy and legislation. As before, the Dutch spies saw it all happen, and the AIVD and MIVD warned their respective American partners.

The attacks persisted. Also targeted by Cozy Bear was the Joint Chiefs of Staff – the principal US military advisory body, constituting the most senior officers of the US Navy, Air Force and Army. So ferocious was this cyberattack, and so thoroughly compromised the American servers, that entire sections of the network had to be shut down. For eleven days America's military leaders were unable to access their work mailboxes.

At this point, the AIVD's hacking team had been inside the building on Red Square for a year. And still their spy post went unnoticed. Thanks to the security camera screenshots, they were also homing in on the group's members. Though their number varied, there were rarely more than ten. Among them, the AIVD recognised spies from Russia's Foreign Intelligence Service, the SVR, which specialised in military, strategic and economic espionage. Its chief was appointed by President Vladimir Putin, who could also give the SVR orders in secret, without informing Russian parliament.

Cozy Bear's attacks on the American government didn't let up. After the Russian annexation of Crimea and US counteraction in the form of sanctions, their intensity only increased. In the summer of 2015, the hackers opened their assault on the Democratic Party, and the AIVD team saw it happen in real time. Once again, the Dutch intelligence agencies alerted their American colleagues.

In September, an FBI agent phoned the Democratic National Committee to warn that Russian hackers were inside their network. He was put through to the help desk, where the call was answered by Yared Tamene, an IT support contractor. He knew next to nothing about cyberattacks. After hanging up with the FBI, he googled 'APT29',

'Cozy Bear' and 'Dukes', as the Russian hacker group is also known. He glanced at the network's system logs for signs of a breach. But, as the *New York Times* later reported, he never really took a serious look, even when the same FBI agent continued to call in the weeks following. In fact, Tamene wasn't sure the man was really an FBI agent at all.

As a result, nothing happened. The FBI's cautionary phone calls came to nothing. The Russians stayed inside the network, reading emails and internal DNC documents. Forty-four years after the break-in at the party's Watergate headquarters, the Democrats were being raided again. In 1972, the five burglars were caught in the act and their boss, Republican President Richard Nixon, was forced to resign two years later. This time around, the Netherlands saw the burglars but the Democrats did nothing. The AVID looked on in disbelief as the Russians were left to do as they pleased.

Having laid the groundwork and done its own extensive spying, nine months later Cozy Bear passed the baton to Fancy Bear, a group allied to Russia's military intelligence agency GRU. Fancy Bear proceeded to steal tens of thousands of emails from the DNC network. It sent them to a go-between, who turned them over to the whistleblower platform WikiLeaks, which released them. It was only at this point, after the emails went public and proved detrimental to Democratic nominee Hillary Clinton's presidential election campaign, that the party finally took the warnings seriously. An in-depth internal investigation followed, but by that time it was too late. Russia had interfered in the American presidential elections.

*

Message from Eelco: 'Coffee?'

Eelco and I were in daily contact. Texting back and forth, we exchanged theories on what the Netherlands might have seen of the DNC hack, shared new ideas, told each other about meetings we'd set up. Often, we also spoke on the phone briefly in the evening. We talked through countless scenarios, trying to nail down what actually had happened, but rarely came up with anything concrete.

Anytime we had news, we met in our usual spot. As when Eelco got confirmation from his US sources that, yes, Holland had provided key information about the DNC hack to American intelligence. Excited, we considered what this could mean. We drew up a list of potential new sources – diplomatic sources, intelligence sources, American sources. People who could reasonably be expected to know.

For some, all we had was a job title. An embassy liaison, say. We made a second list of people we could ask for names. In the following weeks we arranged sham meetings with several of them, ostensibly to talk about some other topic. Casually, we'd fish for a source's name. In one case, we already had a first name. This ploy worked: one person took the bait and supplied the full name. But then we had to find him. We tried Google, social media, public records. All our searches came up empty. After weeks of digging, we finally turned up an address in an old register. Since it was foreign, we asked a good contact to send this potential source a letter.

On and on it dragged, for months. Conversations yielded mere crumbs. Sources refused to open up. At four months and counting, we decided to take a chance and booked a flight to Washington DC. Without any clear plan, we called up every digital expert and former intelligence worker we could think of and asked to talk. In the end, we got meetings with about ten people. We also decided to pay a visit to the recently retired national intelligence director, James Clapper, at his home. If the Dutch agencies had supplied useful information to the Americans, our thinking went, the big boss of American intelligence ought to know. Clapper, imposing even in his gardening clothes, stared from his doorway while we introduced ourselves as journalists from Holland – and then flew into a rage. 'Never in fifty years,' he snarled, had journalists showed up at his house, and he wouldn't stand for it now. 'Get out!' he shouted. We beat a hasty retreat.

Our other meetings in Washington yielded two new nuggets of information. One: the AIVD and the MIVD had indeed been spying on the Russian hacker group Cozy Bear. Two: because of that, the two Dutch agencies saw the Russian hacks on the US State Department, the White House and the Joint Chiefs of Staff. So valuable was the

Dutch assistance that the Americans had sent 'cake and flowers' to the AIVD headquarters. The Netherlands also got valuable intel in return, about Mali, for instance, North Korea and Iran.

Armed with these insights, we continued our work back home. Through an encrypted channel we eventually gathered more details and, seven months later, finally had our story ready to go. But then, just when we wanted to ask the AIVD and the US Embassy for a comment before going to press, I received a disturbing text message.

10

Pornography and Rolls-Royce

Suddenly, they were out. For three years, the AIVD spy post in Cozy Bear's network went unnoticed. And then one day, the connection disappeared. The Dutch spying on Red Square was over.

What had happened? In April 2017, while speaking at a security convention, deputy director of the NSA Richard Ledgett let slip that a 'Western ally' had helped his agency boot the Russians out of the US State Department. The Dutch were livid at the American indiscretion. 'Very upsetting', 'aggravating', 'typical American arrogance', sources later called it. MIVD boss Pieter Bindt and his AIVD counterpart Rob Bertholee reproached their American colleagues. Why jeopardise so valuable an operation by talking about it publicly at a conference? Relations with US intelligence, already shaky since the Snowden revelations and Donald Trump's election, took another hit.

Six years separated the panic at Dutch certificate authority DigiNotar and the loss of the AIVD's spy post on Red Square. In those six years, the world had become a very different place. In 2011, Facebook was not yet king, Osama bin Laden still posed a bigger threat than any cyber army and smartphones were still just a neat gadget.

Back then, DigiNotar was chalked up as an unfortunate incident, never to be repeated. Talk of 'digital threats' only got you blank looks. The Netherlands had no national cyber security centre, nor did its intelligence agencies have separate cyber units. We had only Interior Minister Piet Hein Donner, a respected jurist, trying to reassure the country.

Six years later, American tech giants Apple, Google, Microsoft, Amazon and Facebook were the most powerful corporations on earth, Russian hackers had successfully meddled in the US presidential elections and smartphones were at the centre of our lives. If you left home without yours, you went back to get it.

Now there were threats on all sides. China, Iran, the US, Russia, the UK: all of them were spying. All of them were stealing information and using it to influence populations. In the Netherlands, the NCSC was not only up and running but growing fast. It employed hundreds of people. On big monitors they could clock exactly when the Chinese workday started: when the graphs recording cyberattacks spiked. By 2015 and 2016, the AIVD and MIVD's warnings were growing more insistent. Cyberspies were inundating the country. Brazil, Vietnam, India ... everyone was doing it.

Two days before Eelco and my story about the AIVD's long-time spy presence in Moscow went to press, I got a 7 a.m. text from my telecom provider. 'Success. You've changed your VPN settings. We'll apply the changes as soon as possible.'

I went straight to the newspaper's IT department. 'No,' said a young man in a T-shirt, 'we've made no changes to your connection.' I phoned my telecom, but they couldn't place the notification either. I called a good intelligence source who had experience with cyberspying. 'Huib, this is a red line,' he said. 'The timing, just before your publication of a major story, can't be a fluke. Get a new phone and a new SIM card, pronto.'

A month earlier, I had just got home from Washington DC and, with the AIVD piece almost done, the router in my apartment had died. Just as before my trip to Rio de Janeiro four years ago, it suddenly flatlined; I could get no signal at all. Before, I'd put it down to coincidence. Now, paired with this weird text, I wasn't so sure.

Were these two events somehow linked? I took the router to an IT specialist, just to be sure, but my phone was what really worried me. If someone was messing with my cell service, that presented an immediate problem. It meant my calls and texts weren't secure. Most unsettling was that I couldn't look this threat in the eye. I had no idea where it was coming from.

It could be UK or US intelligence. Even Russia. Or – more likely? – the AIVD. Sources said the Dutch agency would be extremely nervous about our publishing this story. They didn't want their methods splashed across the front page. And it was even more sensitive in this case, because the method in question was hacking. For the AIVD, hacking was a secret weapon they'd honed years before. They were also afraid of the Russian counter-reaction. If it got out that the AIVD had been snooping inside one of the best-known Russian hacking groups for three whole years, that would be explosive news. Worse, for the Russians it would be a very public loss of face, since they steadfastly denied the existence of any such hacker groups. There was a real chance the Russian government would seek payback. Just as it did in 2013, when a Dutch diplomat in Moscow was targeted after a political spat with the Netherlands. Onno Elderenbosch was assaulted, tied up and his apartment ransacked.

Eelco and I published our story at nine in the evening on Thursday 25 January 2018, and it was instantly picked up by media around the world. Internationally, it was relevant. That the FBI had opened an investigation into Russian interference in the 2016 elections was as a result of warnings from the AIVD. Now, for the first time, it was clear why the US had been so sure of the Kremlin's involvement: Holland had told them so. All the big global media outlets ran the story, and their keen interest felt overwhelming. When I switched on my cell the next morning it could barely cope with all the texts, emails and alerts buzzing in.

Over at the Dutch Ministry of General Affairs, people were breaking out in hives, reported one source. They feared Russian reprisal. Our sources didn't feel safe. Some went quiet for weeks. One was so scared he wouldn't meet for months. Someone close to the police told me the High Tech Crime Unit was banning people from talking to the media at all. Police personnel were also told they couldn't meet the press, especially journalists from my paper, *de Volkskrant*, and Eelco's TV news show.

Following our publication, the AIVD launched an internal security investigation into the leak. There's a high price to pay for disclosing state secrets, and the agency wanted a name. Investigators phoned and questioned current and former employees, but there were too few leads. In the end, the internal inquiry concluded this classified intelligence hadn't been leaked from within the AIVD. It must have come from a foreign state.

Meanwhile, I was still trying to understand what had happened to my phone. It was a fairly new iPhone and I'd religiously installed the latest updates. Plus, iPhones are tough to hack, even for the AIVD. To begin with, they'd need a hole in the software. The newer the model and its operating system, the harder and more expensive that is. Information about an unknown vulnerability in the newest model iPhone's OS can easily cost agencies a million bucks. And while that's fine for a serious terrorist, I'm just a journalist.

Hacking wasn't the problem either. Though I'd never discover who was behind it, the text I'd received mentioned a VPN connection. Most likely that meant the connection at my telecom provider. As the Belgacom incident had revealed, more and more providers are using VPNs. Agencies are looking for ways to crack them. Was an agency messing with that VPN connection in an attempt to get its hands on the content of my phone? If so, which agency?

*

At the head of the twenty-foot conference table, the Russian millionaire slams down his fist. He thrusts out his head, brown eyes glaring at us in fury. For twenty minutes, Aleksej Gubarev, aged thirty-six, has kept himself in check. Now, he barks at us, in English, 'I have zero point zero contact with Russian security services. I talk to no one. Ever.' Then he subsides back into his chair.

Gubarev had just taken my *Volkskrant* colleague Tom Kreling and me on a tour of his company, Webzilla. It occupies a grey office block rising several storeys along an unkempt, busy road in the Cypriot coastal town of Limassol. The place is deserted on this Saturday in January 2017. One hand in the trouser pocket of his blue linen suit, the stocky businessman leads us around, briskly pointing out the beanbag seats, the wooden dragons, the game consoles, as if showing us his relics will deflect our unwanted questions.

It was a journalist at the *Wall Street Journal* who first put me onto Gubarev. This American had flown to Amsterdam over Christmas after getting his hands on an explosive file: a report by a British ex-spy about Donald Trump and his Russian contacts. The report contained spectacular details – that the Kremlin had a video of Trump watching while prostitutes urinated on a bed in a Moscow hotel, for example – and also included an interesting paragraph about a Dutch internet service provider called Webzilla.

According to this report, Webzilla and its owner, Aleksej Gubarev, had 'facilitated' the Russian hacks of the Democratic National Committee. That is, the hackers had used Webzilla's network. It alleged Gubarev knew what was happening and was himself a spy for the Russian FSB. But the American journalist couldn't find many leads for all the theories in this report, so he decided to try his luck in Holland. He boarded a plane to Amsterdam and invited himself to *de Volkskrant*. That's how we met.

I'd just begun to feel that I understood the mechanics of cyber espionage. From the British spying at Belgacom to the Chinese spies at Rheinmetall, there were always some common denominators. First, the spies used a trick to get inside, often a phishing email. Next, they brought in a virus, then they stole information. I'd scarcely given any thought to the role of companies that might be facilitating them. But here was this American journalist claiming that a Dutch company had helped Russians hack the United States.

Hosting providers like Webzilla supply two services: storage and transport. They're the warehouses and traffic interchanges of the internet. Like physical storage companies, they rent out space. Only, rather than furniture or moving boxes, that space is for emails and documents. They also provide transport. As at any physical interchange, traffic comes and goes. The hosting provider's servers let organisations send and save emails and retain documents and information. Websites also lease space so that data packets can reach them.

Put simply, no hosting providers would mean no internet. Hosting companies come in all shapes and sizes. There's Leaseweb, a fairly large and well-known Dutch provider. Lesser known are companies like Worldstream, King Servers and Webzilla. Webzilla is a special case, because it started out with no servers of its own. Instead, Gubarev leased them mainly from Leaseweb and then sublet the server space to his own customers. Gubarev's unique selling point was offering a full package: besides server space he also promised maintenance and service. He always had technical experts onsite to fix potential disruptions. To return to the motoring analogy: Gubarev offered not only a nice, tarmacked road, but also breakdown service. Customers were assured that any disruptions would be fixed in fifteen minutes or less.

This was a profitable business. Gubarev's company took off and by 2016 was posting $50 million in annual revenue. His customers, with whom he kept in touch personally, were based mostly in Eastern Europe and Russia. What they did with the server space was their own business. Much as with companies that rent storage units, an owner has no say over what people can and can't put in. But what if one of those servers is consistently used for criminal internet traffic? Can the owner still shrug off responsibility? What if you find out one particular customer's storage units are *always* used to store weapons?

It's here that you begin to see distinctions between hosting providers. Some, like Leaseweb, started out with shady reputations. They barely looked at what customers did. Before 2007, Leaseweb servers were regularly used to distribute spam and child pornography. After 2007, the company employed staff to root out illicit activity. It designated a police contact and police could ask to examine individual machines or order Leaseweb to deny access to data.

Ten years later, the company that had long hosted European internet traffic to the 'PornHub' website – though they did also have classier customers, such as Heineken – had become a solid partner for the police. Their data centre outside Haarlem still had an old Dell server with IDD-brand-tapping software, so anytime the police wanted to intercept a customer's data they only had to hand over a court order and the tapping could begin.

The only problem with this is working out who is renting servers for malicious ends. Under Dutch law, a hosting provider can't look inside its computers, just as a physical storage company can't install cameras in its units. More and more governments are approaching this by trying to monitor traffic going through providers. But this isn't without risks.

What's at stake is illustrated by an incident in 2012. Around Queen's Day, a national holiday in the Netherlands, a group of anarchists in the eastern city of Nijmegen put a festival poster online captioned 'Hang the Queen'. The police saw it just after midnight. Within an hour the public prosecutor's office was on the phone to Leaseweb, whose servers hosted the anarchist website. Take it offline now, the company was told.

Leaseweb refused. Plenty of people want stuff taken down, they said; they wanted to see an official order stating why. It arrived at five the next afternoon and the website was disconnected for two hours. But the authorities don't want to get tangled up in this red tape every time. In December 2018, the Dutch Justice Minister Ferdinand Grapperhaus announced he wanted to be able to impose administrative sanctions on hosting providers that didn't take down child pornography within twenty-four hours.

The European Union has a comparable policy on terrorist content. Privacy watchdogs and hosting companies now fear the Dutch and European governments will expand such penalties to things like hate speech, incitement and fake news. Or, say, a disagreeable post about a head of state. If providers could no longer refuse requests to remove content, that would give authorities a powerful censorship tool.

Governments are trying in all kinds of ways to strengthen their grip on the internet. In 2013, the FBI approached Leaseweb offering half a million dollars in exchange for installing a black box that would give them permanent access to the provider's servers. Leaseweb refused. In March 2019, the European Parliament passed the controversial Article 17 of the EU Copyright Directive, requiring that a large share of content people post on sites like Facebook and YouTube be filtered for copyright violations. Privacy advocates such as the foundation Bits of Freedom worry this marks a first step in the normalisation of internet censorship.

But there's also a counter-argument. Some hosting companies deliberately turn a deaf ear to law enforcement, or build their business models on attracting crooks. Notorious is the Dutch company Ecatel, singled out by the independent research organisation HostExploit in 2010 as cybercriminals' preferred hosting provider. According to government sources, Ecatel's co-owners responded slowly if at all to requests to investigate or shut down servers. In 2018 the company wound up with a court injunction ordering it to remove illegal Premier League streams within thirty minutes of notifications.

What, then, about Webzilla? Where does the blue-linen-suited Gubarev's hosting firm fall? Is it closer to Leaseweb, or more Ecatel? It doesn't look good that the multimillion-dollar business has been registered under some unusual mailing addresses. Such as a rundown cottage in the forest at the Midland Parc Country Club outside Amersfoort, owned by an old lady who lives two hours away. Or a now boarded-up house in a seedy suburb of the same city. Or the home of an employee of a horticultural packing plant who'd never even heard of Webzilla. Why would a professional outfit be using addresses like these?

There are many more questions. Such as, what led Gubarev to move to Cyprus, an island off the Turkish coast, at the age of twenty-two and without bothering to finish his technical degree in Siberia? Why did he also incorporate his holding company XBT in Cyprus, a hotbed of spies and well-known haven for creative tax-evasion schemes? Why does he keep in touch with customers personally rather than leaving that to his employees? How did his firm accrue a fortune in just ten years on a hosting provider's slim profit margins? How can he afford a white Rolls-Royce Ghost and an eighty-foot yacht?

*

An email arrives from Jochem Steman, Gubarev's right-hand man: 'We want firm agreements – in writing – that you won't publish without our consent.' It's just before our meeting with Gubarev and Tom Kreling and I are sitting in our hotel lobby in Limassol talking through the questions we want to ask.

But it looks like we'll have to get past Steman first. Steman is Webzilla's Dutch chief commercial officer and he's got some sweeping conditions. We're not allowed to write about anything other than Webzilla and he wants the right to veto our text. After some back and forth, in which we try to explain in calls and messages that that's not how freedom of the press works, Steman drops his demands moments before the interview.

At a quarter to eleven that morning we drive our hire car out to the office of XBT Holding, where Gubarev and Steman await us. I've been around to every possible intelligence source, trying to glean something about Webzilla. If it's true that such a critical link in the internet is facilitating attacks on Western organisations, the name should at least ring a bell. You could compare it to a mosque that's funding terrorists – the endangerment is that big and that bad. But no matter whom I call – police sources, intelligence sources, technical experts – no one has any answers. They search for words to make it clear to me they genuinely don't know.

Which is weird. Webzilla leases 15 million euros' worth of servers – thousands of computers – from a Dutch data centre and subleases that webspace to customers in Eastern Europe and Russia. Nobody knows who they are or what the servers are being used for. It's not even clear what, if anything, the NCSC – set up to defend the Netherlands against digital threats – knows about Webzilla. I get it: you can't barge inside businesses and poke around in their computers. But what if Webzilla is engaging in deliberate sabotage?

Another example is Dutch King Servers. It's owned by a twenty-six-year-old Russian who lives in western Siberia, near the Mongolian border. He leases about a thousand computer servers in an industrial park in the Dutch town of Dronten, which he in turn subleases mostly to operators of porn sites.

King Servers has a bad reputation and has been implicated in large-scale child pornography, malware and cyberattacks. Any time Dutch police show up at King Servers with an injunction, they can only hope the Russian in the Siberian outback will be willing to disconnect that customer. Beyond a polite request, there's not much they can do. And there's no point asking Russia, which doesn't extradite its own nationals.

In the summer of 2016, when Russian hackers attacked voting systems in Arizona and Illinois, the FBI discovered six of the eight IP address they used belonged to King Servers. Coincidence or not? Working out the exact nature of the company's involvement proved impossibly complicated. Hackers can rent lots of different servers, they can use VPN connections and the anonymous Tor network and then they may wind up going through King Servers, or they may just outsource to criminals with servers of their own. The argument that if they used King Servers, then King Servers abetted the attack doesn't hold up. It's possible, but it could just as easily be a coincidence. Web traffic is like road traffic that way: you wouldn't expect a transport authority to know exactly who's on all the country's road at every moment of the day. Companies like King Servers and Webzilla, meanwhile, compare themselves to the postal service: all they do is carry parcels from point A to point B. They can't open them up. Hence, they don't know what's inside them.

Most likely, this is why my sources don't know anything about Webzilla. Web traffic is variable and tough to pin down and cybercriminals and state-sponsored hackers use this to their advantage. That makes the Netherlands, with its multitude of data centres and important links to the rest of the world, especially vulnerable. The fast networks ordinary people use to share, work and text are used by other entities to spy and attack.

When I ask the NCSC how they prevent foreign agents from appropriating hosting service providers, the answer is unsatisfactory. The organisation that works towards 'a safe, open and stable information society' does not, I'm told, bother with hosting companies. True, they're what underpins the internet, yet Holland doesn't class them with the kind of 'critical infrastructure' whose failure could cause serious societal upheaval.

The solution, in typical Dutch fashion, is self-regulation. The Dutch Independent Post and Telecommunications Authority and national police say they try to hold hosting companies accountable, but how exactly do you do that when the owners terminate their Dutch residence (Ecatel), live in Russia (King Servers) or are registered in Cyprus (Webzilla)?

In contrast to Webzilla, Kaspersky is a familiar name. American distrust of the Russian antivirus provider sharpened after another incident in 2016, when espionage files from an NSA staffer's PC were discovered in the hands of Russian spies. That this staffer's computer was protected by Kaspersky software could be no accident, the Americans decided. US media promptly began claiming Kaspersky's antivirus software was the ultimate Russian spy tool, programmed to automatically ferret out secret documents on millions of computers and feed them to the Russians.

*

In the Netherlands, the AIVD also continued to keep tabs on Kaspersky. Concerns had persisted ever since that joint CIA operation in an Amsterdam hotel.

Then Israel broke into Kaspersky's systems and reported Russian hackers were using computers with Kaspersky software to search for classified documents. With many local governments as well as Dutch telecom giant KPN using this software, the AIVD wanted to judge for itself how much of a risk the company posed.

First, the AIVD needed a place from which to spy. It settled on a big data centre just outside Haarlem, where Kaspersky had some 'update servers'. These were machines it leased from Leaseweb and from which Kaspersky customers could download antivirus updates.

According to my sources, the AIVD wanted to know who had access to these servers. It wasn't the antivirus software they distrusted – that was good and robust – but the Russian connection. Russian spies were already attacking the Netherlands across a broad front. Municipal and ministerial departments were constantly under fire. In early 2017, hackers from Cozy Bear even began targeting the department housing the prime minister's office. Using cleverly composed emails they attempted to lure officials onto bogus websites, but never did manage to get inside the internal systems.

Were these Russian spies, who were clearly well informed about their Dutch targets, getting help from Kaspersky? One theory at the AIVD was that the update servers in Haarlem gave Kaspersky's Russian team a direct portal from Russia to the Netherlands. What was happening at these portals? Were Russian spies using them to tack their own spyware onto the updates? And did the update servers link to any information about Dutch customers that spies could use?

To get some definitive answers, in January 2015 the AIVD sent one of its technical experts to the Haarlem data centre on a precarious mission: to snoop without Kaspersky catching on. It was deliberately scheduled around the Russian new year, when the Russians were likely to be distracted. In order to gain physical access to one of the servers, some adjustments were needed to the machine itself. Nobody else could know what the AIVD was doing. It took the operative an hour and a half to finish the job, then he hurried off the premises.

What this operation turned up isn't exactly clear. Sources close to the AIVD said it had its own intel about Kaspersky, but nothing solid pointing to espionage. Which makes it all the more mysterious why the Dutch administration decided a few years later to bar Kaspersky antivirus software from central government systems. This decision came in the wake of a similar ban in the US. Did that mean the AIVD had indications Kaspersky was spying after all? I went back to my sources. The decision, they said, was made by the national security and counter-terrorism co-ordinator following high-level talks in which the AIVD had been unable to present any incriminating intelligence concerning Kaspersky. Nevertheless, the counter-terrorism unit and administration wanted to take these precautionary measures.

This situation illustrates how companies can find themselves caught in the middle of an escalating cyberwar. Kaspersky has one tremendous weakness: its head office is in Moscow. That's enough to trigger all kinds of wild theories – like one that claims the company's CEO was trained by the KGB and therefore must work for the Russian secret police. The part about the training is true enough, but Kaspersky wasn't established until years later. There's no connection. Then there's the one about the kidnapping by the FSB of CEO Eugene Kaspersky's twenty-year-old son and his release a few days later. Sceptics claim this peculiarly clumsy kidnapping attempt has all the hallmarks of a Russian spy set-up and was meant to put pressure on the CEO. But again, there's not a shred of evidence to back it up.

American legal experts say Kaspersky is obliged by specific Russian legislation to hand customer data over to Russian spy services and allow them access to its systems. Kaspersky itself and international legal experts counter that these specific laws do not apply to the company. It's true, though, that Kaspersky assists law enforcement services in cybercrime investigations, both within and outside Russia. Just like Fox-IT does in Holland. Or Mandiant in the United States.

Other European countries like France, Belgium and Germany didn't join in banning Kaspersky. Would they continue to use its software if Western agencies could present hard evidence of co-operation with Russian spying? KPN, the Dutch telecom giant, also elected to ignore the government's internal ban. According to its IT specialists, Kaspersky offers the best protection. However, to prevent spying, they made sure the antivirus software couldn't connect to external servers, effectively cocooning Kaspersky inside the KPN network.

It's rather ironic. Kaspersky protects computers against spy attacks, but when the fighting intensifies it's banned.

Where does Gubarev figure in this conflict? How does he account for the slew of spy viruses transmitted through his servers? What does he know about his customers?

*

Gubarev charges around the deserted building until we finally reach his office. On one wall hangs a painting of a gold dragon, a gift from a business connection. There's a workout bench with weights in the centre of the room, and a record player with a pile of Michael Jackson albums lying next to it. 'I have everything of his,' Gubarev says, expressionless. Then he walks through to the adjoining conference room and sits down at the head of the table.

Aleksej Gubarev – distant nephew and namesake of a now deceased Russian astronaut and national hero – was born in the Siberian town of Ust-Ilimsk. His father was a logger who felled more than an acre of timber a month for export to Japan and China. After secondary school, Gubarev started a maths degree at the acclaimed Novosibirsk State University, but dropped out when his wife fell pregnant and he became a father at the age of twenty.

To support his family, Gubarev began working as an 'internet business consultant' and eventually started his own company, in Cyprus. Why Cyprus? 'Because I couldn't afford it in Moscow.' Once on the island, he realised it wasn't a bad place to live. 'I got a loan at just six per cent, bought a house and moved my family here.' Apparently there is nothing more to it than that.

Gubarev can't understand why people don't believe him. Young Russian builds million-dollar business on a simple product in ten years. What's so unusual about that, he wonders angrily. 'I built this company from the ground up. The competition's just not good enough.'

We lay out our questions. Jochem Steman – large eyes, slicked-back hair – makes a show of shaking his head from time to time, as though it defies belief that journalists could doubt his boss's integrity. Is it true that Gubarev personally keeps in touch with all his customers, considering there are so many? 'People trust me,' Gubarev replies.

Is there any chance he may have unknowingly co-operated in Russian attacks on the US Democratic Party? Gubarev shakes his head. 'With us, you pay by credit card or bank transfer. Every transaction with a customer is on paper.' Has he checked his servers anytime recently for suspicious data traffic? 'No. It's not even allowed. I have thirty-seven thousand servers worldwide. Legally, we can't touch them.'

Less than an hour later we shake hands, put away our notepads and let Gubarev steer us towards the lift. There we say goodbye and moments later Tom and I are walking through the rear exit. Back outside, we exchange a brief look. Are we convinced of his innocence? No, but we also have no evidence to prove otherwise.

Two years after this meeting, an American journalist tipped me off about a report by an ex-FBI cyber expert. I hadn't thought about Gubarev for some time. Now, with a court case pending, this former agent had done some digging on Gubarev's companies.

According to the forty-page report, Gubarev's servers were routinely used by Russian criminals. Also for attacks by Russia's Fancy Bear and Cozy Bear espionage groups. All told, the Russian entrepreneur had received 400,000 complaints about malicious web traffic hosted by his servers, which he largely ignored. Instead, he blithely continued leasing thousands of servers to customers without the faintest idea how they were being used.

Even experts were astonished at how many criminal cyberattacks had been carried out through his servers. 'The scale of the cybercrime is too big to put down to coincidence,' said one who'd worked at a hosting provider and read the report. 'Attracting criminals and government hackers seems to be a business strategy for Gubarev.' At the Regional Internet Registry for Europe, an independent non-profit that allocates webspace, the report caused consternation. Webzilla and all its subsidiaries, it concluded, had facilitated malicious hacking activities. A member of the RIPE Anti-Abuse Working Group bemoaned the fact that 'The industry generally [...] has a clear and evident problem that traditional "self-policing" is not solving.'

Reading the FBI agent's report, I was stunned. It was abundantly clear that a Dutch firm had been turning a blind eye to illegal hacking activities. By this time, that same company had built a second data centre outside Amsterdam and would be leasing still more web servers. Apparently, nothing can be done to stop it. Gubarev keeps getting richer; he still vehemently denies all allegations of connections to Russian intelligence and his servers hosting cyberattacks and says he's not, by law, allowed to inspect the traffic on his servers.

At this point, you may be wondering how much this impacts the average citizen. Does it really matter that society is more vulnerable because criminals and countries can strike undetected? That question was answered in the spring of 2017.

11

Fishing with Dynamite

René de Vries is driving his ocean-blue Tesla on the A13 to Rotterdam when he gets a WhatsApp message from a co-worker. The fifty-six-year-old port warden is on his way to the World Port Center, the nerve centre of Europe's largest seaport. Glancing at his phone, he reads that there's a problem at the APM terminals.

De Vries can't place the message right away. Of course he's familiar with APM. A global container-terminal operating company with revenues topping $4 billion a year, it has its own terminals in the port's Maasvlakte 1 and 2, where the world's largest container vessels dock. APM's colossal blue cranes lift containers off those ships and deposit them onto the beds of waiting lorries.

Not a minute later, De Vries' phone rings. It's someone from Maersk, APM's owner. 'Nothing is working any more,' the man reports. 'Cameras, cranes, barriers: everything's down.'

De Vries tries to assimilate this information as he turns his car into the port's parking garage next to the city's iconic Erasmus Bridge. He rushes to the lift and presses the button that will take him up to the Port Center's 'incident room' on the nineteenth floor, overlooking Rotterdam.

There, the manager tells him that with both APM terminals down he can't let any more vessels enter the port. From where they're standing, De Vries can just about make out the terminals, twenty-five miles away. But the computer monitors show what's happening clearly enough. The Europort has come to a standstill. Maritime traffic is blocked. Off the Hook of Holland, the sea is filled with tiny specks, each one a waiting ship.

De Vries looks around the office. Monitors, telephones and laptops are everywhere, and fifteen people are frantically making calls. Rotterdam's police chief Frank Paauw has been informed. So has the city's mayor, Ahmed Aboutaleb.

A Port Authority patrol boat speeds out to the terminals. Customs is close behind. Right now, billions in shipments are stuck ashore with nowhere to go. And, as the minutes tick by, traffic is also backing up on the N15 motorway, the port's main access road. Dozens of lorries with goods to load and unload are stuck outside the gate.

Up in the incident room, screens show three of the port's five terminals are completely down. But why? Is it a blackout? Or – De Vries is gripped by a sudden fear – is this an attack? 'Should we be worried about looting?' one frightened employee asks.

Above all, De Vries is thinking about all those stalled containers. Inside might be a store's summer collection. New phones and laptops. Or, far worse: perishable fruit and vegetables. What's more, most of the goods coming through here are bound for places deeper inside Europe.

René de Vries is a veteran cop. He's no stranger to crime. Stabbings, burglars caught in the act, threats and intimidation – he's seen it all. But on this Tuesday, 27 June 2017 he has no idea what's going on. With a fire aboard a ship or a hazardous leak, at least the situation is clear, the problem definable. But what's happening now is utterly intangible.

For the moment, he can't do much beyond securing the port. Seaport police and customs are patrolling the area. Some truck drivers have turned their vehicles around, others look for a place to spend the night locally or bed down in their cabs. How long this will last is anybody's guess. When De Vries gets back behind the wheel of his Tesla that night, an uncanny feeling comes over him. The normally bustling port is eerily still.

*

It's not just the Port of Rotterdam that is debilitated. That same Tuesday 27 June, one organisation after another stutters to a standstill. Parcel service TNT Express, pharmaceutical company MSD, steel manufacturer Evraz, big British marketing group WPP, Russian oil giant Rosneft, an American hospital – all are suddenly helpless.

The culprit is an unknown virus, later to be christened 'NotPetya'. Ruthlessly it strikes in France, India, Great Britain, Poland, Germany, damaging systems all over the world. 'Companies worldwide paralysed,' headlines Holland's *RTL Nieuws*. 'What is it and how can it be stopped?' asks the *Guardian* in Britain. 'A global ransomware attack,' opens the Dutch national nightly newscast. On the scene in Rotterdam's port, a reporter confirms that not a single European country has been spared. 'Do we know anything yet about where this virus came from?' the newscaster asks. 'No,' answers the reporter, APM's blue cranes motionless in the background. 'We have no idea. And that's the trouble. Even if you track down one malicious source, there could be another even more malicious behind that, and another and another all across the world and the internet.'

Experts, reporters, staff at affected companies: nobody could explain what happened that fateful Tuesday. In the space of a few hours, hundreds of thousands of computers were infected and systems in at least sixty-five countries crashed. Parcels couldn't be delivered, doctors couldn't look up medical data and ordinary people couldn't use their money. Never before had a cyberattack wreaked such havoc.

In the days that followed I filled my notepad with questions. Who launched this attack, and why? How could Rotterdam's port be thrown into such disorder? Was this the prelude to a digital war?

Where normally sources and experts can offer some sort of explanation, this time they were just as feverishly scrambling for answers. It seemed no one had seen this coming. And what was worse, something similar had happened just a month earlier, when computers across 150 countries turned black. In Britain, the disruption was so severe that National Health Service hospitals could only treat emergency patients. Ambulances couldn't be dispatched, thousands of operations had to be put on hold, MRI scanners didn't work and blood labs no longer had refrigeration.

Were these two attacks connected? As before, PCs rebooted themselves to a blank screen with only the message: 'Ooops, your important files are encrypted.' In affected offices, computers blinked off as in a chain reaction. Monitors across whole departments went black. One by one, in rapid succession. Workers who saw it happen and frantically ran around unplugging machines were too late. It was that fast. Rebooting was pointless. The computers were locked and unresponsive.

The message that popped up on tens of thousands of monitors indicated ransomware. For $300, people's files would be restored, the attackers said. But as those who transferred the money swiftly discovered, they weren't. Their computers systems had been shattered.

If I wanted to work out what happened in the Port of Rotterdam, I'd have to pin down the origin of the global breakdown first. To find ground zero of the attack.

*

Cybersecurity firms that tracked these infections noted something peculiar: most were in Ukraine. In fact, that country accounted for more than 90 per cent of affected systems. Banks were down, card payments impossible, metros out of service and ditto the airports, post offices and even the Chernobyl nuclear clean-up site.

To understand what had happened, my colleague Tom Kreling and I took a plane to Kiev. We wanted to visit SCM, the country's largest corporation and parent of Ukraine telecom Ukrtelecom, headquartered in the city's famed St Michael's Monastery. There we met Jock Mendoza Wilson, a boyish Scot, who told us about that fateful day.

A little before one o'clock in the afternoon, Wilson's assistant Knesia stormed into the room shouting at him to shut off his computer. Without missing a beat, he leaned to the left and tore the white network cable from its socket. Then he just sat there, suspended, as though perhaps he could hear if the invader had made it into his computer or was still dangling from the network cable.

The IT department called. 'SCM's been hit and no one's allowed to touch their computer.' Wilson recalled the emails he'd meant to send, the project he'd spent four months on that could well be lost. It was only after he'd crossed the marble foyer, dropped into the seat of the car waiting outside and asked the driver to translate the Russian news on the radio that he realised the entire country was down.

Out in the streets there was a strange silence. The kind of calm you'd expect on a Sunday, not a weekday evening, and certainly not on the eve of 28 June, a national public holiday. Wilson was worried. *Can I still get my money? Can aeroplanes still take off and land?* Questions swirled around in his head.

Back home, he looked at what was being reported by Western media. The BBC said a number of companies in Germany, the Netherlands and the US had been hit. He phoned friends and business connections. Wilson had never before experienced a cyberattack, and even after all this time the memory of it still stirs a sense of dread. An awareness of how helpless he is without electricity, water and hospitals. How dependent on telephones, computers, airports and money. Despairing, he wondered: *What's next?*

The economic impact on Ukraine was devastating, Dmytro Shymkiv told us at his office in the nearby presidential palace. According to this former Microsoft Ukraine CEO, now chief technical adviser to President Petro Poroshenko, the virus affected '10 per cent' of the country's systems. Some banks had to replace every single computer. That's because of the way the virus spread – through networks – so every time another computer was powered up, disaster struck again. Ukrsotsbank resorted to using fire alarms to warn its thousands of employees not to restart their PCs.

'Officially, there were something like twelve thousand infected PCs, but it went far beyond that,' said Shymkiv. 'Some companies lost sixty to eighty per cent of their IT infrastructure.'

While the presidential adviser fished a tie from his desk drawer – his boss, President Poroshenko, was holding a conference call with Vladimir Putin and his staffers needed to look the part – we reconstructed the 27 June attack. Shymkiv outlined what he knew of events leading up to it. We listened, hoping for clues to who was behind it and why. And also, just maybe, to explain the crippling of the Port of Rotterdam. To start, Shymkiv explained about M.E.Doc. M.E.Doc is a package of business accounting software developed by a small Kiev-based family firm called Intellect Service. It's widely used in Ukraine for bookkeeping and tax filing. Eighty per cent of organisations had it.

Unfortunately, this company that supplied software for a million PCs was not as robustly secured as, say, American software giants. Shymkiv explained that hackers organised an extended campaign against Intellect Service which ultimately enabled them to break in.

In April, three months before the 27 June attack, they sabotaged the M.E.Doc update process. This gave them a powerful capability to tack their own software onto the next update. Software to let them spy. When users ran one of the next M.E.Doc updates, they unwittingly also installed a piece of spyware. 'Four hundred thousand companies use M.E.Doc. And an accounting system contains all a company's valuable information,' continued Shymkiv. For the hackers, this was a veritable goldmine.

For two months, all they did was spy. But then the hackers changed tack. Even though they could have used the software to observe organisations for months, if not years, they were playing for higher stakes. On the eve of Ukraine's Constitution Day, they unleashed a sabotage virus. The goal: chaos. By spreading through the M.E.Doc software, the virus was assured of infecting the greatest possible number of victims in their enemy. Ukraine.

Pushing back his heavy desk chair, Dmytro Shymkiv excused himself. He couldn't keep the president waiting. One last question, we said: who were these people? 'Who's interested in our financial data and out to destroy companies?' Shymkiv countered. 'It's the classic Russian approach. You don't just burn down the house, but the whole village.'

Cybersecurity firms and affected governments worldwide have echoed Shymkiv's analysis. The virus started in M.E.Doc and then spread like wildfire around the globe. But who were these allegedly Russian hackers? And what did they want?

*

With Russian cyberattacks, I always assumed one of two possibilities. Either it was Cozy Bear – the cyber espionage group the AIVD had watched for years – or Fancy Bear. Cozy Bear is part of Russia's SVR security service, while Fancy Bear takes its orders from its military intelligence service, the GRU.

According to my sources, it definitely wasn't Cozy Bear. And probably not Fancy Bear either. Apparently, my picture of the Russian hacking scene was outdated. I needed people to fill me in. For starters, people from the MIVD, which closely monitored Fancy Bear. Did the Dutch military intelligence agency know anything about the cyberattack on Ukraine?

Sources said the MIVD had been keeping track of online hacking activity at the GRU since 2014. For a long time, cybersecurity firms and agencies lumped these hackers with Fancy Bear, but in truth that label was too broad. Looking at their activity more closely, it was clear there were really two distinct groups of military hackers. There was Unit 26165, and Unit 74455. The first specialised in spying, the second in sabotage and destruction. Their targets matched up perfectly with those of the Russian government. That is, NATO countries, Eastern European administrations and the Kremlin's political foes.

The MIVD had long been apprehensive about the more aggressive Unit 74455. Then, in early 2015, agency specialists discovered an attack server. It was in an industrial park in Meppel, a town in the Netherlands' rural north-east. In an expanse of pastureland cut by the railway line from Zwolle to Groningen sat a Dutch-owned data centre stacked with servers. To one, the MIVD had followed a trail of suspicious traffic. When specialists tapped it and looked at the logs, they got a shock.

Russian hackers had been using the server to stage attacks in Eastern Europe. They'd attempted to infiltrate power stations and implant malware. They'd successfully invaded Ukrainian television networks and released a virus to overwrite data, thus wiping out documents, video and audio files and making it impossible for journalists to report on local elections. This was the first time the MIVD saw just what Unit 74455 could do. That it could harness the internet with the intent to destabilise a country and create upheaval.

Later that year, Ukraine was targeted again. It was winter – 23 December 2015. That afternoon, an employee of a western Ukraine power distribution centre was at his PC when suddenly the cursor came to life on its own. Though he hadn't touched his mouse, it clicked open a window and took a substation offline. Thousands of households were plunged into darkness.

As the American magazine *Wired* later reported, the employee jumped to grab his mouse. But no matter what he did, it remained unresponsive and stubbornly continued taking electrical substations offline. With every click, thousands of households went dark. Though he tried to stop the cursor's progress, he could only watch as the computer logged him out. When he attempted to log in again, he couldn't. The invisible attacker had changed his password. All he could do was look on helplessly as the country's power went out.

One by one, almost sixty electrical substations were taken down that cold December night. More than 230,000 households were left without lights or heat. Backup facilities were disabled, too. Meanwhile, the power centre's phone systems were inundated with thousands of computer-generated calls, making it impossible for customers to get through. All told, 103 towns and cities in Ukraine went completely dark and another 186 had partial blackouts. After six hours without power, engineers managed to restore the systems manually. But since the attackers had damaged network software as well, disruptions continued for weeks afterwards.

Even with dozens of specialists worldwide investigating, it took months to piece together what had happened. From the initial reconstruction it was clear the cyberattack had been carefully planned and choreographed. First, phishing emails were sent to IT workers at power distribution centres. The emails installed malware which let the hackers breach organisational networks. That placed them within one step of computers that actually controlled the grid.

These control systems weren't accessible from just any office network – they were too important for that. So, to get inside, the attackers had to think of something else. Within the office networks, they went in search of login names and passwords of employees authorised to access the systems. It took several months of sifting through data, but eventually they had what they needed. And then it was just a matter of waiting for the opportune moment: for a cold December night.

Ukrainian and Western security services blamed Russia for the attack. So did the MIVD. Specifically, the Dutch agency believed it to be the work of Unit 74455, which had already attempted to breach power stations via Meppel earlier that year.

Meanwhile, the GRU's other unit, 26165, hadn't limited itself to spying. Its hackers were also targeting Ukraine and they weren't being subtle about it. On Wednesday 1 November 2017, workers at several embassies in The Hague opened their mailboxes to find a message from the Embassy of Ukraine. 'Urgent,' read the subject line.

Dear Sir/Madam!
Please, read the document about recent terrorist attack in New York.
Regards,
Ukraine Embassy.

Attached to the email was a Word file with the name 'New York Attack By ISIS'. This attack had occurred the day before, when a man drove his pickup truck onto a Manhattan cycle path, killing eight people. Based on the email address – emb_nl@mfa.gov.ua – which looked real enough, the sender appeared to be the Ukraine Embassy itself.

Those who clicked on the attached Word document saw a pop-up box with the question: 'This document contains fields that may refer to other files. Do you want to update the fields in this document?' If they clicked 'Yes', it opened a program to access Windows settings. An invisible file was then retrieved from a GRU website, which in turn installed a backdoor through which the hackers could enter the embassy's systems in The Hague.

The domain used to stage this cyberattack – netmediaresources.com – had been registered by GRU hackers on 19 October, thirteen days before the phishing email. The infected Word file had been created four days earlier and updated right after the New York City truck attack. If a recipient clicked, the GRU was in. If nobody clicked, they moved on to their next victim. How many embassies were actually infected remains unknown.

These hackers became world famous a few months later when a pair of them, accompanied by two intelligence agents, took a plane from Moscow to Amsterdam. A diplomatic staffer from the Russian Embassy in The Hague picked them up from Schiphol Airport. The group's arrival set alarm bells ringing at the MIVD, which closely monitored the movements of some Russian diplomats. Among other things, they tracked phones and embassy cars. The MIVD would fix minuscule GPS trackers onto the underside of vehicles, which it could either read out manually – by physically taking them off at intervals – or using an automated system, by parking an MIVD car alongside.

Russia had an urgent reason for flying the foursome to Holland. The GRU was under scrutiny following an incident in Britain a few weeks earlier. In Salisbury, Wiltshire, a man and his daughter had been found sitting side by side on a park bench, both gravely ill, their bodies convulsing, eyes rolling, arms jerking. Passers-by thought they were drug addicts, but police called to the scene quickly grasped the severity of the situation. The man – a Russian former spy named Sergei Skripal – and his daughter had been poisoned with a deadly nerve agent. Though in bad shape when discovered, they ultimately recovered.

From the outset, Russia denied any involvement, but as the weeks went by, a growing pile of evidence suggested otherwise. The British government made a convincing case that GRU operatives were responsible for the attack. When it called in the international Organisation for the Prohibition of Chemical Weapons (OPCW) to help investigate the nerve agent, the Russians got nervous. Putin didn't want any surprises. That's when hackers at the GRU started going after the Hague-based OPCW.

They started off by sending emails to dozens of OPCW employees, to both their work and personal addresses, giving them subject lines that tied in with the organisation's work. The emails came with attachments or contained links to external websites. But these hacking attempts failed. It was then that two GRU agents and two hackers were dispatched in person to The Hague. The whole thing was very last-minute. Just days earlier they'd still been furiously googling information about the OPCW. On arriving at Schiphol, the four hired a Citroën C3 in which they spent several days canvassing the area around the OPCW's premises in The Hague. On Friday 13 April, they parked their car in a lot right outside the OPCW building. In the boot was specialist equipment they'd brought along to hack Wi-Fi connections and an antenna to attract web traffic. Since the OPCW had no added security measures, like two-step authentication, this was all they'd need to get into the network. After trailing the four GRU operatives for days, it was in this parking lot that the MIVD decided to step in.

They caught the Russians off guard. Running towards the car, the MIVD saw one grab his phone and attempt to smash it. But he only managed to crack the screen. The Dutch agents were able to prevent further damage and immediately confiscated it along with everything else in the vehicle, including stacks of banknotes amounting to

€40,000, phones, laptops containing incriminating intel and train tickets to Bern in Switzerland. Since the Russians were travelling on diplomatic passports, and the MIVD has no authorisation to make arrests anyway, the men were herded onto a plane back to Moscow that same day.

Some six months later, the head of the MIVD and the Dutch Defence Minister released details of this operation. Such openness by the Dutch authorities about a thwarted hacking plot was extraordinary. But the Americans had forced their hand by moving to prosecute the GRU team for a series of hacks, including that attempt on the OPCW. Pictures shown at the Dutch press conference of the Russians arriving in Amsterdam's airport made news around the world. 'How the Dutch foiled Russian "cyber-attack" on OPCW' was how the BBC reported it, while the *Washington Post* had 'Russian hackers were caught in the act'.

What the MIVD didn't share at this press conference was that the OPCW wasn't the only thing that brought the GRU to The Hague. The team had also spent a night in a hotel in Noordwijk, a nearby seaside town and the headquarters of the European Space Agency. They took their hacking apparatus to Rotterdam and loitered around the public prosecution office, where a criminal inquiry was being conducted into the flight MH17 crash. Though they had been following them all this time, the MIVD didn't stop them from approaching the public prosecution office, so presumably the hackers never got close enough to eavesdrop.

It was in 2015 that the MIVD first noticed changes in how Russian hackers were operating. After the annexation of Crimea, their methods became cruder, more unpredictable. Unit 74455 was using the internet to stage military actions against power stations, media outlets and railway companies. If Russia was behind the 27 June assault, this unit was doing the work. As military tensions with Russia intensified, Ukraine found itself the target of more frequent and heavy cyberattacks, such as those on the Ministry of Finance just when yearly bonuses were being distributed, and strategically timed blackouts.

The United States and Great Britain later laid the blame with Russia. That accusation was to have tremendous consequences.

*

After the NotPetya attack, multinational snack manufacturer Mondelez – owner of big-name brands like Oreo – had to replace 1,700 servers and 24,000 laptop computers. It filed a $100 million claim with US-based insurer Zurich American. Normally, cyberattacks were covered, but in this case the insurance company contended it was an 'act of war'. Claim denied.

Other companies also faced colossal damage. American pharmaceutical giant Merck put it at $870 million. According to the White House, the global impact could even exceed $10 billion.

Part of the blame for all these losses lay with the United States itself. After the Snowden leak, there were at least two other major breaches of US classified information. Among the data stolen on those occasions were powerful hacking weapons created by the NSA and CIA. These tools were the new weapons of the modern age, designed to exploit unknown vulnerabilities to penetrate computer and phone security. And those weapons ended up in the hands of a hacking ring.

Say you have a tool that lets you take over any Windows PC. A tool like that would pose a security threat to all web users, everywhere in the world. This is a technique the NSA calls 'fishing with dynamite'. And that's just what one of the stolen hacking weapons did. It was a lethal exploit that leveraged a security leak in Windows to let the NSA take control of Windows systems and install malware. The NSA had used it to spy for at least five years. For a long time after the theft, the agency did nothing. Not until it seemed like the stolen malware might be dumped online did the NSA beg Microsoft to make a patch, because otherwise the damage would be monumental.

In the spring of 2017, Microsoft released a Windows update with the recommendation that it be installed as quickly as possible. Immediately afterwards, the NSA's malware was published by a hacking group. The first attack followed in May, with ransomware employing that very exploit. Windows users who'd failed to perform the update were soon regretting it. In the Netherlands, systems at Q-Park parking garages stopped working. So did information signs at German railway stations. Entire automotive factories were shut down. Also British hospitals, where patients had to be evacuated. In an attack ultimately attributed to North Korea, the cyberweapon had swung back to strike the West like a boomerang. But the real blow was still to come.

Only a month later, the next devastating cyber virus was circling the globe. Among the victims this time were the Port of Rotterdam, hospitals in the US and control systems at the Chernobyl site. The fact that the weapon hopscotched from one Windows computer to another helps explain why this sabotage virus leaped from Ukraine to other countries and didn't just affect organisations that had M.E.Doc. Global shipping giant Maersk worked with the accounting software in Ukraine. So when Russian hackers released the virus into M.E.Doc, it also snaked its way through linked networks to Copenhagen and, from there, to its subsidiary APM Terminals in Rotterdam.

Now that we know the cause, only one question remains: why was the Port of Rotterdam so dramatically affected? At some companies, only machines with M.E.Doc installed went black. But at APM Terminals, everything was knocked out. That's not what you'd expect from a major industry player and critical link in global shipping.

The reason why is as simple as it is ironic: people at APM didn't see the need for digital security. Physical security? Certainly. They had plenty of sturdy fences and round-the-clock guards. Entry to the terminals required a whole registration procedure plus fingerprints. But digitally, things were a mess. Up until 2015, the Terminal Operating System had no antivirus protection at all. Connections to other organisations – like its parent, Maersk – weren't shielded by any firewall. Nobody, it turned out, was checking if people were authorised to access critical operational systems. Nor had they bothered with penetration tests, which reveal holes in an organisation's digital security. APM, it seemed, was still operating in a pre-digital era.

A year before the attack, security experts had explicitly warned company management about the poor security of their critical Terminal Operating System. APM leadership didn't care to fix it, because upgrading the network would require briefly shutting down the terminals. And the company's executives hadn't wanted to do that. Managers within the organisation knew next to nothing about IT systems. Experts who were rushed in after the fact needed days to get all APM's systems back up and running. Things were so bad that one of them wrote a code just to be able to get the cranes working again. The tall blue arms finally came back online that Friday night, almost four days after the attack.

APM wasn't the only company whose sloppy security was exposed by the two viruses that struck in the spring of 2017. Two months after Microsoft's urgent warning, scores of organisations still hadn't bothered to install the Windows patch. Including my own employer, DPG Media. When the first virus tore around the world one Friday in May, our IT department did nothing. One weekend passed, and then another. Still no update. It wasn't until the next Monday afternoon that an alarming email went out saying there'd be an update soon. Attitudes like these speak to a broader problem: we simply don't want to take cybersecurity seriously.

Like the hack at telecom provider KPN and the crisis at certificate authority DigiNotar, the complete paralysis of Europe's biggest shipping port was a reality check. Once again, we witnessed how a single weak spot can bring an entire country crashing down. It also teaches us a frightening new lesson. Not only are there hacker groups out there that understand the potential of these weaknesses, but they're also willing to use them to strike at their opponents. Whatever the consequences.

Part IV

Who Will Protect Us?

12

The Perfect Weapon

Fences, cameras, reflective glass: Madrid's U-tad, a private technology institute on the city's outskirts, is the antithesis of an open campus. My colleague Tom Kreling and I follow a security guard up stairs and down corridors to a spacious meeting room overlooking the ring road. Already seated are two men – managers at Zed Group, the software company that owns this private university. The guard isn't for show. Without meaning to, these two Spaniards have ended up inside a spy world.

It all started in 2009, one of them begins. He's got short hair brushed up in front, glasses and a sharpish nose. We'll call him Carlos. The other has greying hair and is wearing a white shirt. He'll be Julio. Because of the recent threats to them and their families, they will only share their story anonymously. Surrounded by stacks of documents, they flip open their laptops.

In 2009, their company was growing fast. It was buying up competitors in different countries. That year also marked a digital watershed. It was when people started using social media. The world discovered Twitter, sharing videos on YouTube became a thing and Facebook made a profit for the first time. All this changed the way people used the web. It became more personal and more shared. Julio and Carlos began hearing from customers – mainly telecoms, with hundreds of customers of their own – about the new pitfalls of this social media landscape. Complaints on Twitter or Facebook could wreck a company's image. 'People would do things like post a bad review of a place they'd never been to blackmail a business,' Julio explains. 'Then they'd offer to remove the complaint in exchange for free services.' Customers asked Julio and Carlos if they could help.

Julio and Carlos turned to Zed Group's data analysts and software engineers. Could they design something to signal when a social media storm was brewing that might be harmful to a company? And that could then nudge that storm in a different direction, or even deflect it altogether? Step one was to unravel what makes a post get more attention. But Twitter and Facebook don't give out their algorithms, so the team needed a workaround. They decided to post tweets and messages of their own and look at what happened.

This tactic, they hoped, would give them a handle on the mechanics of the American tech firms. How many tweets and retweets did it take to get a post trending? What got certain stories singled out? How many shares and retweets were needed for Facebook and Twitter to log activity as co-ordinated, and hence spam?

After experimenting for several months, the software engineers knew how Twitter and Facebook boost posts, what makes them go viral and how to influence those trends. Now they could write a code of their own to detect when an organisation was at risk of drawing negative publicity. 'We called it SNAP,' says Julio. Short for 'Social Networks Analysis Platform'.

Customers could input terms that were 'negative' for their business and the software searched for any occurrences of those words in association with the brand. SNAP also signalled whenever negative posts scored a high number of views. That implied an attack. 'And once we could do that,' says Carlos, 'we came up with the counter-weapon.'

*

Detecting an attack is only part of the battle. Diffusing it is more complicated. The team went back to their code and worked out two different ideas. One used bots – hundreds of fake accounts controlled by one entity – to give tweets an unusual amount of attention. Twitter and Facebook would see this anomalous activity, mark it as manipulation and take it all down, including the original post. Julio grins: 'Very effective.'

The other idea was craftier: 'To deflect attention with a tweet of our own that went viral.' How much attention is needed to get a post trending and overwhelm the negativity? Turns out it's easier than you'd think. Give a post the right attention from a couple of hundred accounts and it can be trending within half a day. According to Julio, 'You can rank in the top ten trending topics in Spain with only three hundred accounts.'

This method worked best if the accounts belonged to real people. That way, Twitter and Facebook didn't suspect bots. Carlos and Julio built an app that their customers' employees could install on their phones. The app let SNAP access their Twitter accounts, so anytime their employer wanted to mount a Twitter campaign, they got a notification and could click to post the suggested tweet. The software optimised the timing and logged the effects. Employees who were up and active on social media early in the morning got the notification first thing, night owls got it later in the day. All to make campaigns look as authentic as possible. Carlos: 'A company like Telefonica has fifteen hundred people working in its call centre alone. If a third do it, that's more than enough people to get a topic trending at any given moment.'

The two Spaniards noticed this strategy was most effective on Twitter. It was less group-oriented than Facebook, which worked better with their campaigns. 'Twitter feeds off controversy,' explains Julio. 'Their algorithm isn't as tough on a little manipulation.' After four years of analysis, trials, tests and building, SNAP was ready for its debut. The first tranche of customers signed up, and even the Spanish administration under then Prime Minister Mariano Rajoy, which was apparently having a hard time with troll accounts in Venezuela, expressed an interest in late 2013.

*

Six months after this the 2014 European Parliament elections took place. Prime Minister Rajoy's People's Party (Partido Popular) wanted to use SNAP to shape public sentiment online. 'That's when we offered SNAP for free to the PSOE, the socialist party, to protect the democratic process,' says Carlos. 'It would have been unfair if only one party had had this weapon.' Both parties took full advantage of SNAP and over a period of three years used it to run hundreds of campaigns. On 5 May 2016, for example, Prime Minister Rajoy was interviewed on Spanish radio station Cadena SER and the party mounted a social media campaign to get the hashtag #RajoyEnLaSer ('Rajoy on the SER') trending.

Party employees got a notification from the app telling them to post a tweet. The text was pre-programmed, but the poster could tailor it if they wanted, so long as they used the right hashtag. That the prime minister would be on the radio wasn't exactly historic news, but that wasn't the point of SNAP. Rather, it was about subtle promotion. About getting a topic trending to draw the spotlight off other messages. About focusing attention on a positive event and fuelling the perception that Rajoy enjoyed wide support. 'Used properly,' says Julio, 'it's a potent and effective weapon.'

As SNAP grew in Spain, Julio and Carlos continued refining the software. For each new customer they did a detailed analysis first to chart tweeting behaviour around specific topics, and only then did they bring in SNAP. Thanks to machine learning, the program also progressively fine-tuned itself.

*

While SNAP was expanding, cracks started to appear at Zed Group. The company had been growing fast and was working with partners in Russia and former Soviet bloc countries to fund its growth. One investor was Alfa Group, owned by Russian multibillionaire and oligarch Mikhail Fridman, who had stakes in the oil and telecom industries and a supermarket chain. Zed Group's CEO Javier Pérez Dolset regularly visited Russia. He dined with Fridman on several occasions and was even invited to the latter's private hammam.

Zed Group's CEO also met Yevgeny Prigozhin, a businessman and caterer to Vladimir Putin. Prigozhin had a special status at the Kremlin, having worked his way up from selling hotdogs to running a food empire that supplied everything from school lunches to state banquets – including for the dinners Putin so loved to host for foreign leaders at his luxury restaurant. Over time, Prigozhin also scaled the hierarchy of the Kremlin.

Then came 2017. Bloomberg News published an article about the Russian Internet Research Agency (IRA) in St Petersburg. 'We were stunned,' says Julio, looking back. The piece set out in minute detail how Russian online manipulation worked. How hundreds of young Russians were spreading disinformation from a tower block on the outskirts of St Petersburg (see also Chapter 9). But what really grabbed their attention, says Carlos, 'was that the algorithm and accounts' behaviour were identical to SNAP'.

How was this possible, the two Spaniards wondered. Had someone stolen their software? They tried to figure it out, searching in public sources and doing their own research. In a Russian paper, the *Novaja Gazeta*, they read that a Russian police colonel had established the Internet Research Agency in late 2013 and that this colonel had close ties to Prigozhin – the real person in charge, according to Russian investigative journalists. The team leader was someone from his catering company Concord. And there were emails showing that an accountant at Concord had effected payments to the Internet Research Agency. The whole point of the IRA, the Spaniards realised, was to get young Russians to sing the praises of President Putin so that Prigozhin could curry favour with his big boss.

No one knows how the Russians replicated SNAP, and at such speed. 'It took us four years, with two hundred software engineers, to build SNAP. What are the odds of them creating a similar product in just a few weeks?'

Julio and Carlos confirmed that during the separate meetings their CEO Pérez Dolset had with Fridman and Prigozhin while he was in Russia, SNAP had been discussed. Staffers from the Alfa Group had visited Madrid to learn more about SNAP before Alfa's investment in the company.

But no hard conclusions have been drawn about this, and neither Alfa Group nor Fridman responded to questions about their involvement in SNAP and the meetings with Javier Pérez Dolset.

*

It was time for a counter-attack. Knowing SNAP as they did, Julio and Carlos also knew how to expose the online manipulation. As they saw it, it was their moral duty to track the effects of their invention and stop the trolls. Carlos remembers, 'We saw a whole lot about MH17. MH17's the only campaign the Russians always kept up.' In the first days after the crash, the IRA posted more than 100,000 tweets blaming Ukraine for shooting down the passenger aircraft. Most were via bots – lots of automated accounts controlled by one person. This form of 'influencing' was relatively easy to spot.

But then it got more sophisticated. Obviously, the Russians were learning, too. From having bots bombard the web with an alternative theory to get that trending, now they switched to using more personalised accounts. Julio and Carlos pull up Excel sheets filled with Twitter handles. Like @jenn_abrams, whose profile identified her as a Trump supporter from Virginia. Registered in the United States, she was an active participant in online discussions and took a hard line on immigrants ('You come to my country and want me to change my traditions because you don't like them') but for instance also tweeted (falsely) that CNN in Boston had briefly broadcast thirty minutes of porn one day by mistake.

Well attuned to controversial issues, she tweeted about abortion, immigrants, Hillary Clinton, left-wing fascists and Obama, and was convincing enough to garner 70,000 followers. Some of her tweets even got news coverage and were quoted by the likes of Yahoo, the BBC and the *Washington Post*. Even the former US ambassador in Moscow, Michael McFaul, responded to her tweets.

The longer Julio and Carlos looked, the odder it all became. For example, they saw the same tweeters were also promoting foreign media outlets in places like Iran, Venezuela and Russia. There, too, the influencing was subtle. The Spanish edition of *Russia Today*, for instance, published an article about the flight MH17 investigation, with a headline suggesting Dutch investigators felt defeated by the case's complexity. In reality, it concerned a minor technical facet of the investigation, but with the help of Venezuelan accounts the headline became world news. Carlos: 'We managed to map about ten per cent of the IRA's activities. It doesn't take much to shape public sentiment: two thousand accounts in the United States, six hundred in England, three or four hundred in Holland. We estimate that right now Russia has around five to six thousand.' A figure that goes up by a couple hundred every month.

Did Russia steal SNAP from Spain? These are the facts. Two software engineers from Zed's Russian branch quit their jobs to work for the IRA. Whenever Julio and Carlos talk to former IRA employees, they're warned off: 'Don't investigate. The Russians will come after you.' International experts, including the FBI, have said they suspect the IRA is using 'foreign software' to manipulate social media. And after the Russian meddling in the 2016 US elections, the FBI indicted Prigozhin for his involvement with the IRA. Julio admits, 'Without meaning to, we created the perfect weapon.'

*

The disinformation Julio and Carlos saw mostly originated in Russia and Venezuela – with a significant uptick around the referendum on Catalan independence. But it's not only Russia and Venezuela that are using the weapon. In September 2019, researchers at Oxford University reported the use of 'computational propaganda to shape public attitudes via social media' in seventy countries. Up 150 per cent in two years.

And not just in countries with authoritarian regimes. Among those seventy countries are forty-five democracies in which political parties are using online propaganda tools. Israel has a force of 400 people who are driving the online climate, Vietnam 10,000 and Ukraine 20,000. Some are active not only inside their own borders, but beyond them as well. According to the Oxford report, China is the new major player – deploying an estimated 300,000 to two million 'cyber troops' on social media – and Facebook even tops Twitter as a platform for spreading disinformation. Philip Howard, professor at the Oxford Internet Institute and one of the report's authors, said elsewhere that the 'scope of these campaigns raises critical concerns for modern democracy'.

That goes for European countries, too, where the Oxford study shows Facebook is also providing a platform for manipulation. In Austria, for example, the SPÖ Social Democratic Party set up two Facebook pages aimed at discrediting political rivals in October 2016. And in the Netherlands, an investigation by the *NRC* newspaper uncovered how the political party Denk was mobilising dozens of fake accounts – generating at least 1,600 posts and thousands of shares and likes – to spread its own message and undermine opponents.

*

Zed Group pulled the plug on SNAP in July 2017 after disagreements with its Russian business partners. Julio and Carlos won't use it any longer. 'Too dangerous,' they say. But their quest didn't end with the Russian trolls. The deeper their work took them into social media campaigns, the more they began to make out the overarching context. 'A good online campaign comes with real influencing,' says Carlos. 'With real political power.'

By which he means that social media campaigns serve a political end. Venezuelan and Russian trolls support the Catalan movement because they think weakening Spain is to their advantage. To effectively target that manipulation, they need to know the country and have connections there. The moment Julio and Carlos realised that, other links emerged. Such as that whenever Russian accounts came online in African countries, Prigozhin and his cronies tended to be nearby. In 2019, Libyan authorities arrested two Russian 'consultants' with close ties to Prigozhin. They'd come to Libya to meet with ousted dictator Muammar Gaddafi's son, who was planning to run in the country's presidential elections and already had backing from Moscow.

The two men were carrying laptops and flash drives identifying them as part of Fabrika Trollei – 'troll factory' in Russian – which, according to the Libyan charges, 'specialises in influencing elections that are to be held in several African states'. Fabrika Trollei is actually a collection of political and media organisations connected to Prigozhin. According to sources cited by Bloomberg, Prigozhin had been in touch with Gaddafi's son and was also active in Madagascar, where Russia was running another disinformation campaign. There, Russians worked with locals to set up Facebook accounts that looked as authentic as possible – that weighed in on the right issues in the native language. And that, Julio and Carlos agree, 'is what makes them so effective and difficult to detect'.

*

But even this is only skimming the surface. Leaning towards us across the conference table, Carlos continues, 'When we mapped the campaigns onto the travel patterns of Russian intelligence officers and cash flows, we saw even more.' Such as a poisoned arms dealer in Bulgaria, they tell us, a coup attempt in Montenegro, the murder of a Chechen in Berlin. All thought to be the work of a Russian unit on a mission of destabilisation. The further they looked, the stranger their research got. They can't give us more details, however, or tell us much about contacts with European law enforcement – 'that's risky'. But they can show us documents on judicial investigations and examples of those cash flows, along with the passport of a Russian involved in subversive activities in African countries. The very next day, we see the international press are reporting that same man's arrest for meddling in elections.

Now, because of SNAP, Julio and Carlos find themselves in a sinister world. 'A new playing field has arisen on which conflicts and wars are being fought. On this playing field, attackers can shape public sentiment using false information and plunge countries into chaos.' Neither of them believe Western countries are sufficiently equipped to deal with this new reality. Asked if SNAP has taught them anything, Julio reflects, 'I saw the incredible potential of technology. Now I mainly see the dark side.'

13

Fighting without Rules

Five years ago, I wanted to investigate the dangers of digitisation. Today, I'm at a leaving party for Ronald Prins amid spies, government ministers and top officials who are waging an online battle every day. Some I've talked to before; most I know by name. If the Dutch spy world had a face, this would be it.

Though never shy of the spotlight, Ronald Prins stands uncomfortably at a raised wooden table, dressed for the occasion in a blue suit and tie. The venue is a museum overlooking the Scheveningen shoreline, just outside The Hague. One by one, people file past and warmly shake his hand: AIVD director Rob Bertholee, former Defence Minister Jeanine Hennis, National Police chief Erik Akerboom.

It's a Thursday afternoon, 8 March 2018. Two weeks from now, the Netherlands will be casting its vote in a historic non-binding public referendum on a bill to grant more surveillance powers to the Dutch intelligence agencies. The proposed legislation has sparked fierce controversy. Opponents invoke the spectre of the old East German Stasi, warning that Big Brother could soon be watching us all. Their main objection is to the random tapping of internet traffic that would be permitted under the new law, which is being likened to a dragnet.

Those in favour stress the law will make the country safer. Under the old law, the Dutch agencies couldn't tap the internet whenever they wanted, even though the vast majority of modern communication goes through those cables. Granting agencies these broader powers is crucial, therefore, to obtain useful intelligence about terrorists and spying states.

Ronald Prins is in the thick of this battle. He spent a year working at the AIVD, is a noted expert and supports the new law. He was also recently chosen to sit on an independent committee charged with overseeing Dutch intelligence work. But he has drawn criticism for this as well, because how can someone who was once employed by the AIVD objectively judge its operations? In the run-up to the referendum, there has been renewed censure of Prins's appointment. Walking around this reception, however, you wouldn't know it. The spy directors and government leaders who grab seafood hors d'oeuvres from platters aren't worried about the outcome of the vote: the Dutch agencies sorely need this new legislation and, to their thinking, the public is sure to be on board.

I'm the only journalist here, and wasn't even sure I ought to attend. Routinely I get invitations to conferences, seminars and leaving parties. Mostly, I decline. A symposium on 'Challenges of the Future' with captains of industry? No thanks. A political party working group to talk about the cyber challenges of tomorrow? I'll pass. It comes down to journalistic relevance. To put it bluntly: will I learn something new?

In this instance, the journalistic value is apparent. Prins's firm Fox-IT is a global leader. Among its clients are seven of America's ten biggest banks, both Dutch intelligence agencies, NASA and NATO. Fox-IT encrypts the minutes of the Dutch government's executive council and supplies the hardware that lets officials make calls securely. With people from the AIVD, the MIVD and Defence attending, a reception for Prins promises an interesting guest list.

Some journalists believe you should maintain distance from your subjects. But I want to get close. I want to know what drives a person, why they decide one way or another, and if they're honest. That's why I've been following Ronald Prins all these years, because there's no way you can write about the digital world and ignore the unruly fiftysomething who's been involved in so many major espionage affairs. According to the US magazine *Politico*, which ranked him among its Class of 2019's twenty-eight most influential Europeans, he's 'the spy's spy [...] at the nerve center of digital security in the Netherlands, at a time when the country is fast becoming one of the West's most powerful cyberintelligence powers'.

Prins thinks like a hacker and behaves like an entrepreneur. As someone who needs his freedom, the AIVD, with all its rules and hierarchy, felt more like a straitjacket. Though he has good contacts there, he's equally at ease in a student debate, at a meeting of Shell oil executives or attending a hackathon. While his versatility generates valuable publicity for Fox-IT, it is also Prins's Achilles heel: for the hacker community he's too tight with government, for the government he's too much of a loose cannon.

He's known to flirt with the fast life. At Fox-IT, his pass card number is 007, and callers who are put on hold get the familiar James Bond theme piped into their ears. His friends even organised a Bond-style bash when Prins turned forty. In 2013, when the NSA affair blew up, he decided it would be funny to claim an email address blatantly similar to that of NSA director Keith Alexander, keith.alexander@nsa.org; only the domain letters differed. Emails sent to that address wound up in Prins's inbox. His employees take his pranks as a given. Whenever they see unusual activity on their networks, they know it's one of two things – either serious hackers, or their boss up to something illegal.

And Prins is hooked on action. At his house in Scheveningen he keeps a collection of walkie-talkies so he'll be the first to know whenever the coastguard goes out on a rescue mission. Or, if a Syrian chemicals shipment arrives at Rotterdam Airport, he and his wife are right there, watching through the gates. Once, in 2007, he was in his car on the dual carriageway, his children in the back, when he saw a motorcade of dark brown removal vans with a police escort ahead. Knowing the AIVD was just then moving from Leidschendam to its new headquarters in Zoetermeer, and guessing this might be an agency convoy, he put his foot down and joined the line. As they left the road, armoured vehicles cut him off on the exit and masked agents approached his car, hands on their guns. Prins immediately rolled down the back windows. Upon seeing his children, the agents relaxed. On that occasion, Prins got off with a warning.

Occasionally, his antics do get him into trouble. He has lost his driving licence for speeding several times. And once he was held by the police for flying his drone over a fireworks display. None of that has hurt Fox-IT. As digitisation spread, its business thrived, and in 2015 the British NCC Group paid €133 million to acquire the firm co-founded by Prins, leaving him €40 million richer.

In a wisecracking speech, Prins says he could have done without this official farewell. Three years after Fox-IT was bought up by the British, he is moving on to share his digital expertise where it's more urgently needed. Places like the national Electoral Council, the Dutch Safety Board and the Financial Markets Authority. Characteristically frank and outspoken – his wife says even his family is sometimes shocked by his bluntness – the hacking expert jokes in Dutch about the conservatism of NCC Group, his firm's new owner. Their British chairman Chris Stone is in the audience. Prins: 'He can't understand what I'm saying anyway.'

*

Events like this have a high insider quotient: if you're there, you belong. Everyone is approachable. What strikes me during every conversation I have is that the people in charge of espionage and keeping our country safe are anxious, too. 'Wherever we look, we find traces of spying. And we're not even looking everywhere,' says one. Another: 'There's no high-tech company the Chinese haven't been inside.' And another: 'I wonder sometimes where this arms race is leading.' Paradoxically, while agencies know more, they're less certain these days than ever. One intelligence worker tells me he keeps a stash of banknotes at home so he'll still be able to pay for food and petrol if payment systems are taken out by a cyberattack.

The ways agency people talk and behave are shaped by the organisation they serve. AIVD agents are cautious and tight-lipped. On the whole, they don't like mingling with outsiders. For them, the world splits into two categories: 'inside' for everything that's part of the AIVD, 'outside' for everything that's not. At some point, seeing me chatting with one of his own, AIVD chief Rob Bertholee hurries over to interrupt. Half playfully, half seriously, he warns, 'Don't give away too much!'

People from the MIVD are more open and direct, but there's also a strong element of hierarchy and group dynamics at work. They discuss the ongoing cyberwar in military jargon, talking about adversaries' 'offensive potential', the 'reconnaissance' they've gathered, the operational details they're not allowed to share, and intelligence meant for 'the principal' – either the prime minister or president. For them, the world is a perpetual game of Stratego.

The imperative to expand powers for the AIVD and MIVD is obvious to all the officials here. To keep the country safe, government needs to surveil the digital world as it does the physical one. Cyber espionage has now become the top priority at the MIVD and a main focus for the AIVD, alongside terrorism. Without this new law, the agencies won't be able to investigate whether malicious software is spreading from one place in Holland to another. Say, if they find Iranian malware at a Dutch university, they can't scan the whole country's internet traffic for more signs of it. Which means they can't strike back as hard at foreign spying either.

Privacy is basically a non-issue for this crowd. Not when citizens are voluntarily handing over their personal data to American giants like Facebook and Google. Holiday snapshots, phone numbers, home addresses, workplace screenshots and dating profiles divulging the most intimate details – people are already sharing so much of their private lives, whereas what the agencies want is access to the more obscure communications of specific actors they know far less about. Their faith in the government and its rules runs so deep that experts can't even conceive that these powers might be abused. 'We're not Facebook,' explains someone in intelligence. In their speeches, leaders underline why security matters. Former Defence chief Hennis recalls 'how timid' she was on taking her seat in the Dutch House of Representatives in 2010. Coming from the European Parliament, where she'd earned her stripes as a privacy advocate, now she was overseeing national security and the Dutch police force. She quickly lost her naive perception of digital threats, she notes. In his speech, Erik Akerboom remembers the DigiNotar hack as being a wake-up call; the moment when he suddenly understood just how vulnerable society is.

*

I have mixed feelings about the new surveillance law and referendum vote. I believe the public officials and policymakers attending Ronald Prins's leaving party are genuinely motivated to defend the Netherlands against catastrophe. Their fears makes sense. A hack of sensitive documents could spark a social revolution, our private conversations are conducted over Chinese devices and fake news is corroding journalism. The internet has set in chain an arms race with grave consequences for democracy, for safety and security and for journalism, even if most people don't see it that way.

Is the new law a solution, or is the Netherlands merely fanning cyber aggression? The law will certainly give Dutch agencies a stronger grip on the internet. With it, they'll be able to tap and filter internet traffic at different entry points, like KPN, the country's main telecom provider. The MIVD is already inside more than a thousand foreign computer systems and this new legislation will enable it to extend that reach. But the problem is: on what moral grounds can you demand other countries stop spying on you when your country is doing it, too?

The AIVD, meanwhile, is expanding its digital presence within the Netherlands. If it wants a target's emails, it hacks a network provider. To do that, it needs to break through the provider's security at a weak spot in their software. The agency's hackers might search for such a weakness themselves, but the AIVD can also buy them on the exploit market (exploits are known software security holes) – a shadowy market worth millions that's making the internet increasingly unsecure. Here, again, there are virtually no rules: Western countries can buy exploits wherever they want, like an open trade in enriched uranium.

Characteristically, the Netherlands' solution is one of compromise between the governing parties, under which intelligence agencies won't be allowed to buy exploits from contractors who also sell weapons to dubious regimes. But how do we define 'dubious'? One of the most notable suppliers, the Israeli NSO Group, sells spyware to the United Arab Emirates (UAE), a country that heavily suppresses freedom of speech. Does that qualify as dubious? What if the Emir of the UAE wiretaps journalists and dissidents using this Israeli software, as has actually happened? Does that cross the line?

The law to enlarge cybersecurity therefore also curbs a free internet. And there are more incongruities. Public interest has centred mainly on the 'dragnet' capabilities the law would give agencies to filter internet traffic on a massive scale. This is a serious extension of surveillance powers that will be balanced by strict safeguards. Yet the safeguards are less strict for hacking, which is where things are really escalating.

A week before the public referendum, the yes vote looks set to win. But then, on the eve of the election, polls show a flip. In the final count, the no vote narrowly wins by 49.4 per cent, against 46.5 per cent in favour. The administration responds with promises to do some fine-tuning, but as far as hacking powers go there's no change.

Later that year, the AIVD wants to carry out a bulk hack, retrieving the data of millions of people to access those of only a few suspects. According to sources, they want to hack KPN's email server. But, in this particular instance at least, the Investigatory Powers Commission (TIB) charged with oversight rejects the agency's request.

*

The referendum forces me into an unfamiliar position. Friends, colleagues and other journalists all ask me what they ought to vote. For them, like many others, the digital world is abstract and intangible, but also increasingly pervasive. Tax-filing, transit information, financial transactions – everything is digital. They want me to advise them. Will this law help or harm our safety?

The truth is, I don't know. In a succession of newspaper pieces I've written about this new law, I try to set out in concrete scenarios what it will mean in practice: how tapping works, where agencies will be allowed to do it and its impact on the everyday lives of ordinary citizens. But advice is tricky. I began investigating the digital world as an outsider and was gradually initiated by sources. I explain, examine, expose. Now, suddenly, I'm being expected to express my personal opinion.

And there's another reason for my hesitance. The better I come to understand the internet and the risks, the knottier the problem. To shield society from spies and foreign hackers, agencies need surveillance powers that put a strain on free society. The outcome of the referendum illustrates this: on the one hand, people realise that security services need new capabilities, but on the other they're afraid their civil liberties will suffer. Does the new law mark a step towards a surveillance state? It's a legitimate question.

Such hesitancy is also characteristically Western. National intelligence and security agencies can no longer count on popular support. There's a limit. An open society simply can't take more internet surveillance. It's not the job of democratically elected governments to separate fake news from news fact. Or to spread disinformation of its own. Authoritarian regimes like China and Russia have no such qualms. Back in 2000, US President Bill Clinton described how much the internet was changing America: 'we are already an open society. Imagine how much it could change China [...] China has been trying to crack down on the Internet. Good luck!' he joked. 'That's sort of like trying to nail Jell-O to the wall.'

But China has done it. The country is shielded from foreign hacks yet can strike ruthlessly at whim. Chinese hackers know their government will protect them, as do hackers in Russia and Iran. The internet is a powerful weapon for them, both to surveil their own populations and to spy and sabotage abroad. What's more, they have a strategic advantage in the war against Western powers, because they're not being forced to wage it with their hands tied behind their backs. We may all be fighting the same battle, but some countries are fighting it by different rules.

It's only after the referendum vote that the perfect metaphor for our relationship to digitisation occurs to me. Digitisation is like the use of antibiotics. Antibiotics are great. When administered with judgement and care, there are almost no drawbacks. But overuse and abuse them, and the public health consequences are disastrous. With our immune systems already weakened, antibiotics roll out the red carpet for invaders that burrow like parasites in the most vulnerable spots and wreak irrevocable damage. The question is, have we already passed that critical juncture?

In embracing social media and smartphones, we've also let in risks. The devices we use daily are putting us under fire. And we can't just strike back. Our governments won't put up troll factories to spread disinformation or train tens of thousands of hackers. But doing nothing isn't an option either, and so we march another step closer to the point of no return.

This battleground is no longer a place of tech nerds and pioneers. Evgeny Morozov, an American writer and one of the most interesting thinkers on digitisation, explains how the cyber world has become our bedrock: 'What used to be playfully described as "cyberspace" – something immaterial, virtual and ephemeral – has grown into the economy's most capital-intensive industry, interconnected by material data centers, undersea data cables and a sensor infrastructure that envelops our cities,' he writes. 'In 2018, the four biggest digital giants – Google, Facebook, Amazon and Microsoft – made more capital investments (a combined 77.6 billion dollars) than the four biggest oil corporations – Shell, Exxon, BP and Chevron (a combined

71.5 billion dollars) [...] Such staggering figures will I hope disabuse anyone still stuck on the idea that there's something immaterial – or indeed virtual – about the whole enterprise.'

The digital world is like the monetary world, just as enmeshed in modern society and at the same time just as opaque. And the threats certainly aren't coming from China and Russia alone.

*

Gemalto was a French company that made SIM cards. Incorporated in the Netherlands for its favourable tax regime, the firm manufactured about two billion SIM cards a year for 450 telecom clients. To encrypt communication, SIM cards have a secret key, or 'Ki', burned onto them, which is also stored in a telecom database. If someone were to steal these keys, they would be able to make their own SIM cards, pose as somebody else or decrypt intercepted phone traffic. Of course, Gemalto had measures to prevent that.

But then, in 2015, news came out that the American NSA and British GCHQ were deep inside the card manufacturer's network. '[We] believe we have their entire network,' British spies wrote in a classified document that US-based *The Intercept* published on its website. They had penetrated 'authentication servers' to obtain Kis, tantamount to the holy grail for intelligence services, which meant they could sweep up millions of automated keys and use them to decrypt intercepted phone calls. The NSA had even created a special system that could process fifty million of these keys per second.

The goal of the theft was to get encryption keys for newer cell technologies like 3G, 4G and LTE. Because the old 2G technology had all kinds of security flaws, the US and UK could already decrypt that traffic. But not so the latest generation of cell communication. 'Gaining access to a database of keys is pretty much game over for cellular encryption,' American cryptography specialist Matthew Green told *The Intercept*, and 'bad news for phone security. Really bad news.'

This led to major concerns in the Netherlands. Gemalto made SIM cards for Holland's three main network providers: Vodafone,

T-Mobile and KPN. Vodafone being the carrier used by members of parliament, the House automation office issued a recommendation that all members replace their SIM cards – only to have it inexplicably retracted by Ronald Plasterk, the minister responsible, the very same day.

Six anxious days later, Gemalto presented the findings of its own investigation into the hack. The firm said it believed the UK and US had 'probably' breached its networks – but only its office networks, which 'could not have resulted in a massive theft of SIM encryption keys'. It's the standard response when companies are hacked: deny if at all possible, otherwise downplay the scale and hence the damage. Even '[i]n the case of an eventual [sic] key theft,' Gemalto asserted, the agencies would only have been 'able to spy on communications on second generation 2G mobile networks'.

It was an extraordinary statement. The NSA documents show in black and white that UK and US intelligence got their hands on millions of keys, granting them full access, and that they were inside the authentication servers. And it wasn't 2G but 3G, 4G and LTE that they were after. Yet Gemalto insisted it wasn't possible. How can a company be so sure after investigating for only a week? Look at Belgacom, KPN and DigiNotar: if you want to get to the bottom of spying, you employ recognised experts who then take months to complete their research. Why wasn't Gemalto calling in security expertise?

How certain can we be that Dutch SIM cards are secure? None of the sources I spoke to knew, or was willing to say. Not until four years later, in the spring of 2019, did I turn up two people who were willing, on the condition of absolute anonymity, to say more.

Both sources – one worked in telecom and the other in intelligence – told me exactly the same story. When news of the hack broke, network providers and the AIVD began surveying the domestic risks. The AIVD's National Communication Security Bureau (NBV), which advises telecoms on data security, co-ordinated the investigation. The telecoms also did research of their own. But both the AIVD and providers came up against the same problem: Gemalto would tell them next to nothing. According to the telecom source: 'We asked Gemalto repeatedly to provide detailed information about the seriousness of the hack. How deep inside the network did the UK and US get? We never received that information.'

The AIVD and the providers were left grasping at straws. And evidently they had no authority to force Gemalto to come clean. With no specific details about the hack, they had no way of knowing if Dutch SIM cards were safe. The AIVD saw no point in replacing House members' SIM cards. If they didn't know just which encryption keys the UK and US had in their possession, new SIM cards could be equally at risk. 'Let's not be naive about what the UK and the US are capable of,' warned my intelligence source.

Neither the country's network providers nor the intelligence agency know if Dutch telecommunication is safe. Maybe it is – but, then again, maybe it isn't. Gemalto illustrates yet another of the consequences of digitisation: an interdependency of products and services that's impossible to fathom. That those products and services can also be hijacked by spies means the prying eyes and ears of foreign states could be everywhere.

In 2018 and 2019, similar misgivings emerged over products manufactured by the Chinese company Huawei. They, too, occupy critical points in Holland's infrastructure, deep inside the providers that direct all Dutch phone and email traffic. Huawei's hardware is encapsulated in telecom networks which are continually on the lookout for outgoing data. In the spring of 2019, a path from Huawei to Dutch customer data was discovered at KPN, whose clients include the Ministry of Defence. It was a path only Huawei could access. The AIVD investigated possible links with Chinese state-sponsored espionage, but the complexity defied a decisive answer. Yes, China's spying everywhere and using customer data like KPN's to do it. But had Huawei in fact passed that data on to Chinese spies? One source put it like this: 'The liquor cabinet's open, the liquor's gone, somebody's got the liquor – but does that mean he's the one who stole it?'

Espionage is tough to prove, and Huawei categorically denies any links, saying, 'In every country where we do business, we comply with laws and regulations and protect the privacy of our customers. Cyber security has always been our top priority.' Huawei is a corporate behemoth that has 70,000 people doing research and development on a daily basis. That's the population of a small city. British specialists have been investigating the Chinese giant's devices for years, but are unable to say for certain whether China's government will use Huawei to spy. They have come across security leaks, both serious and less so, but don't know if there is any intent behind them. Huawei has such a multitude of different product lines and models that there's no single blueprint. And this problem isn't unique to Huawei. Sweden's Ericsson supplies crucial telecom hardware to the Netherlands but refuses to reveal their products' source code. Products manufactured by Cisco in the US have backdoors actually built in to give American intelligence services access. The crux of the problem is that European societies are becoming increasingly dependent on products and technologies from countries, like China and the United States, that are also spying on a tremendous scale.

*

How should countries deal with these new vulnerabilities? This dilemma was brought into sharp focus by events in the US in 2020. As Americans geared up for national elections, everyone was worried about a repeat of 2016, when Russia launched a broad campaign to influence the election outcome. All the federal agencies were consequently on high alert to prevent foreign meddling in the presidential race between Joe Biden and Donald Trump.

After Biden's victory and no apparent attempts by the Russians to interfere, the country let out a collective sigh of relief. Until a month later, in December 2020, when the American cybersecurity firm FireEye issued a disturbing report: Russian hackers had managed to penetrate major American corporations and government agencies. The scale of the hack was among the largest and, as it turned out, most successful ever. Even with its astronomical budget, the NSA's Cyber Command was evidently powerless to stop it.

It was ingeniously done. In 2019, the hackers had breached a software company in Texas called SolarWinds, whose IT resources-management software Orion is used throughout American industry and government. To this software, the hackers added a malicious code.

When SolarWinds released an update for Orion in March of that year, the 18,000 SolarWinds customers that installed it also installed the hackers' code. Among them, American corporations like Cisco and Microsoft. Also the US departments of the Treasury, Energy and Homeland Security. And even the Defense Department, including the NSA itself, and the Justice Department. All were victims of the hack. What's more, because the hackers' methods were so clever and advanced, and because they could actually make their malware disappear in some cases, they were able to do their work undisturbed for months. While American cyber specialists were trawling the internet for Russian influencing during the election campaign, hackers from the SVR, Russia's Foreign Intelligence Service and part of the same group as Cozy Bear, were executing a takeover in American industry and government. Some organisations will never even know they were victims, and mapping the hack's full scale will take many more years.

Some US senators called for an immediate counter-attack. Democrat Richard Durbin said it was 'virtually a declaration of war by Russia on the United States'. Microsoft CEO Brad Smith argued that, 'This is not "espionage as usual"' but, rather, 'an attack on [...] the world's critical infrastructure.' Others, like cryptographer Bruce Schneier and political science professor Thomas Rid, maintained it was a case of classic espionage. And doesn't the US do that, too? The speed and the scale may have changed by virtue of the internet, but the goal is the same: to gather intelligence. What if every hack by one country were followed by tit-for-tat counter-attacks targeting one another's infrastructure? Where would the escalation end?

These are the dilemmas Western countries are grappling with. On the one hand, there's the alarm about proliferating cyberattacks.

Gone are the days when state actors used the internet only to spy. The internet has been weaponised. Now, it's being wielded to influence public sentiment in other countries, to spread conspiracy theories about the origins of the Covid-19 virus, to take out power grids or damage equipment in foreign nuclear plants.

On the other hand, Western countries bear just as much of the blame and are likewise exploiting the potential. In 2018, as *Yahoo News* later revealed, US President Donald Trump secretly authorised the CIA to carry out covert cyber operations that 'gave the agency very specific authorities to really take the fight offensively to a handful of adversarial countries', including China, Russia, North Korea and Iran. Not to spy, but to sabotage. That's *Die Hard*, not *Ocean's Eleven*.

Experts have been warning for years that there will come a time when attacks carried out online, by hackers, do real physical damage. The CIA's cyber operations and Russia's Unit 74455 have proved these predictions right. What they're engaged in are acts of war. The West is just as guilty: the Stuxnet attack on Iran in 2007 was also an act of war, and the fabrication and subsequent loss of control of dangerous hacking weapons like it are fuel for further escalation. After the devastating attack on Iran, none other than former CIA director Michael Hayden – who was leading the organisation in the run-up to Stuxnet – warned, 'This has a whiff of August 1945.' Then, it was a bomb of annihilating power that killed tens of thousands of people; now, it's a sabotage virus that worms its way inside and destroys systems. The blast of an atom bomb can't be missed, but a sabotage virus strikes silently and leaves no casualties – at least, not yet.

For armed conflicts, we have international rules of war. For digital assaults, we don't. What's more, prosecution can be impossible, because while physical confrontations leave a trail, cyber actions are much harder to detect and easier to deny. The CIA deploys hacking weapons that mask their origin, and can even manipulate the time zone or keyboard settings to look like they were coded on the opposite side of the globe by someone typing on a Russian keyboard. Committees at the United Nations are working to devise norms of conduct that can prevent cyber escalation, but several countries, including China and Russia, have already withdrawn.

It's not only a case of fighting by a different rulebook. Russia is staking out its own battlefield and experimenting with disconnecting the whole country from the World Wide Web. That would let it fall back on its domestic internet in the event of a cyber crisis or, say, if it were to release an offensive cyberweapon and didn't want to suffer the consequences at home. In 2018, Dutch researchers discovered the destructive 'Triton' virus wreaking havoc in power stations and petrochemical and nuclear plants in Central Europe. Triton is thought to have been crafted by Russia and was first unleashed in Saudi Arabia in 2017. The malware targets plant safety shutdown systems designed to defend against life-threatening disasters. If Russia has its own internet, it will be shielded from that kind of attack.

But there's not always a clear line between espionage and sabotage or subversion, just as it's not always clear when striking back is justified. In the autumn of 2020, while the European Medicines Agency (EMA) was working on the approval of the Pfizer/BioNTech and Moderna Covid-19 vaccines, Russian hackers moved to infiltrate the EMA network. Employees received cleverly composed emails appearing to be from colleagues; if they clicked on the enclosed link or attachment, it deposited an implant that let the hackers read all their messages. The hackers, who were part of Cozy Bear and probably also behind the SolarWinds affair, eventually saw a ZIP file go by containing a 'new user token'. Before new employees can access EMA's office network, they have to activate two-step authentication. To do this, EMA sends an access token to an employee's email address, the employee opens the link, enters their credentials and, using an app, connects their smartphone for two-step authentication, after which the app generates a unique access code.

Seeing that ZIP file, the Russians intercepted it and linked it to a device of their own. At this point, the system should have spat out an error message, since it can't generate multiple tokens for the same user. But, according to sources, that setting had been disabled by

EMA itself, leaving it vulnerable to exploitation. Nobody subsequently noticed that one employee was logging on using multiple devices, and neither did any of EMA's firewalls register suspicious logon attempts.

That gave the Russians access to EMA's internal network for weeks. Rather than being interested in the Pfizer/BioNTech and Moderna vaccines as such, it seems they wanted to know which countries were ordering doses and in what quantities, sources say. According to one, it was 'classic economic espionage'.

Later, though, all kinds of EMA documents surfaced on a Russian internet forum claiming to provide 'Evidences of BIG DATA SCAM of Pfizer's vaccines'. Among them were confidential emails, procedural approval documents, comments from EMA employees and correspondence with the EU from November which revealed that EMA was being pressured by the European Commission to expedite approval of the vaccines, and in any case not lag too far behind the American FDA. The documents were arranged together and with elements cut and spliced in a way that was clearly intended to sow doubt about the safety and reliability of the Western vaccines.

Is this a case of classic espionage, or manipulation? When does one become the other? And, when manipulation happens, what constitutes a proportionate response? Sabotaging Russia's power grid? Hacking Cozy Bear? In the aftermath of the SolarWinds hack, critics pointed to the flawed security of networks in the US. Why did no one notice Russian hackers were rooting around US government departments? Instead of fanning the flames of offensive aggression, shouldn't the United States be investing more in defensive capabilities, and in analysing which software could leave the government open to attack? The Russian infiltration at SolarWinds was 'low-hanging fruit', observes a Dutch intelligence source. 'There are dozens more companies like it.' And if EMA arbitrarily impairs its own systems security, isn't it wilfully making itself vulnerable to spying? Don't companies and organisations have a greater responsibility to bear?

The multitude of internet connections and their high speed, combined with the open nature of Dutch society, have made the

Netherlands a particularly attractive target. At the same time, its intelligence and security services are recognised as being among the best in the world. A 2020 study by the Harvard Belfer Center placed the Netherlands fifth in a ranking of 'the most comprehensive cyber powers', after the United States, China, the United Kingdom and Russia. The Dutch Defence Ministry's Cyber Command unit can 'attack, manipulate or disable adversary systems'. Its intelligence and security services, the AIVD and MIVD, can hack computer systems in other countries. Their Joint Sigint Cyber Unit had amassed a workforce of 700 by 2019, its hacking team growing from five people in 2014 to fifty. These days, an intelligence source tells me, Dutch agencies could 'easily' craft their own Regin virus – that advanced, many-headed hydra which lurked unnoticed inside Belgacom for years.

The Netherlands is locked in ongoing cyber combat with chiefly North Korea, China, Iran and Russia, and not a day goes by without some online skirmish. On this new battleground, it is intelligence agencies that have to defend the front line. Most persistent and worrisome, sources say, are the attacks from Russia, whose implants have been found at sensitive points in Holland's infrastructure. In an autumn 2018 news broadcast, Dutch Defence Minister Ank Bijleveld characterised the digital tensions with Russia as 'a form of war'. But it's a silent one – a war that no one sees.

So what happens if information systems come under attack: who will protect the networks that process all of citizens' personal data? Several incidents in 2019 proved that even Holland's most privacy-sensitive systems are not secure. At a child support services office in Utrecht, hackers made off with the files of more than 3,000 vulnerable children, containing information about mental disorders and details of sexual abuse. A phishing attack at a hospital in Apeldoorn led to a breach of all their patient data. And at a hospital in Amsterdam, students were found to have been browsing through people's medical files for months.

Every step we take, corporate interests and government organisations are collecting our data. Cameras register where people walk and park, businesses register the products customers buy, debt collectors how creditworthy they are and pharmacies which medicines they use. The Dutch police have a database that stores pictures of 1.3 million citizens – almost 8 per cent of the population. But people are also giving their own data away. On sites like Facebook and Google, and to ancestry sites such as MyHeritage, an Israeli commercial platform to which millions of people voluntarily supply their family histories and genetic material.

In the hands of surveillance agencies, these mountains of data pose a threat to democracy. First to be affected are usually political activists, minorities and other disadvantaged groups. The NSA in the US and GCHQ in the UK already compile lists of the names of citizens who support WikiLeaks. China uses a gigantic network of cameras equipped with facial recognition to track the movements of millions of Muslims. Turkey uses spyware supplied by the German–British Gamma Group to keep tabs on its protestors and dissidents.

The more things escalate, the closer the prospect of physical harm. In 2019, a Dutch investigative TV programme raised the alarm over domestic infrastructure found to be vulnerable to cyberattacks by foreign states. The country's 'physical safety' is in jeopardy, it said: 'Tunnels, bridges, locks and dams are not secure against cyberattacks.' The Dutch National Coordinator for Security and Counterterrorism (NCTV) came to a similar conclusion in its 2019 annual assessment. 'Disruption of society looms,' it wrote: 'The digital threat to national security is permanent' and has the potential to impair 'Dutch autonomy and independence.' The question is: how does the country intend to protect itself?

In 2015, the heads of the AIVD, MIVD and NCTV convened in secret to address this question and came out with a recommendation to allocate € 340 million to national cybersecurity. Prime Minister Mark Rutte and his administration said no. Instead, a task force was formed, which developed a strategy, which bore fruit, some years later, in a 'policy agenda'. This speaks to a kind of cavalier attitude that leads some sources to blame a generation gap: the politicians in their forties and fifties making these decisions about cybersecurity grew up without computers and smartphones, have little affinity with digital tools and don't grasp the vulnerabilities. Take the cabinet member (Ronald Plasterk again) who had to replace his work phone after installing the controversial Telegram instant messaging service on it. Or the refusal of some cabinet officials to use their extra-secure Tiger telephones to encrypt calls.

Another problem is that no one actually feels responsible for digitisation. It's a perfect example of a problem of many hands, where everyone's responsible for a small piece but no one's looking after the whole. In the Netherlands, that responsibility is spread out across five government departments. Compare this to the situation in Belgium and Sweden, where digital affairs has a department of its own.

Co-operation between government and industry has also been rocky. Following Russia's interference in the 2016 US elections, a short-term joint effort was launched to prevent Russia from influencing the Dutch elections in early 2017. Fox-IT, Northwave, Deloitte and other firms were asked to keep an eye on their clients' systems, and that led them to notice new hacking techniques. The Dutch AIVD and MIVD discovered still other forms of Russian malware. But plans to consolidate this business and intelligence data ultimately hit a dead end when the AIVD, though expecting to get information from the companies, refused to share what it had learned. The companies instantly lost interest.

This failed co-operation is symptomatic of a disjointed approach to digitisation overall: of embracing the benefits but ignoring the risks. Just as we message, share and like but neglect to install password managers or decent antivirus software on our laptops. The result is like driving a car without airbags.

The Dutch cabinet's self-proclaimed ambition 'to be the digital leader for Europe' stands in stark contrast to its real investments in cybersecurity. While hundreds of millions are spent on new IT projects that successively fail to achieve what they set out to achieve – for the Ministry of Defence: €900 million; for the Tax and Customs Administration: 203 million; for the national resident registration system: 100 million; for the judicial system: 200 million; for the Food and Consumer Product Safety Authority: 65 million – there's no money for good security.

Instead of the €340 million needed, investments in cybersecurity are made piecemeal to plug the worst security leaks, like duct-taping the hold of a sinking ship. This was also the conclusion reached in a report commissioned from PostNL CEO Herna Verhagen ahead of the 2017 Dutch parliamentary elections, on how to keep the country's head above the 'digital water'. There is a '[w]orrying increase in cyber threats,' she warned. 'Large-scale societal destabilisation could ensue.'

The severity of those threats is increasing across the board, she wrote in the report, from the kinds of cybercrime that directly affect the general populace – in 2015, reported cybercrimes for the first time ever topped those of bicycle thefts, the prime Dutch mode of transport – to spying and sabotage by foreign states. 'We all regard it as self-evident that there are rules, traffic lights and roundabouts for the purposes of road safety. And that companies supply safe, reliable equipment, food and drinking water to consumers. The security of the digital world should be equally important with [sic] the security and safety of the world around us.'

Verhagen's 'urgent' advice was to strengthen cybersecurity and allocate 10 per cent of the national IT budget – that is, hundreds of millions of euros – for a digital defence system. She also recommended appointing a 'top official' to draw up and implement a 'cybersecurity programme of action'.

The report was presented to Prime Minister Mark Rutte and national employers' federation (VNO-NCW) chair Hans de Boer, who expressed his support for Verhagen's recommendations. 'This issue calls for efforts at every level; in government, in industry and among consumers,' De Boer said. AIVD director Dick Schoof also endorsed the need for action: 'Countries like Germany and the United Kingdom already invest heavily in cybersecurity. The Netherlands shouldn't and can't afford to fall behind.'

But in October 2017, when Mark Rutte unveiled the members of his new third-term cabinet, it quickly became apparent that Verhagen's advice had been tossed aside. The administration earmarked a meagre €95 million for cybersecurity – a far cry from the recommended 10 per cent. 'Papering over the cracks, that's all it is,' one government insider summed up. 'At the higher, strategic level, the importance still isn't getting through.'

*

Throughout the years I investigated this topic, one question went unanswered: who'd tried to get into my routers? Two had died on me. The first time – just before my trip to Brazil in 2013 – I tried pressing different buttons, resetting it, hoping to salvage the device myself. By the time I took it to a repair shop, it was too late; I'd wiped all the evidence, leaving no trace of possible spying, let alone of a perpetrator.

I vowed not to make the same mistake again. Next time, I'd pull the plug and take it straight to an expert. So, when it happened again in late 2017, I decide that this time I'd nail whoever it was. Careful not to press anything, I bagged it up and brought it to a specialist firm.

When I came back after a few months to hear what they'd found, I was feeling optimistic. A young man in jeans let me in, sat down and shook his head. 'I'm sorry to have to disappoint you,' he said, 'but we can't get full access to your router. Only the manufacturer can do that.'

Driving home again on the dual carriageway, I mulled over my dead router and the doomed search for explanations. A lot had changed in the nearly six years separating that first broken router and the disappointing inspection of the second. The scale and the severity of spying have increased, our dependence on the internet has grown and society is even more vulnerable. Now we know that the warnings were justified. But, just as I haven't been able to solve the mystery of my router, we haven't grasped it yet.

EPILOGUE

Before I had put down even a word of this book, the screen on my Dell laptop died. It happened while I was on an island in South East Asia. If the wind was right you could get Wi-Fi, but computer stores were thin on the ground. A trip to the mainland would have taken days, so my colleagues at *de Volkskrant* suggested calling Dell's international support service. My exchanges with their Asia team seemed to go round in circles: support staff couldn't understand my name, didn't recognise the serial number of my laptop and could only help if my machine was registered in Asia.

Oddly enough, the day after that call I got a text message from the team informing me a laptop part was being shipped to me by sea. Which part? Where to? Two days later, a woman who spoke English contacted me through WhatsApp, introducing herself as the sister of the man who'd be bringing the part to me. The day after that, a man with a backpack arrived at the island's one supermarket, asking for me. He spoke three words of English, turned out to have a new computer screen with him, and a quarter of an hour later my laptop was back up and running. Point being: the digital age has its upsides, too.

It's tempting to lay the blame for the failures and dangers of the internet wholly on what companies and governments do or don't do. On Facebook, for allowing the private data of millions of users to be used for political campaigns, on the tech company Clearview AI, which has built a database containing photos of three billion unsuspecting people, on the governments that scan internet traffic, and on the surveillance agencies that are spying all over.

But that's to ignore the role citizens themselves play. Facebook can only exist and grow by virtue of the personal information users *voluntarily* hand over. Were masses of people to cancel their accounts, that would be the end of Facebook. The same with data superpowers like Google: use is voluntary and user data fuels its business. There are privacy-friendlier alternatives that work at least as well and store a whole lot less user data. DuckDuckGo and Startpage.com are two. Similarly, it's a choice to use WhatsApp, when Signal is more secure and works just as well.

In 2020, it's estimated that half the Western world will be impacted by some form of cybercrime or the effects of a data leak. Often, the weak points where criminals strike stem from simple negligence. Like using the same password for different accounts, not updating an app or operating system right away, using passcodes that are too easy to guess and always leaving Wi-Fi or Bluetooth on so anyone can see your laptop or phone. Luckily, there are easy fixes for all this: password managers that generate unique secure passwords, installing updates now instead of later, using six-digit instead of four-digit passcodes – or, safer yet, fingerprint ID – switching off Wi-Fi and Bluetooth when you're not using them, and never connecting to public (read: unsecure) Wi-Fi networks.

There are plenty more tips like these, and all kinds of resources are available to readers looking for ways to protect themselves. *Wired* offers some guidelines on 'How to Protect Your Digital Self'. Other journalists have also published about the risks of the digital age. Kim Zetter has written an excellent book about Stuxnet, *Counting Down to Zero Day*. Nicole Perlroth describes the development of cyberweapons in her fascinating *This Is How They Tell Me the World Ends*, and Andy Greenberg's *Sandworm* dives deep inside the Russian hacking world. To read more about the risks surrounding digitisation, a good place to start is the reporting of Zach Dorfman, Jenna McLaughlin and Ryan Gallagher.

When writing about the world of espionage and intelligence, the question inevitably arises of whose interests the journalist serves. Am I a convenient puppet for the AIVD, put to use by government for its own ends? It would be naive not to consider the possibility. Still, people who are clearly only looking out for government concerns are not terribly interesting to talk to, because they lack the unbiased view that's imperative for a journalist.

There's another important reason I don't think Dutch intelligence and security services are steering my work to suit their own purposes. I write about things they'd prefer to keep secret, about *their* operations. That's also why it takes years to win over a good source: they know they're treading a perilous line. To guard against the possibility of manipulation or my own tunnel vision, I always cross-check information and consult with fellow journalists before going to press. That agencies aren't always pleased with what I uncover is clear from the AIVD's and MIVD's repeated content removal requests citing national security interests, as well as a legal case brought by the AIVD against specific passages of this book. For more about this, see the Author's Note. Another good indicator is that several of my sources have been targeted by the Dutch National Police's Internal Investigation Department.

Anything written about intelligence services will always be received with some degree of scepticism, most especially by fellow journalists. That's partly because the work of intelligence is carried out where no one can see. Epitomising this was one response to the story Eelco Bosch van Rosenthal and I broke about the AIVD's hacking of Cozy Bear in 2018.

It was a piece by a foreign affairs and defence reporter that appeared in the Dutch daily *Trouw*. 'Someone stood to benefit from leaking AIVD operation,' claimed the headline. Based on reactions from the officials involved, the author inferred the AIVD had no plans for 'a manhunt for leaks within the ranks'. He also assumed some connection to the public referendum on the proposed surveillance law, to be held two weeks later. 'It would appear – certainly if no charges are pressed – that the political and administrative heads of the Dutch security services can live with the publication of this particular information.' And: 'It wouldn't be the first intentional leak.'

As I wrote earlier in this book, the AIVD most certainly did conduct an internal security investigation into possible leaks. If the journalist writing in *Trouw* had had his own sources, he could have checked with them himself. And a link between our publication and the referendum was impossible, since the first time Eelco and I heard any snippet of information about this operation was in June 2017, when the Dutch Senate hadn't even approved the bill yet. No one could have known a petition for a referendum would be launched months later, let alone that it would be successful and when that referendum would take place. All of these details were included in our original piece in *de Volkskrant*, but that didn't stop the *Trouw* reporter from spinning his own theory.

Intelligence agencies operate in mysterious ways. That's simply the nature of their work. It was also an important reason for me, in writing this book, to give as detailed and clear as possible an account of my journalistic process.

Author's Note

Writing about the world of security and intelligence is to walk a fine line: sources want as little as possible to be traceable back to them, readers want to know every possible detail. If not a name, then at least a description of some kind. Man or woman? Intelligence insider or not? It's only logical that readers seek some way to parse the information.

But even a description, no matter how superficial or innocuous, can get a source into serious trouble. Phone calls leave digital trails, as do cars and card payments. 'Whatever you do, just don't say I'm in intelligence,' a nervous source may tell me, or 'Don't name the town where we met.' Because, if I write that I saw a source in The Hague on Tuesday, a team of investigators can work out pretty quickly where I talked to that person and who it must have been.

The fact that so few people are quoted directly in this book is an unavoidable and necessary concession when writing about intelligence and security agencies. In Holland, the sentence for leaking state secrets is six years in prison.

Nevertheless, I would like to say something about my sources. This book is based on conversations with 110 people: people who were or are employees of the Dutch General Intelligence and Security Service (AIVD), National Coordinator for Security and Counterterrorism (NCTV), Military Intelligence and Security Service (MIVD), officials in various government departments, security analysts and experts. People I do not regard as sources are spokespersons and press officials or, say, an official who sends me a public report. A source is someone I've seen or spoken to on multiple occasions and who has shared with me information that is not public. A source could also be someone who, rather than actively sharing with me, confirms or denies information I have.

I never record conversations with sources. Though it would vastly simplify my work, my sources know all too well that audio files can easily end up in unintended hands. Instead, I take notes. There is a drawback to this as well, if you're meeting in a public space, because it marks you out as a journalist. Of necessity, my notes are limited to quick scribbles – keywords and phrases, no quotes written out verbatim. Immediately following a meeting I work up my notes and save them in an encrypted file. To check and as far as possible verify information I've gathered, I regularly present passages to other sources to ask if the information is factually accurate.

To a large extent, this forces me to appeal to the trust of my readers. But it's that or nothing: either you write about intelligence actors and what they're up to this way, or you're confined to the information made publicly available by agencies themselves.

Alongside conversations with sources, I've also drawn on a wide array of other material, ranging from state secret documents to confidential political reports and from administrative memos to AIVD and MIVD annual reports and reports published by public and private organisations. To the best of my knowledge, none of the information I have used was hacked.

Several passages in this book are based on pieces I wrote for the Dutch daily newspapers *NRC Handelsblad* and *de Volkskrant*. The chronology of those articles is slightly different from how they are presented here. This is intentional and is due to the fact that the course of my investigative journalism was less smooth and linear than represented in this book. For readability, I've changed the order around in a few cases.

For this same reason, I've done my best to avoid using jargon, technical terms and the names of officials and researchers. I've tried to avoid overusing the term 'cyber' – a favourite policy buzzword – and to use my own characterisations and metaphors. That comes at the risk of simplifying or even oversimplifying some details, such as how hardware and technology work. For example, that the kind of computer server used to sign digital certificates is called an HSM and that up until 2002 the AIVD was called the Domestic Security Service, abbreviated BVD. Where I've written Leaseweb, it's actually EvoSwitch in some cases, from which Leaseweb leases its servers.

This book seeks to present the most readable account of the situations and facts as I was able to ascertain them. Though the final result is drawn from hundreds of conversations, responsibility for that result, as for any omissions, is mine.

The MIVD and AIVD were both given opportunities to review portions of the manuscript before publication and to assess the potential danger to ongoing intelligence operations and/or intelligence employees. The MIVD read chapters 3, 5, 8, 11 and 13 and made two content removal requests. After some consideration I elected to keep both passages, as they are based (in part) on public information.

The AIVD read all chapters of the book and made content removal requests for chapters 2, 3, 8 and 9, mostly in respect of names and information traceable to AIVD employees. To the extent the individuals were not key to the narrative, I agreed to their requests. Two individuals who are still employed by the AIVD are referred to by their first initial in chapters 2, 3 and 8, as is the CIA operative mentioned in chapters 3 and 8. The AIVD also asked for the removal of certain details it deemed top-secret information and that could jeopardise individuals. When I refused on the grounds that the arguments were not convincing, the agency filed and won a lawsuit in July 2019. On penalty of a fine for non-compliance of €25,000 per violation, several details have been generalised or removed from the book.

REFERENCES

1 An Uninvited Guest

NSA tapping figures are from the first Snowden publications
Glenn Greenwald, 'NSA collecting phone records of millions of Verizon customers daily', *Guardian*, 6 June 2013.
Glenn Greenwald and Ewen MacAskill, 'NSA Prism program taps in to user data of Apple, Google and others', *Guardian*, 7 June 2013.

Beverwijk and Katwijk on US list of critical sites
Cablegate, WikiLeaks, cable number: 09STATE15113, December 2010.

2 Total Blackout

Frans Bromet clip about mobile phones in 1998
https://www.youtube.com/watch?v=TNwhIHqM60g

DigiNotar system replica in secured bunker at Schiphol Airport
René Schoenmaker, 'De opkomst en ondergang van DigiNotar', Webwereld.nl, September 2011.

Details about DigiNotar cable, acquisition price etc.
Case of *Vasco vs. DigiNotar Owners*, rechtspraak.nl, 7 August 2014.

Piet Hein Donner press conference on hacking of government websites
YouTube, 3 September 2011.

3 The Switzerland of the Surveillance World

Abdul Qadeer Khan
Jaco Alberts, 'De Nederlandse connectie met de islamitische bom', *de Volkskrant*, 19 November 2011.

BBC China vessel intercepted in Italy
Robin Wright, 'Ship Incident May Have Swayed Libya', *Washington Post*, 1 January 2004.

Iraqi communication systems attacked in 2003
John Markoff and Thom Shanker, 'Halted '03 Iraq Plan Illustrates [U.S] Fear of Cyberwar Risk', *The New York Times*, 1 August 2009.

Natanz and its centrifuges
Kim Zetter, *Counting down to Zero Day: Stuxnet and the Launch of the World's First Digital Weapon*, Broadway Books, 2015.

Casualties resulting from Natanz operation
Kim Zetter and Huib Modderkolk, 'Revealed: How a secret Dutch mole aided the U.S.-Israeli Stuxnet cyberattack on Iran', *Yahoo News*, 2 September 2019.

4 Red Alert

Publication of KPN customer passwords
Colin Hoek and Brenno de Winter, 'Wachtwoorden KPN-klanten gepubliceerd', NU.nl, 10 February 2012.
'Hoogste alarmfase na hack KPN', Nos.nl, 9 February 2012.

5 Bombing SIM Cards

NSA infecting growing number of computers
Ryan Gallagher and Glenn Greenwald, 'How the NSA plans to infect millions of computers with malware', *The Intercept*, 3 December 2014.

NSA figures
Peter Koop, 'Some numbers about NSA's data collection', Electrospaces.net, 15 June 2014.

Dutch Tax Administration collecting parking data
The Netherlands Scientific Council for Government Policy, 'Big Data in een vrije en veilige samenleving', Amsterdam University Press, 28 April 2016.

Chinese chips
Jordan Robertson and Michael Riley, 'The Big Hack: How China Used a Tiny Chip to Infiltrate [U.S]Companies', Bloomberg.com, 10 April 2018.

How the US chooses drone targets
Cora Currier and Peter Maass, 'Firing Blind. Article 6 of 8 from the Drone Papers', *The Intercept*, 15 October 2015.

Bombing SIM cards
Jeremy Scahill and Glenn Greenwald, 'The NSA's secret role in the [U.S.] assassination program', *The Intercept*, 10 February 2014.

Casualties from drone strikes
The Bureau of Investigative Journalism, thebureauinvestigates.com/ projects/drone-war

GCHQ metadata collection figures
Peter Koop, 'Some numbers about NSA's data collection', Electrospaces.net, 5 June 2014.

6 A Many-Headed Hydra

The Greek case
James Bamford, 'A death in Athens', *The Intercept*, 29 September 2015.

Israeli firms that supply surveillance software
James Bamford, 'Shady Companies With Ties to Israel Wiretap the U.S. for the NSA', Wired.com, 4 March 2012.

Israel bugs Bill Clinton and Monica Lewinsky
Gordon Thomas, *Gideon's Spies: The Secret History of the Mossad*, St. Martin's Griffin, 2000.

NSA catalogue
Jacob Appelbaum, Judith Horchert and Christian Stöcker, 'Catalog Advertises NSA Toolbox', *Der Spiegel*, 29 December 2013.

Britain refuses to co-operate in Belgacom investigation
Anouk van Kampen, 'Britten weigerden medewerking aan onderzoek naar hacking Belgacom', *NRC Handelsblad*, 25 October 2018.

Belgium needs NSA
Mitch Prothero, 'Belgium Called in the NSA To Catch Europe's Most Wanted Man', Buzzfeednews.com, 21 August 2016.

8 Conspiracy in Amsterdam

Dutch agencies should share information faster
Niels Rigter, 'VS: informatie na aanslag kwam te laat', *De Telegraaf*, 5 September 2018.

Report on Chinese APT1spy group
Mandiant, *Exposing one of China's Cyber Espionage Units,* fireeye.com/content/dam/fireeye-www/services/pdfs/mandiant-apt1-report.pdf, 19 February 2013.

Chinese spy group strikes in the US
David Barboza, Nicole Perlroth and David E. Sanger, 'Chinese Army Unit Is Seen as Tied to Hacking Against U.S.', *New York Times,* 18 February 2013.

US accuses China of spying
David E. Sanger, 'U.S. Blames China's Military Directly for Cyberattacks', *New York Times,* 6 May 2013.

MIVD employee magazine
Stichting Argus, www.inlichtingendiensten.nl/organisatie/ingelicht

AIVD and MIVD at odds
Bart Olmer, 'Spionnen onder één dak: ruzie', *De Telegraaf,* 28 February 2014.

Yahoo hack by FSB
Vindu Goe and Eric Lichtblau, 'Russian Agents Were Behind Yahoo Hack, U.S. Says', *New York Times,* 15 March 2017.

Russian hacking capabilities
Peter Apps and Jim Finkle, 'Suspected Russian spyware Turla targets Europe, United States', Reuters.com, 7 March 2014.

Russian hackers target Belgium
Mark Eeckhaut and Nikolas Vanhecke, 'Ook België doelwit van Russische hackers', *De Standaard,* 5 October 2018.

Russians and the malware market
Max Goncharov, 'Russian Underground Revisited', Trendmicro.de, 28 April 2014.

9 Caught on Red Square

Tweakers scoop
Olaf van Miltenburg and Joost Schellevis, 'Chipmachinefabrikant ASML is gehackt door Chinese overheid', Tweakers.net, 27 February 2015.

Response to parliamentary questions over Rheinmetall hack
rijksoverheidnl/documenten/kamerstukken/2016/07/01/beantwoording-
    kamervragen-over-het-bericht-nederlands-duits-defensiebedrijf-
    gehackt-door-chinezen

From Ocean's Eleven to Die Hard
Kim Zetter, 'Hacker Lexicon: what are CNE and CAN'?, Wired.com,
    7 June 2016.

Kaspersky investigation into Cozy Bear, aka 'Miniduke'
GReAT, 'Miniduke is back: Nemesis Gemina and the Botgen Studio',
    Kaspersky, 3 July 2014.

New York Times *on Russian troll factory*
Adrian Chen, 'The Agency', New York Times, 2 June 2015.

Investigation by De Groene Amsterdammer *on Russian trolls*
Robert van der Noordaa and Coen van de Ven, 'Het MH17-complot',
    De Groene Amsterdammer, 29 May 2019.

Russian hackers attack voting systems
Bill Whitaker, 'When Russian hackers targeted U.S. election infrastructure',
    CBSNews.com, 17 July 2018.

Russians reading Obama's emails
David E. Sanger and Michael Schmidt, 'Russian Hackers Read Obama's
    Unclassified Emails, Officials Say', New York Times, 25 April 2015.

Russian attack on US Joint Chiefs of Staff
Nancy A. Youssef, 'Russians Hacked Joint Chiefs of Staff',
    TheDailyBeast.com, 4 April 2017.

DNC dismisses FBI warnings
Eric Lipton, David E. Sanger and Scott Shane, 'The Perfect Weapon: How
    Russian Cyberpower Invaded the U.S.', New York Times, 13 December 2016.

10 Pornography and Rolls-Royce

NSA director reveals help of Western ally
Ellen Nakashima,
'New details emerge about 2014 Russian hack of the State Department: It
    was "hand to hand combat"', *Washington Post*, 3 April 2017.

Dutch King Servers involved in Russian hacks
Andrew E. Kramer, 'A Voice Cuts Through, and Adds to, the Intrigue of Russia's Cyberattacks', *New York Times*, 27 September 2016.

US suspects Kaspersky of spying
Nicole Perlroth, 'How Antivirus Software Can Be Turned Into a Tool for Spying', *New York Times*, 1 January 2018.

Former FBI agent report on Gubarev and Webzilla
Matthew Rosenberg, 'Tech Firm in Steele Dossier May Have Been Used by Russian Spies', *New York Times*, 14 March 2019.

11 Fishing with Dynamite

Impact of ransomware on UK hospitals
National Audit Office, 'Investigation: WannaCry cyber attack and the NHS', 25 April 2018.

Effects of NotPetya
Andy Greenberg, 'The Untold Story of NotPetya, the Most Devastating Cyberattack in History', Wired.com, 22 August 2018.

US hospital replaces computers
Jessica Davis, 'West Virginia hospital replaces computers after Petya cyberattack', HealthCareITNews.com, 30 June 2017.

Ukraine power grid attack
Kim Zetter, 'Inside the Cunning, Unprecedented Hack of Ukraine's Power Grid', Wired.com, 3 March 2016.

US and UK blame Russia for NotPetya
Sarah Marsh, 'US joins UK in blaming Russia for NotPetya cyber-attack', *Guardian*, 15 February 2018.

Zurich American refuses to pay out claims
Luke Irwin, '"An act of war": Zurich American refuses to pay out on cyber insurance policy following NotPetya attack', IT Governance Blog, 3 April 2019.

NSA employees fear hacking will cause harm
Ellen Nakashima and Craig Timberg, 'NSA officials worried about the day its potent hacking tool would get loose. Then it did', *Washington Post*, 16 May 2017.

12 The Perfect Weapon

Prigozhin's special status within the Kremlin
Tom Vennink, 'De man die Poetins maaltijden opdient, heeft ook trollen-
en huurlingenlegers', *de Volkskrant*, 15 November 2019.

Jenna Abrams, Russian troll
Caroline Mortimer, 'Jenna Abrams: popular far-right US Twitter account
revealed as a Russian propaganda outlet', *Independent*, 13 November 2017.

Oxford report
Samantha Bradshaw and Philip N. Howard, 'The Global Disinformation
Order', University of Oxford, 2019.

Denk political party and trolls
Andreas Kouwenhoven and Hugo Logtenberg, 'Hoe Denk met "trollen"
politieke tegenstanders monddood probeert te maken', *NRC Handelsblad*,
10 February 2017.

Libya arrests two Russians
Samer Al-Atrush, Ilya Arkhipov and Henry Meyer, 'Libya Uncovers Alleged
Russian Plot to Meddle in African Votes', Bloomberg, 5 July 2019.

13 Fighting without Rules

Ronald Prins
'Ronald Prins. The Spy's Spy', politico.eu/list/politico-28-class-of-2019-
the-ranking/ronald-prins/

Israeli surveillance software used to spy on journalists
Azam Achmed and David D. Kirkpatrick, 'Hacking a Prince, an Emir and a
Journalist to Impress a Client', *New York Times*, 31 August 2018.

Surveillance law referendum opinion polls
I&O research

Bill Clinton speech on China
movies2.nytimes.com/library/world/asia/030900clinton-china-text.html

Opinion piece by Evgeny Morozov
Evgeny Morozov, 'De illusie van het ooit vrije internet', *NRC Handelsblad*,
5 April 2019.

Gemalto response to claim it was hacked
https://www.thalesgroup.com/en/markets/digital-identity-and-security/
press-release/gemalto-presents-the-findings-of-its-investigations-into-
the-alleged-hacking-of-sim-card-encryption-keys

SolarWinds hack
Joe Gould, 'No. 2 Senate Democrat decries alleged Russian hack as "virtual
invasion"', c4isrnet.com, 17 December 2020.
Ken Dilanian, 'Suspected Russian hack: Was it an epic cyber attack or spy
operation?', NBCnews.com, 18 December 2020.

Trump authorises covert CIA operations
Zach Dorfman, Kim Zetter, Jenna McLaughlin and Sean D. Naylor,
'Exclusive: Secret Trump order gives CIA more powers to launch
cyberattacks', News.yahoo.com, 15 July 2020.

Interview with former CIA director Michael Hayden
Paul D. Shinkman, 'Former CIA Director: Cyber Attack Game-Changers
Comparable to Hiroshima', USNews.com, 20 February 2013.

CIA using untraceable hacking weapons
WikiLeaks, *Vault 7: CIA Hacking Tools Revealed*, 7 March 2017.

Research on Triton malware
'*TRITON* Actor *TTP* Profile, Custom Attack Tools, Detections, and
ATT&CK Mapping', FireEye.com, 10 April 2019.

Belfer report
Julia Voo, Irfan Hemani, Simon Jones, Winnona DeSombre, Daniel Cassidy
and Anina Schwarzenbach, *National Cyber Power Index 2020*, Belfer
Center for Science and International Affairs, 2020.

Child support services data leak
Daniël Verlaan, 'Groot datalek bij Jeugdzorg: dossiers duizenden kwetsbare
kinderen gelekt', RTLNieuws.nl, 10 April 2019.

Apeldoorn hospital data leak
'Gelre ziekenhuizen waarschuwt voor datalek na phishingaanval',
Security.nl, 11 December 2018.

Amsterdam hospital patient data leak
Michiel van der Geest, 'Patiëntdossiers in te zien door lek bij ziekenhuis OLVG', *de Volkskrant*, 15 February 2019.

Police database with pictures of 1.3 million people
Wester van Gaal, 'Gezichtsherkenning op de Nederlandse straten: moeten we dat willen?', *Vice*, 18 July 2019.

Turkey using spyware on dissidents
Lorenzo Franceschi-Bicchierai, 'Turkey's Government Tried to Hack Hundreds of Protesters Over Twitter, Researchers Say', *Vice*, 14 March 2018.

TV programme on risks to Dutch infrastructure
Floor Bouma, 'Rekenkamer: ministerie moet cyberveiligheid waterwerken verbeteren', *NRC Handelsblad*, 28 March 2019.

Disruption of society looms
Cyber Security Assessment Netherlands 2019, NCTV.nl, 12 June 2019.

Failed IT projects
Mark Lievisse Adriaanse and Derk Stokmans, 'De overheid en haar ICT-projecten: een structurele worsteling', *NRC Handelsblad*, 19 April 2019.

Verhagen's cybersecurity advisory report
The economic and social need for more cybersecurity, Cybersecuritycouncil.nl, October 2016.

Epilogue

Wired *guidelines on how to protect yourself online*
https://www.wired.com/2017/07/protect-digital-self/

Sources for AIVD scoop
Marno de Boer, 'Iemand had er belang bij om de operatie van de AIVD te laten lekken. Maar wie?', *Trouw*, 27 January 2018.

ACKNOWLEDGEMENTS

My greatest debt of gratitude is to individuals whose names I cannot name. Who put their careers on the line and risked going to jail. Who made time before work to look something up, picked up the phone until late in the evening and never got upset when I hounded them in the middle of family dinners, boat cruises or meetings. Thank you from the bottom of my heart.

I am grateful to the editorial board of *de Volkskrant* for giving me this opportunity and their unconditional faith in me – all the way to the courtroom: Philippe Remarque, Corine de Vries and Pieter Klok. My Dutch publisher, Uitgeverij Podium, was a joy to work with; Joost Nijsen was so confident in me that he thought the book would be in shops a year earlier, and Willemijn Lindhout was unstinting in her support, coaching and guidance. Impressive.

I couldn't have done it without Hugo Logtenberg's drive, encouragement and journalistic compass: 'Details, Huib, mind the details!' Peter de Greef as always kept me on the right track. Tom Kreling was a wonderful travel companion and believed in this book even before I did. Joris Luyendijk opened my eyes to the book's true significance, and his precision and advice contributed to both its urgency and readability.

I also wish to thank Marije Randewijk, Eelco Bosch van Rosenthal, Ruben Maes, Titia Kramer, Mieke Clement, Peter Modderkolk, Jeroen de Bakker, Pieter van Os and Ryan Gallagher for their shoulders to lean upon, cups of coffee, fact checking and places to write. Bonny, Roxy and Lou, I cannot thank you enough: you are the true heroes.

INDEX

A NOTE ON THE AUTHOR

Huib Modderkolk is an investigative journalist for the Dutch national newspaper *de Volkskrant*. He is a frequent guest on the popular talkshow *De Wereld Draait Door*, where he explains the complexities of the digital world. Modderkolk won the Dutch-Belgian investigative award De Loep in 2018. His reports have been taken up by the *New York Times*, *Washington Post*, *Reuters*, *CNN*, *Guardian*, *BBC*, *Der Spiegel*, *France24* and many other media sources. He has collaborated with the *Wall Street Journal*, the *Guardian*, the *New York Times* and *The Intercept*. He lives in Holland.

A NOTE ON THE TYPE

The text of this book is set in Minion, a digital typeface designed by Robert Slimbach in 1990 for Adobe Systems. The name comes from the traditional naming system for type sizes, in which minion is between nonpareil and brevier. It is inspired by late Renaissance-era type.